Feminist Liberation Practice with Latinx Women

This book unearths ancestral wisdom to address the needs of oppressed women in both the Global South and Global North. Focusing on Latinx womxn, it empowers through decoloniality, liberation, *mujerismo*, and *nepantlismo*. As such, Latinx womxn compose their *testimonios*, engage in critical consciousness, and commit to global liberation. *Mujerismo*—a dissident daughter of liberation theology–is a Latinx womanism with anti-patriarchal, anticolonial, anti-neocolonial, and antiracial-gendered colonial orientations. *Mujeristas* appropriate cultural/religious/spiritual symbols to construct empowering new meanings for decolonization and liberation. Feminist liberation practices assist in this process. When Latinx womxn's immigration accentuates inhabiting the cultural borderlands, they enter *Nepantla*—a *place in between*—to reclaim themselves and to heal soul wounds and trauma. Rooted in the *Nahuatl* concept of collective transformation, *Nepantla* encourages the development of psychospiritual abilities. As Latinx womxn engage in *nepantlismo*, they awaken their spiritual faculties to become instruments of courage, resistance, revolution, love, and hope.

This book will be valuable to researchers, therapists, and educators interested in the practice of feminist therapy. The chapters in this book were originally published as a special issue of *Women & Therapy*.

Lillian Comas-Díaz works on multiculturalism, feminism, liberation, and spirituality. A private practitioner and a Clinical Professor at George Washington University's Department of Psychiatry and Behavioral Sciences, she was a faculty member at Yale University Psychiatry Department, where she directed its Hispanic clinic. Additionally, she directed the American Psychological Association Office of Ethnic Minority Affairs. The author/coeditor of 13 books, and 170 scholarly articles; Lillian received multiple awards, including the 2019 American Foundation and APA Association Gold Medal Lifetime for the Practice in Psychology.

Carrie L. Castañeda-Sound is the Director of the Master of Arts in Clinical Psychology with an Emphasis in Marriage and Family Therapy: Evening Format program at Pepperdine University, and a licensed psychologist in California. Her teaching and research interests include Latinx, liberation, and *Mujerista* psychologies. She directs the Language, Culture, and Gender Lab, which involves students in research in the broad areas of language, culture, and gender within the field of psychology and specifically psychotherapy.

Feminist Liberation Practice with Latinx Women

Edited by
Lillian Comas-Díaz
and Carrie L. Castañeda-Sound

LONDON AND NEW YORK

First published 2024
by Routledge
4 Park Square, Milton Park, Abingdon, Oxon OX14 4RN

and by Routledge
605 Third Avenue, New York, NY 10158

Routledge is an imprint of the Taylor & Francis Group, an informa business

Introduction, Chapters 1–7 © 2024 Taylor & Francis
Conclusion © 2024 Lillian Comas-Díaz and Carrie L. Castañeda-Sound

All rights reserved. No part of this book may be reprinted or reproduced or utilised in any form or by any electronic, mechanical, or other means, now known or hereafter invented, including photocopying and recording, or in any information storage or retrieval system, without permission in writing from the publishers.

Trademark notice: Product or corporate names may be trademarks or registered trademarks, and are used only for identification and explanation without intent to infringe.

British Library Cataloguing in Publication Data
A catalogue record for this book is available from the British Library

ISBN13: 978-1-032-63260-5 (hbk)
ISBN13: 978-1-032-63261-2 (pbk)
ISBN13: 978-1-032-63262-9 (ebk)

DOI: 10.4324/9781032632629

Typeset in Minion Pro
by Newgen Publishing UK

Publisher's Note
The publisher accepts responsibility for any inconsistencies that may have arisen during the conversion of this book from journal articles to book chapters, namely the inclusion of journal terminology.

Disclaimer
Every effort has been made to contact copyright holders for their permission to reprint material in this book. The publishers would be grateful to hear from any copyright holder who is not here acknowledged and will undertake to rectify any errors or omissions in future editions of this book.

Contents

Citation Information   vii
Notes on Contributors   ix

Introduction: Feminist Liberation Practice with Latinx Women   1
Carrie L. Castañeda-Sound and Lillian Comas-Díaz

1. A *Mujerista* Liberation Psychology Perspective on *Testimonio* to Cultivate Decolonial Healing   9
Jesica Siham Fernández

2. Nepantla Moments in Therapy: A Clinical Example with Latinx Immigrants   35
Pilar Hernandez-Wolfe

3. Mujerista Psychology: A Case Study Centering Latinx Empowerment in Psychotherapy   53
Marlene L. Cabrera and Carrie L. Castañeda-Sound

4. Anti-Colonial Futures: Indigenous Latinx Women Healing from the Wounds of Racial-Gendered Colonialism   69
Nayeli Y. Chavez-Dueñas, Hector Y. Adames, and Jessica G. Perez-Chavez

5. Abolitionist Feminism, Liberation Psychology, and Latinx Migrant Womxn   85
Daniela Domínguez

6. The Connectivity Bridge – A Clinical Understanding: Postcolonial Therapy with Latinx Women Living in the United States   104
Carmen Inoa Vazquez

7. Why Am I A Woman? Or, Am I? Decolonizing White Feminism and the Latinx Woman Therapist in Academia   126
marcela polanco

Conclusion—Latinx Feminist Liberation Practices: Integration
and R/Evolution 147
Lillian Comas-Díaz and Carrie L. Castañeda-Sound

Index 153

Citation Information

The following chapters were originally published in the journal *Women & Therapy*, volume 45, issue 2–3 (2022). When citing this material, please use the original page numbering for each article, as follows:

Introduction

Feminist Liberation Practice with Latinx Women: Introduction to the Special Issue
Carrie L. Castañeda-Sound and Lillian Comas-Díaz
Women & Therapy, volume 45, issue 2–3 (2022), pp. 123–130

Chapter 1

A Mujerista *Liberation Psychology Perspective on* Testimonio *to Cultivate Decolonial Healing*
Jesica Siham Fernández
Women & Therapy, volume 45, issue 2–3 (2022), pp. 131–156

Chapter 2

Nepantla Moments in Therapy: A Clinical Example With Latinx Immigrants
Pilar Hernandez-Wolfe
Women & Therapy, volume 45, issue 2–3 (2022), pp. 157–174

Chapter 3

Mujerista Psychology: A Case Study Centering Latinx Empowerment in Psychotherapy
Marlene L. Cabrera and Carrie L. Castañeda-Sound
Women & Therapy, volume 45, issue 2–3 (2022), pp. 175–190

Chapter 4

Anti-Colonial Futures: Indigenous Latinx Women Healing from the Wounds of Racial-Gendered Colonialism
Nayeli Y. Chavez-Dueñas, Hector Y. Adames and Jessica G. Perez-Chavez
Women & Therapy, volume 45, issue 2–3 (2022), pp. 191–206

Chapter 5
Abolitionist Feminism, Liberation Psychology, and Latinx Migrant Womxn
Daniela Domínguez
Women & Therapy, volume 45, issue 2-3 (2022), pp. 207–225

Chapter 6
The Connectivity Bridge – A Clinical Understanding: Postcolonial Therapy with Latinx Women Living in the United States
Carmen Inoa Vazquez
Women & Therapy, volume 45, issue 2-3 (2022), pp. 226–247

Chapter 7
Why Am I A Woman? Or, Am I? Decolonizing White Feminism and the Latinx Woman Therapist in Academia
marcela polanco
Women & Therapy, volume 45, issue 2-3 (2022), pp. 248–268

For any permission-related enquiries please visit:
www.tandfonline.com/page/help/permissions

Notes on Contributors

Hector Y. Adames, Department of Counseling Psychology, The Chicago School of Professional Psychology, Chicago, IL, USA; Immigration, Critical Race, And Cultural Equity (IC-RACE) Lab, Chicago, IL, USA.

Marlene L. Cabrera, GSEP Department of Psychology, Pepperdine University, Los Angeles, CA, USA; Miller School of Medicine, Department of Neurology, University of Miami, Miami, FL, USA.

Carrie L. Castañeda-Sound, GSEP Department of Psychology, Pepperdine University, Los Angeles, California, USA.

Nayeli Y. Chavez-Dueñas, Department of Counseling Psychology, The Chicago School of Professional Psychology, Chicago, IL, USA; Immigration, Critical Race, And Cultural Equity (IC-RACE) Lab, Chicago, IL, USA.

Lillian Comas-Díaz, Department of Psychiatry and Behavioral Sciences, George Washington University, USA.

Daniela Domínguez, Counseling Psychology Department, University of San Francisco, San Francisco, CA, USA.

Jesica Siham Fernández, Ethnic Studies Department, Santa Clara University, Santa Clara, CA, USA.

Pilar Hernandez-Wolfe, Couple & Family Therapy Program, Lewis & Clark Graduate School of Education and Counseling, Portland, OR, USA.

Jessica G. Perez-Chavez, Immigration, Critical Race, And Cultural Equity (IC-RACE) Lab, Chicago, IL, USA; University of Wisconsin-Madison, Madison, WI, USA; Cambridge Health Alliance, Harvard Medical School, Boston, MA, USA.

marcela polanco, College of Education, San Diego State University, San Diego, CA, USA.

Carmen Inoa Vazquez, Columbia University, New York, NY, USA.

Introduction: Feminist Liberation Practice with Latinx Women

Carrie L. Castañeda-Sound and Lillian Comas-Díaz

ABSTRACT
This special issue synthesizes the interdisciplinary scholarship and clinical knowledge regarding the application of liberation psychology and feminist approaches with Latinx women. Embracing the approach of decolonization, the authors of this special issue center the intersectionality of Latinxs' identities and experiences and interrogate neocolonial practices that perpetuate marginalization. The articles address oppressive structural and systemic processes, share innovative frameworks and methods (e.g., *testimonios*) of feminist liberation practice, and give voice to narratives that have been erased or silenced.

Introduction

Feminist therapy and liberation psychology share several commonalities. These similarities include the development of critical thinking and a commitment to social change (Lykes & Moane 2009). Although feminist therapy is evolving, presently it does not address the specific needs of women of color and Global South women. To illustrate, mainstream feminist psychology is rooted in neocolonial legacies of hegemonic feminisms, and thus, it is complicit with neocolonial tendencies of hegemonic psychological science (Kurtiş & Adams, 2015). Therefore, Western feminists have been accused of supporting "imperial feminism," due to their unawareness of the effects of racism and imperialism in their assumption of an "international sisterhood" (Amos & Parmar, 1984). Likewise, Filomena Chioma Steady (1987) noted that the topic of racism is threatening to White feminists because it identifies them as possible participants in the oppression of African Americans.

Mainstream feminist scholarly practices tend to be inscribed in relations of power and implicitly support them (Mohanty, 1991). To illustrate, Kuumba (1994) argued that feminism does not address the conditions and struggles of the majority of the women in the world. She identified a serious concern when feminist therapists apply Western based approaches to the conditions and realities of oppressed women in the world. For instance, she argued that Global South women's issues, such as political subjugation, economic exploitation, and cultural domination, cannot be addressed through "women's issues" only. Therefore, Kuumba recommended the inclusion of a historical, dialectical analysis of women's oppression and liberation approaches into feminist practices. Likewise, Mohanty (1991) identified the need for Western feminists to develop strategic coalitions across class, race, and national boundaries. Along these lines, Kurtiş and Adams (2015) declared that feminist psychology is in need of being decolonized. Specifically, Macleod et al, (2020) identified guidelines for a feminist decolonial psychology as: (a) destabilize the patriarchal colonial heritage of mainstream psychological science, (b) connect coloniality of gender with other systems of power, such as globalization, (c) explore topics that connect the link of colonial and gendered power relations, (d) use research methods that fit with feminist decolonial psychology, and (e) focus on issues that enable decolonization.

Feminist liberation therapy emerged to address the needs of oppressed and Global South women. Specifically, feminist liberation therapists aim to examine the needs of marginalized women in the Global South, as well as the contexts of oppressed women in the Global North. Moreover, feminist liberation practices address decolonization, global, and transnational feminism issues (Kurtiş & Adams, 2015). Going beyond an integration of feminism and liberation, Mohanty (2003) stated that feminist liberation therapy is an interdisciplinary approach that expands the applications of emancipatory therapy, including areas such as cultural studies, feminism of color, indigenous healing, psychosocial interventions, and community approaches. Additionally, feminist liberation therapists use psychospirituality (Comas-Díaz, 2016) and artivism (art for the purpose of social justice) (Sandoval & LaTorre, 2008) among many other cultural practices. Indeed, artivism is an important expression of a feminist liberation decolonial practice because it reinterprets history with a critical lens toward Western modernity, due to modernity's androcentric, misogynistic, racist, and Eurocentric nature (Espinosa Miñoso, 2020).

Rooted in liberation psychology (Martín-Baró, 1994), feminist liberation psychologists are dissident daughters of Liberation Theology and as such, commit to holistic healing (Comas-Díaz, 2016). Consequently, feminist liberation therapy emerged from Latinx feminists' criticism of liberation psychology's neglect of Latinx and Global South womxn's issues. Grounded in feminisms of color, such as womanist, *mujerista* (Bryant-Davis & Comas-Díaz, 2016) and *womanista* (Global South feminism) (Chavez-Dueñas & Adames, 2021; Comas-Díaz & Bryant-Davis, 2016) orientations, feminist liberation practices emphasize the recovery of historical memory, decoloniality, interdisciplinarity, intersectionality, communality, social justice activism, solidarity with all oppressed people, transnationality (Enns et al., 2021), connection with the sacred, syncretistic spirituality (Comas-Díaz, 2014), and spiritual activism–social activism with a spiritual vision (Anzaldúa, 2002).

Feminist liberation therapists are in a unique position to address issues of oppressed females, such as racial and ethnic girls, women of color, women with disabilities, lesbian, bisexual, queer, and transgender individuals, poor, migrant, transnational girls and women, socioeconomically challenged women, and aged female populations. Since the number of liberation psychologists is growing (Comas-Díaz & Torres Rivera, 2020), we hope that so do feminist liberation therapists. Thus, feminist liberation practitioners have developed healing approaches beyond the confines of mainstream and feminist psychotherapy modalities. These methods include therapeutic and community healing approaches to address racism, gendered racism, gender-based violence, and structural inequality (Lykes & Moane, 2009), as well as xenophobia, economic exploitation, and sexual orientation marginalization. Specific examples of feminist liberation practices include *testimonio* (first account of people's experiences with oppression, marginalization, victimization, and trauma (Aron, 1992), *autohistoria* (artistic form of expressing one's history/story) (Anzaldúa, 1987, 2002), artivism, Photovoice (femalxs taking photos of their life experiences as an empowering technique) (Women of PhotoVoice/ADMI & Lykes, 2000), and participatory action research practices (Fals Borda & Rahman, 1991; Lykes & Távara, 2020), among others. Moreover, since feminist liberation approaches emphasize communalism and global solidarity, some of these practices include *promotoras* (Latinx women promoting health in their communities) (Lujan, 2009), Healing Circles (Richardson, 2018; Tubbs, 2020), Emotional Emancipation Circles, Spoken Word, Hip Hop, and other Latinx artivism examples (Comas-Díaz, 2019). These practices are inclusive, empowering, transformative, and social justice oriented. To achieve these goals, feminist liberation therapists are infused with global, postcolonial, and decolonial perspectives (Mohanty, 2003). As previously indicated, feminist liberation practitioners need to be fully engaged in the realities of a transnational world (Enns et al., 2021; Mohanty, 2003).

This special issue offers seven articles with diverse illustrations of feminist liberation therapy and healing, grounded in Latinx and Indigenous feminism. These include the voices of Latinxs who actively engage with communities as practitioners, researchers, educators, and/or advocates. All of the authors of this special issue illustrate the deleterious legacy of colonization on mental health and wellness and offer methods and conceptualizations with relevance to women in therapy. A common method and intervention utilized is *testimonio,* which involves personal and collective stories that are contextual, historical, and facilitate critical consciousness.

Testimonios also have relevance outside of clinical settings. Jesica S. Fernández' (2022) article "A *Mujerista* Liberation Psychology Perspective on *Testimonio* to Cultivate Decolonial Healing" incorporates testimonios with the central focus on Latinx womxn, but as a mujerista strategy in a pedagogical setting. This article provides a thorough description of the history and method of testimonios and offers insights to the power of testimonios to reflect current social issues, such as the disparate impact of the COVID-19 pandemic on Latinx communities. The testimonios discussed in the article address issues such as loss of life, loss of employment, and subsequent grief issues. The author explains that *testimonios* hold power and "… that when circulated or shared can contribute to supporting a sense of community, political action, and individual and collective healing" (p.6).

The *testimoniantes* (individuals sharing their stories) shed light on the layers of structural and intersectional forces at play in the lives of Latinx women during the pandemic. Oppression due to social class and documentation status are just two examples, yet they are juxtaposed with the power of radical hope to guide connection and healing through these testimonios.

Pilar Hernández-Wolfe's (2022) article "Nepantla Moments in Therapy: A Clinical Example with Latinx Immigrants" also uses *testimonios*, and she demonstrates healing within the context of feminist liberation psychology. Hernández-Wolfe integrates key concepts from *Epistemologies of the South* and *mujerista* psychology as the theoretical foundation of her clinical work. By co-creating *testimonios*, Hernandez-Wolfe identifies *nepantla* moments with a mother and her daughter in their therapeutic journey. Readers will find the (re)telling of their testimonios both informative and healing, as mother and daughter identify the intergenerational trauma that shaped their lives and relationships.

In "Mujerista Psychology: A Case Study Centering Latinx Empowerment in Psychotherapy," Marlene Cabrera and Carrie Castañeda-Sound also address familial conflict by using a case study to demonstrate how a Latinx client in her 20s navigates intergenerational demands and expectations that are informed by colonial constructs about race, gender and sexuality. The article demonstrates *mujerista* approaches that include reauthoring the life story, living out the *patrón*, envisioning transformation, embracing psycho-spirituality, and naming and engaging in *la lucha* (social justice). This article is a useful demonstration of how mujerista approaches can be applied to create a feminist liberation psychotherapy.

This special issue also includes innovative theoretical framing and recommendations to psychotherapists for working with Indigenous Latinx women. Nayeli Chavez-Dueñas, Hector Adames, and Jessica Perez-Chavez

2022 article "Anti-Colonial Futures: Indigenous Latinx Women Healing from the Wounds of Racial-Gendered Colonialism" incorporates Maya cosmology and the *Intersectionality Awakening Model of Womanista Treatment Approach* (I AM Womanista; Chavez-Dueñas & Adames, 2021). Throughout this article the authors center the history of indigenous Latinas that are often ignored or erased and highlight the resilience and resistance of Latinas in spite of racial-gendered colonialism. Offering guidance to psychotherapists about ways to integrate this ancestral knowledge in the client's journey toward liberation and healing, this article raises necessary conversations about the diversity of Latinas, liberation, and the naming of injustices. Critical to liberatory frameworks, the authors recommend that clinicians assist their clients to envision and work toward a future that "reflects their traditional indigenous culture and not the oppressors" (p. 12).

Daniela Domínguez continues the dialogue about liberation from structural oppression, but within the context of the immigration industrial complex (IIC). In the article titled "Abolition Feminism, Liberation Psychology, and Latinx Migrant Womxn in Detention," she uses the integrated lens of abolition feminism and liberatory frameworks to present a rich discussion of the multiple influences on migration of Latinx women to the United States (e.g., the legacy of U.S. foreign policy and capitalism), as well as gender-based violence, heterosexism, and transphobia. Finally, the author presents actions clinicians can take to resist oppressive legal and detention policies against Latinx immigrant populations. The reflection questions presented at different levels (e.g., individual, mutual aid, institutional, and policy) are a tangible springboard for engaging in community dialogues about prison abolition and liberation, particularly as they relate to Latinx migrant womxn, whose rates of detainment are increasing.

The experience of immigration is a central topic for the final two articles. In "The Connectivity Bridge-A Clinical Understanding: Postcolonial Therapy with Latinx Women Living in the United States," Carmen Inoa Vasquez shares insights about helping Latina immigrants and their descendants heal from intergenerational trauma related to migration. Her article reflects the work in her psychotherapy practice, and she specifically focuses on career women whose "success is not always enough to mitigate the negative effects and stressors brought by this experience" (p. 4). She shares a narrative of one of her clients, who is navigating the pressure to adhere to colonial gender specific behavioral expectations (i.e., *marianismo* and *machismo*), as well as other cultural values (i.e., familism, *orgullo*, and *simpatía*), while also contending with the effects of trauma from her migration.

The final article in this special issue is "Why Am I A Woman? Or, Am I? Decolonizing White Feminism and The Latinx Woman Therapist in

Academia." Sharing her personal narrative, marcela polanco (*this author writes her name in lower case letters*) broadens the lens to tackle postcolonial White feminism and the coloniality of gender and race within academia. Informed by Lugones' (2016) analysis of the "simultaneity of gender, race, capitalism, and Eurocentrism," polanco places herself within this analysis by navigating being the "Object" within academia and within the United States. Readers will also notice the unapologetic use of Spanglish in this article to convey her lived experience and as a lens to examine gendered language and linguistic hierarchy. Such a deliberate use of Spanglish is a conscious way of fighting linguistic terrorism—microaggressions against immigrants due to their accents and linguistic expressions (Anzaldúa, 1987) and as a decolonial and liberation act (Comas-Díaz, in press).

This special issue significantly expands the practice of feminist therapy by incorporating emancipatory, Indigenous, and feminism of color approaches. As such, it shares the perspectives and applications of feminist liberation and decolonial therapy with Latinx womxn. The contributing authors share innovative frameworks and methods of clinical practice, sociopolitical action, and training that exemplify the syncretism of feminism and liberation psychology, giving birth to a feminist liberation therapy. The articles draw from multidisciplinary, scholarly literature, as well as from the lived experience and *sabiduría* (wisdom) of Latinx womxn. The case studies and testimonios are a snapshot, or illustration, of what feminist liberation in therapy looks like and should not be prescriptive. These articles advance an understanding and conceptualization of feminist liberation with Latinx womxn that can inform the training of the next generation of practitioners and shed light on different ways of relating to Latinx clients for professionals in practice and for anyone interested in healing.

References

Anzaldúa, G. E. (1987). *Borderlands/La Frontera: The new Mestiza*. Spinster/Aunt Lute Publishers.

Anzaldúa, G. E. (2002). Now let us shift…the path of conocimiento…inner work, public acts. In G. E. Anzaldúa & AL. Keating (Eds.), *This bridge we call home: Radical visions for transformation* (pp. 540–570). Routledge.

Amos, V., & Parmar, P. (1984). Challenging imperial feminism. *Feminist Review*, 17(1), 3–19. https://doi.org/10.1057/fr.1984.18

Aron, A. (1992). *Testimonio*, a bridge between psychotherapy and sociotherapy. *Women & Therapy*, 13(3), 173–189. https://doi.org/10.1300/J015V13N03_01

Bryant-Davis, T. & Comas-Díaz, L. (Eds.). (2016). *Womanist and mujerista psychologies: Voices of fire, acts of courage*. American Psychological Association.

Cabrera, M., & Castañeda-Sound, C. (2022). Mujerista psychology: A case study centering Latinx empowerment in psychotherapy [Special Issue]. *Women & Therapy*.

Chavez-Dueñas, N. Y., & Adames, H. Y. (2021). Intersectionality awakening model of Womanista: A transnational treatment approach for Latinx women. *Women & Therapy*, *44*(1–2), 83–100. https://doi.org/10.1080/02703149.2020.1775022

Chavez-Dueñas, N. Y., Adames, H. Y., & Perez-Chavez, J. G. (2022). Anti-colonial futures: Indigenous Latinx women healing from the wounds of racial–gendered colonialism [Special Issue]. *Women & Therapy*.

Comas-Díaz, L. (2014). *La Diosa*: Syncretistic folk spirituality among Latinas. In T. Bryant-Davis, A. Austria, D. Kawahara, & D. Willis (Eds.), *Religion and spirituality for diverse women: Foundations of strength and resilience* (pp. 215–231). Praeger/Greenwood.

Comas-Díaz, L. (2016). Mujerista psychospirituality. In T. Bryant-Davis & L. Comas-Diaz (Eds.), *Womanist and mujerista psychologies: Voices of fire, acts of courage* (pp. 149–169). American Psychological Association.

Comas-Díaz, L. (2019). Latina Adolescents at the Cultural Borderlands. In T. Bryant-Davis (Ed.), *Multicultural feminist therapy: Helping adolescent girls of color to thrive* (pp. 155–187). American Psychological Association.

Comas-Díaz, L. (in press). *Decolonization: A personal manifesto*.

Comas-Díaz, L., & Bryant-Davis, T. (2016). Conclusion: Toward global womanist and mujerista psychologies. In T. Bryant-Davis & L. Comas-Diaz (Eds.), *Womanist and mujerista psychologies: Words of fire, acts of courage* (pp. 277–289). American Psychological Association.

Comas-Díaz, L., & Torres Rivera, E. (Eds.). (2020). *Liberation psychology: Theory, method, practice, and social justice*. American Psychological Association Press.

de Sousa Santos, B. (2017). *Epistemologies of the south: Justice against epistemicide*. Routledge/Taylor & Francis.

Domínguez, D. (2022) Abolition feminism, liberation psychology, and Latinx migrant womxn in detention [Special Issue]. *Women & Therapy*.

Enns, C. Z., Comas-Díaz, L., & Bryant-Davis, T. (2021). Transnational feminist theory and practice: An Introduction. *Women & Therapy*, *44*(1-2), 11–26. https://doi.org/10.1080/02703149.2020.1774997

Espinosa Miñoso, Y. (2020, July 1). Why we need decolonial feminism: Differentiation and constitutional domination in western modernity. *Afterall Articles*. https://www.afterall.org/article/why-we-need-decolonial-feminism-differentiation-and-co-constitutional-domination-of-western-modernit

Fals Borda, O., & Rahman, M. A. (1991). *Action and knowledge: Breaking the monopoly of power with participatory action research*. Intermediate Technology Publications; Apex Press. https://doi.org/10.3362/9781780444239

Fernández, J. S. (2022). A *mujerista* liberation psychology perspective on *testimonio* to cultivate decolonial healing [Special Issue]. *Women & Therapy*.

Hernández-Wolfe, P. (2022). Nepantla moments in therapy: A clinical example with Latinx immigrants. [Special Issue]. *Women & Therapy*.

Kuumba, M. B. (1994). The limits of feminism: Decolonizing women's liberation/oppression theory. *Race, Sex & Class*, *1*(2), 85–100. https://www.jstor.org/stable/41680222

Kurtiş, T., & Adams, G. (2015). Decolonizing liberation: Toward a transnational feminist psychology. *Journal of Social and Political Psychology*, *3*(1), 388–413. https://doi.org/10.5964/jspp.v3i1.326

Lujan, J. (2009). "Got Hispanic clients" Get a promotora? *The Internet Journal of Allied Health Sciences and Practice*, *7*(3), 4. https://nsuworks.nova.edu/ijahsp/vol7/iss3/4/

Lykes, M. B., & Moane, G. (2009). Editors' introduction: Whither feminist liberation psychology? Critical explorations of feminist and liberation psychologies for a globalizing world. *Feminism & Psychology*, *19*(3), 283–297. https://doi.org/10.1177/0959353509105620

Lykes, M. B., & Távara, G. (2020). Feminist participatory action research: Co-constructing feminist liberation praxis through dialogic relationality and critical reflexivity. In L. Comas-Díaz & E. Torres Rivera (Eds.), *Liberation psychology: Theory, method, practice, and social justice* (pp. 111–130). American Psychological Association. https://doi.org/10.1037/0000198-007

Macleod, C. I., Bhatia, S., & Liu, W. (2020). Feminisms and decolonizing psychology: Possibilities and challenges. *Feminism & Psychology*, *30*(3), 287–305. https://doi.org/10.1177/0959353520932810

Martín-Baró, I. (1994). *Writings for a liberation psychology: Ignacio Martín-Baró* (A. Aron & S. Corne, Eds. and Trans.). Harvard University Press.

Mohanty, C. T. (1991). Under western eyes: Feminist scholarship and colonial discourses. In C. Mohanty, A. Russo, & L. Torres (Eds.), *Third world women and the politics of feminism* (pp. 51–80). Indiana University Press. http://links.jstor.org/sici?sici=01903659%28198421%2F23%2912%3A3%3C333%3AESA%3E2.0.CO%3B2-Y

Mohanty, C. T. (2003). *Feminism without borders: Decolonizing theory, practicing solidarity.* Duke University Press.

polanco, m. (2022). Why am I a woman? Or am I? Decolonizing white feminism and the Latinx woman therapist in academia. [Special Issue]. *Women & Therapy*.

Richardson, J. L. (2018). Healing circles as black feminist pedagogical interventions. In O. Perlow, D. Wheeler, S. Bethea, and B. Scott (Eds.), *Black women's liberatory pedagogies: Resistance, transformation, and healing within and beyond the academy* (pp. 281–294). Macmillan. https://doi.org/10.1007/978-3-319-65789-9_16

Sandoval, C., & Latorre, G. (2008). Chicana/o artivism: Judy Baca's digital work with youth of color. In A. Everett (Ed.), *Learning, race, and ethnicity: Youth and digital media.* MIT Press.

Steady, F. C. (1987). African feminism: A worldwide perspective. In R. Terborg-Penn, S. Harley, & A. Benton (Eds.), *Women in African and the African diaspora* (pp. 3–14). Howard University Press.

Tubbs, S. (2020). *The Black girls healing circle workbook: A guide to healing through sisterhood & connection* (Vol. 1). Published Independently.

Vazquez, C. I. (2022). Postcolonial therapy with Latinx women living in the United States [Special Issue]. *Women & Therapy*.

Women of PhotoVoice/ADMI, & Lykes, M. B. (2000). *Voices e imagenes: Mujeres Mayas Ixsiles de Chajul/Voices and Images: Mayan Women of Chejul.* Guatemala Magna Terra.

A *Mujerista* Liberation Psychology Perspective on *Testimonio* to Cultivate Decolonial Healing

Jesica Siham Fernández

ABSTRACT
Grounded in a liberation psychology *mujerista* epistemology and a decolonial feminist standpoint, the article describes the development and application of *testimonio* as a resource toward healing. The application of this resource goes beyond the classroom to include clinical settings. By bridging Latin America liberation psychology within LatCrit theory, the article describes *testimonio* as a decolonial feminist *mujerista* strategy to cultivate decolonial healing through storytelling. Healing is conceptualized as a process of reconstituting the self, individually, relationally, and collectively, through life stories. Extending this definition, *decolonial healing* is experiencing community well-being through relational critically reflexive dialogues that facilitate a critical social analysis, mutual reciprocal recognitions, and radical hope. Building on evidence that identifies *testimonio* as a pedagogical and methodological tool, this article purports that the sociopolitical process of *testimoniar* can serve as a therapeutic *mujerista* strategy to support community well-being. The sociopolitical elements of *testimonio* toward decolonial healing experiences, as a potential therapeutic resource, are discussed through a thematic analysis of Latinx students' reflections featured in their *Testimoniando El Presente* essay assignment. *Testimonios* were conducted with their mothers, friends, siblings, or mentors and written within in the context of an online undergraduate course. Through an analysis of Latinx students' written reflections, evidence in support of *mujerista* strategies like *testimonio* that can complement existing decolonial practices and healing therapies are discussed. The conclusion offers an invitation to engage a *mujerista* epistemology, specifically adapting *testimonio* as a resource to support decolonial healing among Latinx students living in precarious times.

During the COVD-19 pandemic I have seen a vulnerable side to her. I was under the assumption that I knew my mom, but she has been my willing participant in various projects during my time in college. I now realized that I only knew my mother, not the woman who took on that role.

Adriana's reflection on Angela's *testimonio*[1]

> My mom was nervous when we began. I explained to her that this was just a conversation about her, not an interview or an assessment. She relaxed a bit and agreed to begin. While her face was at peace, her bouncing up and down on our yoga ball told me that all anxious feelings might not have left her body. My mom and I know each other's "tells." We know how to read each other sometimes better than we can read ourselves. Because of this shared understanding, I didn't expect to learn anything new in this conversation. I was happily surprised.
>
> Andrea's reflections on Elizabeth's testimonio

The social conditions that have ensued from the pandemic locate some of us in a state of grief. A heartache for the lives that have been lost, the physical connections that have been paused, and the projects and possibilities that were compromised or remain unrealized. At the same time, however, individuals and communities are striving to maintain well-being through personal and collective healing experiences, resources, and practices unique to themselves and their communities, traditions, and ancestral knowledge. As the opening epigraphs from Adriana's and Andreas' *testimonios* with their mothers, Angela and Elizabeth, illustrate: when we reveal, we heal. The original reference to this expression is credited to American performing artist and producer, Shawn Corey Carter, professionally known as Jay-Z, who in his song "Kill Jay Z" wrote the following lyric: "But you can't heal what you never reveal." Indeed, the subjective experiences of a person's life, the meaning they ascribe to their social condition in the face of distressing events, and how they leverage personal and relational resources to cultivate a sense of wholeness via the sharing of personal and political stories characterized as *testimonios*, supports a form of healing grounded in *mujerista* liberation psychology (Comas-Díaz, 2020) and a decolonizing standpoint (Cruz & Sonn, 2011; Fernández et al., 2021). Healing is a continuous process and practice of reconstituting the self through life stories or *testimonios* that incorporate experiences of struggle alongside a recognition of one's wholeness, sustained hope, and the transcendence of suffering or grief toward hope and possibility.

Healing is imperative to create radical transformative change. At its most fundamental meaning, healing is the experience of being seen and heard, of feeling and being connected to the self and others, and of experiencing mutual human recognitions that affirm relational radical hope (Chavez-Dueñas et al., 2019; French et al., 2020). While perceived as an individual experience, healing is a collective process and practice; it sustains personal and community well-being by catalyzing change or transformation at multiple levels from the micro to the systemic (Ginwright, 2011, 2015). The conceptual definition of *healing* that informs these claims are grounded in an understanding of healing as embodied, relational, and reflexive—as personal and communal.

Writing within the sociopolitical context of a global pandemic associated with COVID-19, and systemic structural inequities associated with racism, this article describes the use of *testimonio* in an undergraduate college online course to cultivate among Latinx students an experience toward decolonial healing grounded in *mujerista* liberation psychology. By analyzing Latinx student reflections, as written in their *Testimoniando El Presente* essay assignment (see Appendix A), I demonstrate the possibilities of utilizing *testimonio* as a resource to support decolonial healing. As Delgado Bernal et al. (2012) purport, "*testimonio* is a process (methodology), product (inclusive of text, video, performance, or audio), and a way of teaching and learning (pedagogy)" (p. 364). Thus, the resource described can be applied in various settings beyond the classroom; as a pedagogical and methodological tool to a form of clinical intervention. To engage *testimonio* as a *mujerista* liberatory sociopolitical therapeutic intervention is to surface, via the act of *testimoniar*, the personal, political, and social condition of people's lives toward the goal of supporting and cultivating decolonial healing experiences in precarious times.

Setting Intentions

COVID-19, along with the anti-Black racial violence that ensued in the summer of 2020 and the Black Lives Matter Movement that aims to achieve racial freedom, impress upon us the urgencies to transform our institutions in the direction of justice and liberation. A transformation that must uplift and affirm our interdependent humanity to coexist. To support the thriving, dignity, and well-being of communities living in conditions of persistent precarity and systemic marginalization—through collective action, consciousness raising, and challenging the coloniality of power (Mignolo, 2007) entrenched in the *status quo*—is to actualize the fullness of our shared humanity. The circumstances of inequity and disenfranchisement that COVID-19 unveiled and reproduced cannot be understated given its disproportionate impact on communities of color, especially Latinx communities (Fortuna et al., 2020; García et al., 2020). The social, political, and economic conditions that surfaced in relation to COVID-19 underscore the human crisis we found (and still find) ourselves in. Relatedly, it beckons the need to resist individual and collective succumbing to a "new normal." Racism, structural violence, and economic inequity, which contribute to precarious living conditions, should never be normalized nor accepted. If normalized, we risk and compromise the possibilities of experiencing transformative justice and radical systemic change, which are urgently necessary to live well and fully. When we default to normalizing our social condition or place metaphorical blinders around that which we are called to bear witness and listen to but choose not to, possibilities toward self and collective healing are futile.

Therefore, by employing a *mujerista* liberation psychology perspective to reflect and draw connections or threads across Latinx students' *testimonios*, I highlight the nuances, complexities, and contrapuntal voices that each *testimonio* made visible. I describe *testimonio* as a strategy and necessary resource that can be adapted beyond the pedagogical domain. Centering a *mujerista* liberation psychology perspective, I analyze some excerpts from Latinx students' *Testimoniando El Presente* essay assignment to engage with the themes of the special issue on *Feminist Liberation Practice* in the journal *Women & Therapy*. Relatedly, I respond to two interconnected questions that align with these themes: *How do Latinx students engage testimonio as a resource to make visible individual and collective challenges? How does testimonio, aligned with mujerista liberation psychology, facilitate or support an experience toward decolonial healing?* Although the examples draw from the pedagogical elements and outcomes of *testimonio* in an online classroom, I purport that the relational dialogic critical reflexivity that *testimonio* facilitates complements existing decolonial practices and healing therapies within and outside of the classroom space.

The guiding intentions for this article are to demonstrate how *testimonio* as a *mujerista* strategy supports decolonial healing. To build support for this proposal, in what follows I first and foremost honor the work of Latina feminist scholars who engage in *mujerista*, *feminista* traditions of *testimoniar* (Latina Feminist Group, 2001; Moraga & Anzaldua, 1983). Then, I offer a few excerpts from Latinx students' *Testimoniando El Presente* essay assignment to illustrate the power of listening-feeling-witnessing-connecting through story-like statements unique to *testimonio*. I conclude with an invitation, an offering in the form of prompts or guiding questions, to animate deeper critical reflexivity among readers—educators, therapists, healers, health and wellness practitioners, and activist-teacher-scholars. Crafted in the spirit and intention of offering a humanizing resource, it is my hope that the present article can help direct us in efforts to actualize *el buen vivir* (living well) (Ciofalo, 2018; Viera, 2013) via a *mujerista* tradition, like *testimonio*, that has sustained Latinx communities in their pursuits to imagine and forge more humanizing, liberatory just ways of being, living, and experiencing the world.

A *Mujerista* Liberation Psychology Perspective on *Testimonio*

Testimonio is part of a long tradition of feminist storytelling. Grounded in a Latina *feminista* perspective, *testimonio* is a strategy for survivance, resistance, and refusal rooted in Indigenous traditions and Latin American social movements that birthed LatCrit theory and liberation psychology. By Centering Latin America liberation psychology within a decolonial feminist framework, *testimonio* is a *feminista*, specifically a *mujerista* strategy (Comas-Díaz, 2020) that communities have engaged to cultivate healing through storytelling. Prior scholarship attests to the power of *testimonio* as a healing, restorative, and therapeutic practice (Booker, 2002; Chang, 2016; Cienfuegos & Monelli, 1983), as well as a political activism tool to support struggles for justice and liberation (Angueira, 1988; Brabeck, 2003; Pérez Huber, 2009; Silva et al., 2021; Smith, 2010). Building on the well-documented evidence that purports *testimonio* as both a political strategy and therapeutic intervention, I describe *testimonio* through a *mujerista* liberation psychology perspective.

A *mujerista* framework, grounded in the work of feminist Cuban American theologian Ada María Isasi-Díaz (1989, 1994), purports that liberation is a praxis of critically reflexive action: "*mujeristas* will always insist on the need to be actively involved, in the reflective moment of praxis. Without reflection there is no critical awareness, no conscientization, and therefore no possibility of self-definition and liberation" (1989, p. 560). Underscoring the importance of critical reflexivity *as* and *in* action, or a process of de-ideologization (Martín-Baró, 1994), *testimonio* is active, intentional, and relational. *Testimonio* is a process that aims to reclaim experiences, as it recovers or surfaces stories. The Latina Feminist Group, in their edited anthology *Telling to Live: Latina Feminist Testimonios* (2001), use the metaphor of *papelitos guardados* (hidden papers) to describe the unspoken and often silenced stories that hold a significance and value in someone's life. The *papelitos guardados*, the stories that are kept, held, and unheard, are often those yearning to be vocalized and rendered visible. When shared or brought to the surface in a public and affirming context, via relational dialogues, writings, and poetry for example, *testimonios* support the process of cultivating connection and the capacity to experience individual and collective well-being by being in relationship with others. *Testimonio* facilitates the experience of reciprocal recognitions through bearing witness to someone's story of struggle, radical hope, and *sobrevivencia* (survivance, thriving). The *testimonio* illustrate the centrality of cultivating a human connection via stories that honor another person's experience or the fullness of their subjective embodied being.

As an oral tradition that values the power of spoken word, *testimonio* must be understood as a *mujerista* liberation psychology praxis. *Testimonio* is anchored in a sociocultural, embodied, and political practice of (re)telling that allows for pluriversality, as well as multidisciplinary sociohistorical and transnational connections. The stories that are felt in and through the body offer a powerful human rendering of someone's life in a specific moment

(Moraga & Anzaldua, 1983). The self-storying that fosters relationality and connection, through engaging in critical reflexivity with others, can facilitate individual and collective opportunities toward healing. The re-telling of stories is a purposeful and intentional experience that re-humanizes because it renders visible the pain, alongside the desire to heal and transform through collective action. Moreover, the relational mutuality that is fostered through stories, like *testimonios*, can support a sense of community, which is necessary to experience well-being (Chavez-Dueñas et al., 2019; Comas-Díaz, 2006). To remember, resist, and re-exist *with* and *among* others is to honor the power of the word; specifically, the stories that circulate to actualize transformative conditions *of* and *for* liberation.

Testimonio, unlike other oral or narrative approaches, is active, intentional, and relational because it aims to recover, reclaim, and relive experiences that could likely be left untold or silenced. Stories as *testimonios* that when circulated or shared can contribute to supporting a sense of community, political action, and individual and collective healing. Publicly voicing one's story—by sharing, telling, and expressing these in the presence of another person or a collective—can be a liberatory experience because the pain and suffering associated with a struggle is no longer reduced to the private, individual domain. In this way, the story is heard, the person is seen, and the emotion is shared and felt. *Testimonio* is or becomes a collective moment of affirmation and a relational experience that humanizes against a backdrop of structural violence.

The method, process, and practice of *testimoniar* through stories offers an opportunity for deep and meaningful learning that can cultivate modes of being toward healing. *Testimonio* therefore facilitates what Frantz Fanon (1967) described as reciprocal recognitions through bearing witness to someone's story of struggle, resistance, dreams, and *sobrevivencia*. To engage *testimonio* as a methodology is to document via stories the personal, social, and political social conditions of people's lives (Beverley, 2000; Espino et al., 2012; Pérez Huber, 2009; Silva et al., 2021). Beyond a pedagogical tool for learning, however, *testimonio* can serve as resource to support healing processes because it invites the listener and the storyteller to reveal their truths, how they have come to understand themselves and their social condition, along with the pain and possibilities for radical hope-in-action associated with the pursuit of liberation, especially of existing unburned by social suffering.

The storytelling that circulates within and through *testimonio* can support a process of decolonial healing that is grounded in radical hope and re-humanizing encounters with the potential to heal by restoring a sense of community and wholeness. The centrality of cultivating a human connection that honors another person's story, and their whole being, reflects *mujerista* liberation psychology perspective. *Testimonios* are stories that center the self in connection with past and present communities in struggle within the sociohistorical political experiences that when considered as whole can offer a source of affirmation that can begin the journey toward healing (Chavez-Dueñas et al., 2019)—and, as this article purports, decolonial healing. Related to the concept of decolonial love (Maldonado-Torres, 2008; Sandoval, 2000), decolonial healing is a relational process guided by the stories told and witnessed, past and present, and those yet to be that render people as capable of cultivating their own modes of healing within the complexities of their existence. Decolonial healing, as a form of sociopolitical well-being, is possible—fully sensed, experienced, and sustained individually and collectively—through relationships threaded and interlaced *through* and *with* stories that surface challenges and struggles alongside reciprocal recognitions that sustain radical hope-in-action. *Testimonio* can serve as a valuable pedagogical resource toward healing because it allows both the listener and the storyteller to reveal their truths, how they have come to understand themselves and their social condition, along with the pain and radical hope associated with their experiences.

Reflexivity on Pedagogy in the Context of COVID-19

Throughout most of my experiences as an educator, I have approached teaching-learning as a relational decolonial humanizing praxis. My purpose as an educator and learner are to help cultivate and co-create with my students a learning community of reciprocal recognitions of our knowledge and experiences and a sociopolitical consciousness that fosters radical hope and imagination. These were the principles and values that guided the online learning community I co-developed with my students and what we experienced over the course of two quarters in response to swift shift and transition to online learning that ensued under COVID-19. The institutional pedagogical response to COVID-19, however, challenged pedagogical praxis to be more purposeful and intentional about fostering students' well-being alongside their academic thriving. The institutional pressures to adapt courses to meet the demands and urgencies of the university, without fully considering the needs, voices, and concerns of the students, made palpable the neoliberalization of higher education. Amidst these circumstances, I found myself listening to the stories of the many students who were concerned, anxious, and overcome with deep grief over the loss of their college experiences and graduations and the challenges of learning online with limited resources and support.

The up-rootedness and disconnect many students experienced with having to return home, or in some cases not having a home to return to, amplified their concerns and already compromised well-being. Many students, especially Latinx and first-generation college-going, were forced to leave their university housing within an unreasonably short period of time. The lack of institutional guidance and support on how to manage the multiple responsibilities compromised the well-being of students and their families. Without a recourse, some students blended their academics with family responsibilities from caring for ill parents, supporting siblings academically, and tending to the needs of immediate and extended family. Some Latinx students became sole providers and wage earners for their families when a parent, or parents, became unemployed or ill. Listening openly to students' stories of loss and longing, while centering healing as part of our learning, guided and informed my development of the course.

Testimonio Assignment Description and Implementation

The *Testimoniando El Presente* essay assignment was incorporated in my *Chicanx/Latinx Communities* (ETHN 122) online course offered in the 2020 spring and 2021 winter quarters. The assignment provided students with an opportunity to engage in relationally critically reflexive dialogues through the process and method of testimonio. Specifically, the assignment encouraged students to hold space for a member of their family or community to reflect and give voice to their experiences in relation to the pandemic, as well as critical reflexivity via dialogues and a critical sociopolitical analysis of the challenges that were unfolding for them and within their communities in the context of the pandemic and ensuing racial and economic injustices. Students were encouraged to identify a friend, family, or community member with whom they have rapport and to engage them in a dialogue about how they were experiencing COVID-19. Prioritizing the *testimoniantes,* health and well-being were central to this assignment. Therefore, students were given the ten week duration of the quarter to mindfully discern when, how, and with whom they would engage in *testimonio*. To further support this process, the description and guidelines for the assignment were provided to students early in the quarter. This allowed students sufficient time to engage in *testimonio*, provide me with drafts or outlines for feedback on their essay, and then write and share the final assignment with the *testimoniante*.

The structure and format of the assignment submitted by each student varied. For example, some students submitted essays written in the first person, while others were in the third person. Most all assignments featured student threaded reflections, responses, and analyses of the *testimonios*. Where appropriate, relevant literature in LatCrit theory, Latinx Studies, and Critical Race and Ethnic Studies, as well as decolonial feminist theory were referenced. Of most significance was observing students' own stories and experiences being threaded and connected to the *testimoniantes* story. In addition to writing up a reflection in relation to the *testimoniantes' testimonio*, students were encouraged to critically reflect on the experience of witnessing or intentionally listening-connecting to a person's story. Because of this, most students opted to connect with a friend, while others sought out community members and mentors. The majority of the students engaged a family member, specifically a parent or sibling however. Latina students engaged *testimonio* with their mothers, thus supporting the *feminista* tradition that characterizes the process of *testimoniar desde y con el corazón* (to testify from and with the heart).

Based on these student critical reflections, I purport that *testimonio* holds implications beyond pedagogy and methodology. *Testimonio* can be adapted and utilized at a strategy, tool, or resource to cultivate mutual recognitions and radical hope that can help cultivate healing toward restored or sustained well-being. This became most evident a few weeks into the spring quarter when the cumulative impact of the murders of George Floyd, Breonna Taylor, and Ahmaud Arbery and the response and mobilizing by the Black Lives Matter Movement led students to experience extreme levels of stress, anxiety, and racial trauma that further compromised their overall health and well-being. In what follows, I offer selected excerpts from Latinx students' essays to illustrate how *testimonio*, grounded in *mujerista* liberation psychology, can help support experiences toward decolonial healing.

Testimonio as a *Mujerista* Strategy to Cultivate Decolonial Healing

Testimonio, grounded in a *mujerista* tradition of "telling to live,"—of narratives for storying the self—can be adapted and leveraged as a resource to foster individual and collective decolonial healing. By highlighting selected excerpts from students' *Testimoniando El Presente* essay assignment, I demonstrate the possibilities of making space in the classroom for healing through a heart-centered pedagogy. The *testimonio* excerpts I offer are those from students who granted me permission and *confianza* (trust, confidence) to include some of their excerpts. Request for inclusion in this article were made only to Latinx students who fulfilled all assignment requirements and, in some cases, exceeded the expectations by writing longer reflections and analyses that incorporated additional resources beyond those provided in relation to the course. At times, students offered their own reflections in relation to and in connection with the person's *testimonio*. By centering the reflexive relational stories offered as *testimonios*, as well as students' experiences and process of fostering and experiencing a sense of relationality, I purport stories are and can be fundamental resource toward healing that can sustain well-being. I feature some of these *testimonio* excerpts without paraphrasing, redaction, or stylistic edits to center and honor the voice of the *testimoniante*. In reviewing some of the *testimonios*, I discerned three experiences associated with healing: critical social analysis, mutual recognitions, and radical hope. For each one, I offer a description, followed by excerpts from students' assignments, to demonstrate how *testimonio* was utilized to support decolonial healing.

Critical Social Analysis

The capacity to understand how social problems are entrenched in systems and structures of inequity where power and privilege circulate to further marginalize certain communities or limit opportunities characterizes a critical social analysis. Some of the individuals that students engaged in *testimonio* offered a critique of COVID-19 that made visible their frustrations and challenges. Most importantly, however, these critiques were offered through a critical social analysis of the situation they found themselves in and how it tied to other conditions of injustice. In effect, the social conditions under COVID-19 significantly altered the living, working, and well-being of some students' closest family members and friends whom they engaged in *testimonio*.

The impact of COVID-19 on employment and working conditions was identified in the *testimonios* that two students, Adriana and Chris, documented. Adriana's reflections of her *testimonio* with Angela, her mother, makes palpable the challenges of the moment and trying to make a living under COVID-19, especially when unemployed. The absence of formal employment did not minimize the amount of labor some people experienced, however. In fact, some were tasked with taking on additional roles and responsibilities that far exceed their capacities, as Adriana reflects in witnessing a *testimonio* with Angela, her mother:

> My mother is a Mexican immigrant who has been in the United States for the past 23 years, she is now 42. She said: "*He estado aquí 32 años y sigo siendo low income*" (I've been here 32 years and I'm still low income). Like other immigrants, my family came to the United States in pursuit of the very elusive American Dream, an opportunity at a better life. Now she is unemployed, no longer waking up at 4 am to get to her shift in time, then coming home to do household work. Under COVID-19, the weight on her shoulders has not lifted; instead, it has intensified. I asked her if there were any challenges she encountered because of COVID-19, and I could tell that she was frustrated: "*Es difícil por que uno no esta preparada para ser maestra, mamá, y aparte sin poder trabajar. En estos momentos todo tu trabajo dura no sirve para nada por que el gobierno no nos ayuda [no les importa] que todos tengamos necesidades*" (It is difficult because no one is prepared to be a teacher, a mother, and yet be unable to work outside [the home]. Right now all my hard work is useless because the government doesn't help us [they don't care] that we all have needs.)

Angela articulates the challenges of having her responsibilities for caring and providing for her family being magnified under COVID-19. She underscores how these conditions are disproportionately impacting those whom are unemployed. Angela views this as rooted in the structure, the system of government, that inequitably allocates and limits resources, while leaving other families and communities in dire conditions of precarity and economic instability.

Diana's *testimonio* with her daughter Gaby similarly expressed the concerns that Angela described for her family's thriving. In describing their living circumstances and how Diana is applying her skills in innovative and creative ways to sustain her family financially, Gaby begins the *testimonio* by describing her mother's actions:

> Holding a turquoise piece of fabric on one hand, and the other holding a thread and needle, Diana sewed a white yarn into the edges of the fabric as we commenced our discussion. I began by asking what sheltering in place has looked like for her so far. "*I have been making face masks, gardening, looking for ways to earn money like doing the taxes or seeing what help the government is offering,*" she said. My father lost his job as a school bus driver due to the pandemic, leaving my mother concerned for our family's financial well-being. When asked what specific concerns she had in mind, Diana responded, "*that my husband will not get his job. I worry he will get sick and end up in the hospital.*" Despite this, Diana remains hopeful and with a positive attitude, even though adapting to a new routine at home brings challenges of its own.

Diana's husband, who is Gaby's father, like Adriana's mother has become unemployed because of COVID-19. With limited resources and opportunities to seek new employment opportunities in labor industries and sectors, Diana has had to develop new means of providing for her family. To minimize the contagion of COVID-19 that would compromise the health and well-being of people at a greater health and mortality risk, Diana has become an entrepreneur, crafting an independent source of income to modestly contribute to the family. Diana has applied her skills in sewing and gardening, among other activities, to help sustain her family's economic needs and well-being. While the concerns for their health are present and palpable, these fears and worries do not seem to limit Diana's perseverance. The critical social analysis that Diana's *testimonio* illustrates is characterized by her capacity to adapt to a challenging circumstance. At the same time she also garners the persistence, patience, and optimism to direct her skills and knowledge in the service of supporting her family's needs.

Unlike Angela and Diana, whom have had to adapt to new forms of living and coping with circumstances of familial unemployment, conditions exacerbated under COVID-19, other responsibilities emerged for some *testimoniantes* who were employed. Chris, in documenting Ester's *testimonio*, described how additional forms of labor and responsibilities have developed, some with their unique and pressing demands. For some people who are employed, they are often faced with specific challenges associated with their work, as Chris' *testimonio* with Ester, his mother, illustrates. In reflecting upon Ester's *testimonio*, Chris writes:

> My mom brought light to the fact that many aspects of her life have changed completely. She is constantly on Zoom meeting after Zoom meeting even outside of her class period because every day brings new direction from the school district. […] Being creative and having an energetic personality she thought she could use Tik Tok, the ultra-popular social media app, to keep students engaged in class materials. […] When she proposed a similar method through Tik Tok the school shut her idea down.

Ester's innovation and creativity to adapt to the new conditions of her work environment as a teacher and to support student learning characterizes her critical social analysis of the shifting landscapes of education, especially the transition to online teaching. Yet when attempting to introduce a new idea or curriculum that could encourage student engagement, she expressed disappointment with the lack of support by the school's administration and leadership. For Ester, as similarly noted by Angela, the social structure limits her capacity to innovate, adapt, and leverage resources in support of her community of students. This was differentially experienced by Diana who was not formerly employed, however she innovated ways of making financial ends meet. Ester's keen awareness of this institutional challenge characterized her critical social analysis, which Chris was able to demonstrate and reflect upon by rendering her *testimonio*.

The critical social analysis some *testimoniantes* engaged in also involved an awareness of the impact of COVID-19 on students' academic engagement, especially when parents' or a caretaker's health was compromised. Jennifer, in her *testimonio* with Chaley, highlighted the challenges that she's experienced as an educator having to support students' learning, as well as their overall sense of well-being. Specifically, supporting students whose economic family conditions led to them becoming unhoused. Beyond being a teacher, Jennifer had to step into the role of an advocate to help her student's family gain access to housing and other necessary resources. In quoting Jennifer's *testimonio*, Chaley offered the following reflection:

> Jennifer and I also talked about the direct impact of COVID-19 on her students. Sadly, she told me that since most of her students live in the East Side of San Jose, which is still a current hotspot for COVID-19 that hearing stories of new cases from her co-workers and students weekly is common. The problem with this is that most of the students that contract COVID-19 are usually in a household where all have the virus. She notices that once they're infected that their *"success level completely drops off."* What makes this hard is the school's schedule; in order for it to feel less stressful, a class is only given twice a week. Therefore, if a student misses two classes, they're a week behind schedule and they're missing out on a lot of material that will

help them become successful. Then, Jennifer told me that a family impacted by COVID-19 are now homeless because they lost their jobs. Thankfully, the school is working hard on supporting the family as much as they can.

Students' academic experiences with online learning must be contextualized within living conditions and environments where students are located. The students' living conditions that Jennifer described are characteristic of some immigrant Latinx families in low-income and working-class communities, where often more than one family is occupying one housing space. In such compact spaces, it is challenging to engage in social distancing or to isolate someone that has become infected with the virus. This, when combined with the economic precarity several families were already experiencing, furthers stressful environments that amplify the academic disengagement of students. Clearly, it is difficult to fully engage as a student when a parent or love one's health is compromised, when economic instability is experienced, and when one's living situation is altered substantially to the point of becoming unhoused. All of these conditions, however, are entrenched within the inequitable institutional structures, like health care and labor, that do not provide adequate resources and support to immigrant families. Jennifer's critical social analysis of the lack of resources and support provided to certain communities, especially families in the East Side of San Jose, is evident in the disproportioned number of people that have tested positive and have lost their lives to COVID-19. The decreased "success level" that Jennifer observed among her students cannot be decontextualized from the environments that students find themselves in.

Together, the concerns that Angela, Diana, Ester, and Jennifer described in their *testimonios* exemplify the circumstances that unfolded under COVID-19. Each of their *testimonios* demonstrated their critical social analysis as they contextualized the challenges and problems they were experiencing within the structures of power that led to inequities and an unjust, unfair outcome wherein each of them was located. This point was clearly and explicitly made in Katya's *testimonio*:

> Systems not people … Rather than criminalizing undocumented people, free health clinics, like Community Health, are taking community care into their own hands while recognizing the flaws and exclusivity of our health care system.

As workers, caretakers, providers, and human beings—mothers, friends, and teachers—they witnessed and reflected upon the inequities under COVID-19 in their classrooms, homes, and families. In bearing witness to these injustices and inequities, some *testimoniantes*, like Jennifer's, mobilized resources and advocated to provide support to students and their families.

Mutual Recognitions

The experience of witnessing and offering a *testimonio* can be affirming and empowering. *Testimonio* can facilitate a sense of community and guide communities toward organizing and engaging in collective action. These are likely and rather common outcomes of *testimonio* that can inspire efforts and actions toward social change. Yet there are other outcomes that might surface in the process of listening and voicing *testimonio*. The feeling of vulnerability of exposing one's deepest concerns is an outcome of engaging in *testimonio* that can open up the person to unhealed wounds or more pain. Healing as the transcendence of suffering from pain necessitates opening the self, including the sources of pain or grief. When we reveal, we heal, and this contributes to experiences of *being* and *becoming* or feeling whole again and to experience validation through mutual recognition. To be seen and heard is to be recognized. Indeed, to experience mutuality by being understood by another person can be incredibly validating and affirming. The experience of mutual recognitions is in and of itself the act of *testimoniar*, to be a part of a reflexive relational dialogue with another person whose story of pain and joy can be received, and met with humane compassion and care.

In students' *testimonio* excerpts, mutual recognitions surfaced in the process of engaging the assignment. Such experiences were described in the *testimonio* reflections provided by Karla, Adriana, and Andrea. Karla's *testimonio* with her mother, for example, made visible her concern over their family's well-being, and more generally Latinx communities, especially those who are working-class and undocumented. This was a similar concern that was expressed by Diana. Noting the difficulties in responding to her question, Karla quotes her mother's remarks and follows up with a reflection that renders visible their mutual recognition:

> "… because we're [a mixed-status family], life is hard. You know the work that I do, and the work that your dad does. It's not easy, but it's necessary. And it's the only option. So, keep studying and one day you'll be able to help us." At this point while she was saying this, I teared up a little. It always hurts to think of all the silent sacrifices they make each and every day that they don't tell us about. It makes me think about how drastically different my brother's life and mine are.

Through this *testimonio*, Karla acknowledges the challenges of being working-class and an immigrant in a mixed-status family. Karla honors the sacrifices that her parents have made, and in doing so, she also comes to realize how significantly different her life is and has been compared to her mother's. Despite the circumstances unfolding under COVID-19, Karla is able to acknowledge that the resilience that her mother exudes is one that has remained with her as an immigrant in the United States. The resilience that is captured in Karla's mothers' words and subsequently reflected upon characterizes their mutual recognition as mother and daughter.

The expression of mutual recognition was similarly described in Oliveya's *testimonio* with her friend, Katya, who when asked to share her hopes and dreams for the future stated:

> So, I dream to get everyone in touch with their bodies and making the earth the body. I dream to disrupt all individualism, disrupting the idea that we are separate from the earth, disrupting the idea that we are better than someone because that someone somehow was born darker or placed in jail, understanding that those people are just as good as us and those people are us. I think radical knowing that we are all on the same boat, on the same planet, of the same planet. I feel like every time people ask me this question, I think of something different but right now I think our future is in the children. I have seen so many people that are afraid of being creative because they're afraid to fail but failure is a part of life, we need to fail. That's why I love dancing and falling or surfing and falling, I love learning new things because I fail, and my body must learn that that's okay because in school you don't learn that ever. I dream for everyone to be in the dirt, in poetry, in their bodies, everyone seeing each other, actually seeing each other.

Explicit in Katya's *testimonio* is the need, the urgency to experience one's body, to feel connected to all things living and being, and to experience fully a mutual recognition of failure or pain that can lead toward healing, connection, and living fully. What Katya describes characterizes decolonial healing as a process and a practice of experiencing a sense of wholeness, connectivity, and community with the self and with others and to strive to repair that which has been wounded and harmed toward the actualizing of self and collective dignity and well-being. To see one's life as threaded and connected to the lives of others, of those we may not know personally, but whose pain and loss we hold, is an act of mutual recognition. In other words, it is a form of solidarity that is deeper than critical empathy; it is a humanizing encounter.

The humanizing experiences of mutual recognition that Katya described was also echoed by Andrea's mother. Andrea in her *testimonio* with Elizabeth, who like Ester and Jennifer is also a teacher, describes the challenges of being an educator. Through Elizabeth's *testimonio*, Andrea describes how her mother saw her Latinx identity as a Latina educator summon her to take on the responsibility of creating more equitable educational opportunities for her students, similar to Ester. Andrea documents Elizabeth's words:

> When asked what Latinx meant for her in this time, she said: "*It means that I have a responsibility to help my Latinx students. I understand their living situations. I know that some kids are crammed in small spaces. I can be flexible. It's easy for me to have empathy with them.*" My mom has a connection to these students, having shared lived experiences and common cultural practices. This mutuality is something she

always calls on in her teaching, whether in her classroom or from home via Zoom. Without naming *testimonio*, my mom is utilizing this pedagogy by ensuring that her identity and experiences are present in her teaching. What my mom is doing is transformative. She is a Latinx educator who connects with, advocates for, and shows love to Latinx students.

By witnessing, going beyond merely listening to her mother's pedagogical practice, Andrea identifies the mutual recognitions that her mother engaged when she's teaching. Andrea characterizes Elizabeth's pedagogy as rooted in a sociocultural understanding of Latinx students' lives. Engulfed in her teachings are values of care, compassion, and commitment to students' learning, practices that Andrea was able to contextualize and complement through Elizabeth's *testimonio*. Listening to her mother's reflections of what it means to be Latinx and a Latinx educator in this moment underscores Andrea writings that attest to the mutual recognition she holds for her mother. Similarly, these are the mutual recognitions that Elizabeth and Jennifer engaged in with their students, which reflect the essence of *testimonio*. To engage *testimonio* is to be seen, to be heard, and to belong.

Within Latinx communities, and specifically Chicanx, the concept of "*in lak'ech*" has figured prominently in poetry, literature, popular culture, and quotidian expressions. *In lak'ech*, an expression that Chicano playwright Valdez made known in an excerpt from his poem, *Pensamiento Serpentino* (1994) has come to signify precisely what the theme of mutual recognitions exemplifies. That is, you are my other me, *tu eres mi otro yo*. This mutuality, the reciprocal human recognition of being one with the other, is what Adriana described when reflecting on her mother's *testimonio*, writing and reflecting on their relationality she states:

> My mom calls me "*mamá*" and I call her "*mami*", to me this is a sign of respect and love. She sees me as an individual but also as an incarnation of her. She has bestowed on me her trust, her love, and the responsibility to care for my siblings. [...] I am her and she is me, the concept of *in lak'ech* is one that I hope to abide by, as my mom has done so much for me that I could only hope to advocate for her, my community, and womxn who share similar stories.

The indivisibility that Adriana describes with her mother, Angela, reflects an important dimension of *testimonio*, which is seeing ourselves as being connected to and equally seen and heard by another. To presume that by listening to someone's *testimonio* we are passive is to misunderstand the significance of *testimonio* as a pedagogical and political tool and most of all as a valuable resource toward experiences for decolonial healing. To witness, not as a spectator or observer, but rather as a fellow companion, an accomplice, *un acompañante* is to allow one to connect, lean in, and be invited into one's life and knowing. The invitation to open and connect is one of vulnerability and of possibility for connections and bridging that can likely heal and transform conditions of oppression. This is possible when we are in the presence of those whom we love and come to love and embrace as fellow beings regardless of our kinship. It is in the experience of mutual human recognition where we can experience a feeling of oneness, the relational embodiment of *in lak'ech*.

Radical Hope

Cultivating opportunities for connection are fundamental to building a collective memory that can serve as an antidote against hopelessness. In an edited anthology, featuring writers, activists, and artists, De Robertis (2017) characterizes hope as an experience of remembering the past to recognize or make meaning of the present as one imagines new opportunities and possibilities for the future. By simultaneously reflecting on the past, yet reimagining toward the future, people are able to cultivate the optimist and agency to leverage their resources, such as their community's strengths and assets, and to bring about change conducive to supporting individual and collective healing (Chavez-Dueñas et al., 2019; Mosley et al., 2020). Envisioning something other than what is painfully experienced as oppressive is essential to developing what Ginwright (2008, 2011) describes as radical hope.

Testimonios, because of their relational and introspective elements, can facilitate the process of critically reflecting in order to envision, imagine, and dream anew. The shared experiences for mutual recognition and understanding, which *testimonio* facilitates, can lead to a sense of community that can restore health and healing. The experience of decolonial healing among Latinx students and *testimoniantes* was characterized by moments where relational critical reflexivity was possible. In turn, this sparked radical hope among them, evidenced in some of the reflections Latinx students offered in relation to the *testimonios* they documented. Maria, for example, when reflecting on her motivations for engaging *testimonio* with Luis, her brother, described a desire to establish an emotional connection that honored their individual as well as shared struggles, which Maria reflects upon in writing and stating her intentions:

> I wanted to use this *testimonio* as a way to establish an emotional connection with my brother during this pandemic where we are both internally struggling. My hope was making sure my brother knew that his voice and experience are valid, making sure his *papelitos guardados* are unfolded so that he can heal, and convey a narrative of personal, political, and social realities.

Maria's desire to hold space for her brother to process the internal struggles, as well as sense of pain or grief associated with COVID-19, is evidenced in her reflection. Guided in this intention, Maria describes Luis' process of unraveling, of reflecting, and in the process hoping her brother can experience some sense of well-being that can ultimately lead to healing. Utilizing *testimonio* as a strategy to help her brother acknowledge and talk about his emotions and feelings allowed both Maria and Luis to connect in ways that perhaps they had not been able to do so previously or at least not with a degree of depth. By ensuring that Luis' *papelitos guardados,* the unspoken and untold stories, would be brought to the surface or become "unfolded" over the course of the *testimonio,* Maria strived to support brother's healing process.

Healing, like the wielding of hope, while often described as an individual affective state or condition of being, is a relational experience that requires being in the presence of others. In other words, of experiencing mutual recognitions through validation and affirmations, and even holding space for others, as the previously described excerpts have shown. By encountering each other's pain alongside one's dreams, radical hope can be cultivated. It is this experience of dreaming toward healing and hope which Katya described in her *testimonio,* sharing with Oliveya through the following statement:

> I feel like they're all under the same umbrella. I feel like I'm getting better at dreaming, all the activists that I've been into talk about the power of dreaming. Radical hope and radical dreaming fits into every single category of life. I have a radical hope that everyone I know will be able to be loved and to accept love. I have so many dreams for my sister that connect with the rest of the world like more disability services, more awareness of brain injuries and how prevalent they are and how connected and interwoven and not necessarily separate they are to mental illness. My dream for that would be more awareness for disabilities, for all marginalized communities. I think that awareness that comes with compassion, not just awareness that is shoved in your face. Something I've been working on and asking myself is to envision a world where people listen and if I hold that vision in my head which, is so hard to dream because it seems impossible that people that are privileged and protected will hear us or will hear people that need to be heard, that's a big dream. I dream of somehow connecting people to compassion and allowing them to sit with discomfort and knowing that within discomfort there is beautiful unity and existence.

Hope, specifically the radical hope that Katya describes, is one that is grounded in a critical social analysis of the personal and collective experiences of struggle. The recognition of inequity and injustice as felt and experienced by another, while individually felt when consider within a broader social context is also a collective wound. Such recognition can often become the catalyst that can lead to imagining and engaging in actions that could potentially lead to transformation, change, and justice—to creating something otherwise. Indeed, it is the radical hope that Katya describes, which is grounded in mutual recognitions, that can serve to cultivate opportunities for decolonial healing not as an individual process, but as a relational, collective, and ongoing practice of dreaming to heal. Decolonial imaginings as dreams that can restore hope in action.

Acknowledging the present moment, the interdependence with others, humans, and all things living, appeared to be an important sentiment present in Diana's *testimonio*. Radical hope was intrinsically connected to and reinforced by experiences that affirmed a sense of mutuality and being one with life. In response to Gaby's inquiry about what it means to exist in this moment and what her hopes are for the future, Diana offered a grounding reflection:

> When you ask me who I am, I am a woman with many qualities. And I want to get better, I want to learn more, and be a better person. Being human means I integrate myself into everything that has life on this Earth.

The integration that Diana described as guiding her approach and view toward life and her sense of being integrated with life and the earth seemed to underscore her radical hope. Although Diana acknowledged that times are dire and uncertain, she also believed that these could offer opportunities for growth and learning. The expansiveness of the self that Diana described served as a mechanism for adapting and confronting the pandemic context, at the same time as she acknowledged her skills, strengths, and "*many qualities*," which she leveraged to support her family. In doing so, she was also fostering a sense of hope and healing anchored in what she could do to contribute the thriving of her family. For Diana the concerns are there, yet the radical hope overshadows these, guiding her action and fueling her optimism as source of healing that was made visible in her *testimonio* with Gaby.

Radical hope while fomented through an optimistic perspective that is guided by relationships, connections, and actions can also surface through the recognition and acceptance of pain in order to move through a more restorative sense of being. The naming of pain validates the suffering of others via mutual recognitions of grief, which when transcended can lead to healing. The transcending, however, is not about getting over the pain. On the contrary, it is about facing and confronting its sources in order to transgress and deconstruct the structures that contribute to the cause of injustice. The process of deconstructing that which oppresses and indeed presses upon people's lives and well-being involves the development of a critical social analysis of the conditions that must be challenged and resisted, especially when livelihoods and futures for a better tomorrow are at stake. It is this experience of radical hope which Chris and Andrea documented in their *testimonios* with their mothers. To provide evidence in support of this point, in his closing reflections, Chris offered the following in relation to Ester's *testimonio*:

Because now the future is uncertain for students who had been planning to go to college, workers who have lost their jobs, and really for most everyone around the world. Ester, my mother, hopes that everybody will be able to find opportunities that will help them stay on their feet, but also hopes that they are able to follow their dreams. In a time where people are more focused on surviving than their dreams she notes that this can be hard. She has faith in the fact that out of struggles creativity thrives.

Characterized as faith, the hope that Ester described for a better, more promising future is grounded in her willing capacity to see that amidst the challenges there is still hope and opportunity. Ester acknowledges the difficulties of the present moment yet embraces these challenges as opportunities for innovation and creativity that can serve as anchors for cultivating the radical hope that is necessary to envision a better tomorrow. Such expressed sentiments resonate with those offered by Katya and Diana. It is this relentless sense of hope that can foster experiences toward decolonial healing because even in the most tumultuous of times one can still dream and participate in the actualizing of a better, more just, and human present-future.

The act of dreaming alone is not sufficient to actualize justice. Yet it provides an important source of inspiration and motivation to act toward redressing injustices and minimize suffering and oppressions. Doing so can lead to more humanizing positive social conditions aimed toward healing. The intentions for hopeful times ahead when followed by action can bring about the restoration of well-being, which is an experience Andrea documented through Elizabeth's *testimonio*, thereby offering the following statement:

> The final question I asked, "*What are your hopes and dreams for you and your community?*" offered an opening for a space of positive reflection. It was beautiful to see how quickly my mom was able to conjure her hopes and dreams. She had them readily available, showing that she holds them close and is able to easily access this positivity. She went down a mental list of the people she holds close and loves dearly. She had dreams for them. She had dreams for herself. She had dreams for the world. Taking into account the transformative work that she has done within herself and for others, I have no doubt that she will do everything in her power to get closer to making those dreams a reality each and every day. And that gives me hope.

Andrea's reflection of her mother's response attests to the significance of radical hope, one that is mutual, reciprocal, and relational. Radical hope serves as an anchor to the agency that must be summoned when social conditions frame or position Latinx communities as lacking power and will. Yet, as Angela's earlier remarks demonstrate, there is strength in the face of adversity and vulnerability. Elizabeth's *testimonio*, consistent with Ester's and Diana's, illustrates how even in the most challenging of times, dreams cannot be wilted and hope must remain. Radical hope must be summoned with purposefulness to guide actions conducive to bringing to life that which is imagined as transformative and just. The radical hope that characterized Elizabeth's reflections cannot be understated, and neither can the radical hope by others who offered their *testimonio*.

As the excerpts featured illustrate radical hope, Latinx communities are actively leveraging their resources as teachers, mothers, siblings, and caretakers to support those around them. In the case of educators, Latinx women are encouraging the learning and academic success of their students by caring from them as more than just students and considering their home and family circumstances. In their own ways and within their respective contexts and positionalities as educators, Ester, Elizabeth, and Jennifer, like Angela, Diana, Katya, and Luis, are experiencing the challenges of COVID-19. Yet they are not acquiescing and succumbing to the difficulties their experiencing. On the contrary, through their critical social analysis, reciprocal recognitions with students and others similarly impacted by COVID-19, and radical hope, they are reframing the moment as one of optimism, innovation, and possibilities for transformation, systemic change, and justice. A transformation that honors the dignity, humanity, and labor of communities institutionally marginalized—Latinx who are on the peripheries of being seen, heard, and fully cared for in a society that has inadequately served their needs, thriving and possibilities to experience well-being.

Concluding *Reflexiones* on Decolonial Healing

In this article, I described the *Testimoniando El Presente* essay assignment that students were encouraged to pursue to process and document their family and/or communities' experiences, as well as their own personal stories of precarity, as well as hope amidst COVID-19 and racialized forms of violence. By encouraging students to connect course content with *testimoniantes*' stories, as well as their own reflections and experiences, the assignment sought to facilitate opportunities to engage in critical reflexivity through a critical social analysis of the unfolding conditions impacting their lives. Moreover, through this relational dialogic critically reflexive process of witnessing, listening, and writing, Latinx students sought to foster opportunities toward decolonial healing among themselves and those they engaged in *testimonio*.

As the *testimonios* provided by the Latinx students demonstrate, the process of healing cannot be done in isolation. Healing calls us to engage in a relational critically reflexive dialogue, an introspective, personal, and communal process of being heard. Witnessing in the context of a *testimonio* experience is about seeing the other person fully; it is precisely about those moments of mutual recognition that contextualize the social conditions of oppression through a critical social analysis that can help us understand the *why* to the problems noted and *how* to create change. The radical hope that Latinx students brought to the surface in their documenting of their loved one's *testimonio* demonstrates the affirmation and validation they facilitated, which helped the *testimoniante* reflect and process the current moment. In doing so, there was a realization, a process of surrendering, embracing, and cultivating decolonial healing through the recognition that while their current times are dire, better ones will come.

Drawing from selected Latinx student *testimonio* excerpts, I have offered educators, practitioners, and therapists, and anyone concerned with community connected well-being, grounded in practices toward healing and decoloniality, an invitation. The invitation is for us to consider how *mujerista* liberation psychology perspectives—which have been foundational in informing my scholarly and pedagogical training—can be utilized and adapted beyond the pedagogical and academic sphere to support healing, specifically to aid communities, particularly Latinx students, in journeys toward decolonial healing. I purport that as educators we can and in fact must make space in the classroom, as well as other relational settings, for modes of decolonial healing that thread learning with dialogic critical reflexivity. We can and must cultivate decolonial healing across multiple settings, especially contexts that are oriented toward supporting our individual and collective well-being. Under the context of a global pandemic, the refusal to proceed business as usual within our respective locations, especially as educators or practitioners, can motivate us into innovation or creativity to develop resources or strategies for responding, engaging, and, most importantly, cultivating healing.

As an educator, community-engaged researcher, grounded in a decolonial feminist praxis, I encourage us to consider *testimonios* as one possible tool to aid us in documenting, resisting, and healing from, through, and with each other during these pandemic times. The sociopolitical context associated with the tumultuous conditions and precarities of the present yet unfolding moment under COVID-19, along with its ramified impact, calls us to engage and connect in innovative creative ways. In assigning the *Testimoniando El Presente* essay assignment for documenting the impact of COVID-19 on Latinx communities, I strived to bridge the pedagogical and sociopolitical elements of narrative practices and traditions with *mujerista* liberation psychology and decolonial feminist epistemologies. Through the assignment, Latinx students engaged in and offered their individual and collective testament to the impact of COVID-19 within their families and communities. Moreover, they offered a rendering of the struggles and grief, but above all the humanizing radical hope that bound them together.

Healing is an experience of wholesomeness, of being seen and heard, affirmed and valued as human being. It is an imperative experience and a response that resists succumbing to grief and loss. Amidst conditions of exclusion, disenfranchisement, and othering, which are often experienced among institutionally marginalized communities, specifically Latinx families and communities in the United States, radical healing practices—*esperanza, fe, y animo* (hope, faith, and encouragement, even courage)—are antidotes to oppression. As Mosley and colleagues (2020) write, "radical healing involves becoming whole in the face of historical and ongoing experiences oppression" (p. 28). To heal is to render visible the pain, which evokes a past, and memories associated with it, in order to reconfigure new modes of existing that can alleviate the conditions that cause hurt and loss. Healing is an ongoing process of relationality that requires listening, witnessing, and holding space for others (Comas-Díaz, 2006, 2020).

Mujerista traditions and practices, like stories, hold invaluable potential for restoring our sense of humanity, solidarity, and love, all of which are fundamental to experience modes of decolonial healing (Isasi-Díaz, 1989, 1994). The decolonial healing that is characterized in the featured *testimonios* illustrate a *mujerista* liberatory standpoint that honors *el poder de la palabra* (the power of words), which I underscore has its foundations in decolonial feminist and Indigenous practices, traditions, and cosmovisions. This honoring is an important step for supporting communities in struggle demanding justice, as well as humanizing the communities whose stories are left unheard or communities are not afforded the platforms to speak for themselves and be heard on their terms. By offering my reflections on the assignment—from its development, implementation, and outcomes to the significance and impact it had on Latinx students—it is my intention that as educators and practitioners, we can turn to *mujerista* epistemologies, grounded in liberation psychology and decolonial feminisms, for *sabiduria* (wisdom) to aid us and our communities in our journey toward decolonial healing.

We must envision and act to create an anti-oppressive, just, and humanizing present-future. To do so, we must engage forms of embodied relational knowledge and sociocultural traditions for liberation. *Testimonio* as a *mujerista* resource toward decolonial healing facilitates a relational dialogic critical reflexivity that aligns with or can accompany healing practices, therapies, and clinical interventions. Specifically, *testimonio* can help guide pedagogical and therapeutic processes of teaching-learning-connecting to actualize liberatory conditions that affirm humanity. To *testimoniar* is to amplify individual and collective stories, to strengthen and uplift communities, and to restore the fullness of our humanity and human potential.

Note

1. In keeping with *testimonio* tradition of honoring people's stories, or the spoken narrative and words of each person, some Latinx students and their *testimoniante* preferred I use their first name. In such cases, they granted me consent to do so and were provided with several drafts of this paper in order to ensure they were comfortable and in agreement with the excepts I feature. Few Latinx students and *testimoniantes*, however, choose a pseudonym.

ORCID

Jesica Siham Fernández http://orcid.org/0000-0002-5513-7413

References

Angueira, K. (1988). To make the personal political: The use of testimony as a consciousness-raising tool against sexual aggression in Puerto Rico. *The Oral History Review*, 16(2), 65–93. https://doi.org/10.1093/ohr/16.2.65

Beverley, J. (2000). Testimonio, subalternity, and narrative authority. In N. K. Denzin & Y. S. Lincoln (Eds.), *Handbook of qualitative research* (pp. 555–565). Sage.

Booker, M. (2002). Stories of violence: Use of testimony in a support group for Latin American battered women. In L. H. Collins, M. R. Dunlap, & J. C. Chrisler (Eds.), *Charting a new course for feminist psychology* (pp. 307–321). Prager.

Brabeck, K. (2003). *Testimonio*: A strategy for collective resistance, cultural survival and building solidarity. *Feminism & Psychology*, 13(2), 252–258. https://doi.org/10.1177/0959353503013002009

Chang, H. (2016). Autoethnography in health research: Growing pains? *Qualitative Health Research*, 26(4), 443–451. https://doi.org/10.1177/1049732315627432

Chavez-Dueñas, N. Y., Adames, H. Y., Pérez-Chavez, J. G., & Salas, S. P. (2019). Healing ethno-racial trauma in Latinx immigrant communities: Cultivating hope, resistance, and action. *The American Psychologist*, 74(1), 49–62. https://doi.org/10.1037/amp0000289

Cienfuegos, A. J., & Monelli, C. (1983). The testimony of political repression as a therapeutic instrument. *The American Journal of Orthopsychiatry*, 53(1), 43–51. https://doi.org/10.1111/j.1939-0025.1983.tb03348.x

Ciofalo, N. (2018). Indigenous women's ways of knowing and healing in Mexico. *Women & Therapy*, 41(1-2), 52–68. https://doi.org/10.1080/02703149.2017.1323478

Comas-Díaz, L. (2006). Latino healing: The integration of ethnic psychology into psychotherapy. *Psychotherapy: Theory, Research, Practice, Training*, 43(4), 436.

Comas-Díaz, L. (2020). Journey to psychology: A mujerista testimonio. *Women & Therapy*, 43(1-2), 157–169. https://doi.org/10.1080/02703149.2019.1684676

Cruz, M. R., & Sonn, C. C. (2011). (De) colonizing culture in community psychology: Reflections from critical social science. *American Journal of Community Psychology*, 47(1-2), 203–214. https://doi.org/10.1007/s10464-010-9378-x

De Robertis, C. (2017). *Radical hope: Letters of love and dissent in dangerous times*. Vintage Books.

Delgado Bernal, D., Burciaga, R., & Flores Carmona, J. (2012). Chicana/Latina *testimonios*: Mapping the methodological, pedagogical, and political. *Equity & Excellence in Education*, 45(3), 363–372. https://doi.org/10.1080/10665684.2012.698149

Espino, M. M., Vega, I. I., Rendón, L. I., Ranero, J. J., & Muñiz, M. M. (2012). The process of *reflexión* in bridging *testimonios* across lived experience. *Equity & Excellence in Education, 45*(3), 444–459. https://doi.org/10.1080/10665684.2012.698188

Fanon, F. (1967). *Black skin, White masks*. Grove Press.

Fernández, J. S., Sonn, C. C., Carolissen, R., & Stevens, G. (2021). Roots and routes toward decoloniality within and outside psychology praxis. *Review of General Psychology., 25*(4), 354–368. https://doi.org/10.1177/10892680211002437

Fortuna, L. R., Tolou-Shams, M., Robles-Ramamurthy, B., & Porche, M. V. (2020). Inequity and the disproportionate impact of COVID-19 on communities of color in the United States: The need for a trauma-informed social justice response. *Psychological Trauma: Theory, Research, Practice & Policy, 12*(5), 443–445. https://doi.org/10.1037/tra0000889

French, B. H., Lewis, J. A., Mosley, D. V., Adames, H. Y., Chavez-Dueñas, N. Y., Chen, G. A., & Neville, H. A. (2020). Toward a psychological framework of radical healing in communities of color. *The Counseling Psychologist, 48*(1), 14–46. https://doi.org/10.1177/0011000019843506

Garcia, M. A., Homan, P. A., García, C., & Brown, T. H. (2020). The color of COVID-19: Structural racism and the pandemic's disproportionate impact on older racial and ethnic minorities. *The Journals of Gerontology: Social Sciences Series B, 76*(3), 75–80.

Ginwright, S. (2008). Collective radical imagination: Youth participatory action research and the art of emancipatory knowledge. In J. Cammarota & M. Fine (Eds.), *Revolutionizing education: Youth participatory action research in motion* (pp. 13–22). Routledge.

Ginwright, S. (2011). Hope, healing, and care. *Liberal Education, 97*(2), 34–39.

Ginwright, S. (2015). *Hope and healing in urban education: How urban activists and teachers are reclaiming matters of the heart*. Routledge.

Isasi-Díaz, A. M. (1989). *Mujeristas: A name of our own!! The Christian century*. http://www.religion-online.org/article/mujeristas-a-name-of-our-own/

Isasi-Díaz, A. M. (1994). *Mujeristas*: A name of our own. Sisters struggling in the spirit. In N. B. Lewis (Ed.), *A women of color theological anthology* (pp. 126–138). Women's Ministries Program, Presbyterian Church (USA).

Latina Feminist Group. (2001). *Telling to live: Latina feminist testimonies*. Durham, NC: Duke University Press.

Maldonado-Torres, N. (2008). *Against war: Views from the underside of modernity*. Duke University Press.

Martín-Baró, I. (1994). *Writings for a liberation psychology*. Harvard University Press.

Mignolo, W. D. (2007). Introduction: Coloniality of power and de-colonial thinking. *Cultural Studies, 21*(2–3), 155–167. https://doi.org/10.1080/09502380601162498

Moraga, C., & Anzaldua, G. (Eds.). (1983). *This bridge called my back: Writings by radical women of color*. Kitchen Table Press.

Mosley, D. V., Neville, H. A., Chavez-Dueñas, N. Y., Adames, H. Y., Lewis, J. A., & French, B. H. (2020). Radical hope in revolting times: Proposing a culturally relevant psychological framework. *Social & Personality Psychology Compass, 14*(1), 1–12.

Pérez Huber, L. (2009). Disrupting apartheid of knowledge: *Testimonio* as methodology in Latina/o critical race research in education. *International Journal of Qualitative Studies in Education, 22*(6), 639–654. https://doi.org/10.1080/09518390903333863

Sandoval, C. (2000). *Methodology of the oppressed*. University of Minnesota.

Silva, J. M., Fernández, J. S., & Nguyen, A. (2021). "And now we resist": Three testimonios on the importance of decoloniality within psychology. *Journal of Social Issues, 78*(2), 388–412.

Smith, K. M. (2010). Female voice and female text: *Testimonio* as a form of resistance in Latin America. *Florida Atlantic Comparative Studies Journal, 12*, 21–38.

Valdez, L. (1994). *Luis Valdez—early works: Actos, Bernabé and Pensamieno Serpentino*. Arte Public Press.

Viera, E. (2013). *Construyendo psicología política latinoamericana desde la psicología de la liberación*. Revista Electrónica de Psicología Política, 30, 37–56.

Appendix A

Testimoniando El Presente essay assignment
Assignment description

Stories hold wisdom. We can learn so much about ourselves and others, as well as about our past, present and future when we listen to those who have seen and lived through so much more beyond this moment. Therefore, please engage in the *Testimoniando El Presente* essay assignment by engaging *testimonio* with someone in your family and/or community. Prior to engaging *testimonio*, carefully read and reflect upon the following article:

- Delgado Bernal, D., Burciaga, R., & Flores Carmona, J. (2012). Chicana/Latina *testimonios*: Mapping the methodological, pedagogical, and political. *Equity & Excellence in Education, 45*(3), 363–372.

After a close reading of the article, you are encouraged to develop your own questions or prompts, or engage *testimonio* as a free-form reflexive dialogue—as an intentional conversation.

If, however, you would prefer to offer more structure, you are welcome to modify the following guided questions:

1. What are you experiencing and/or feeling in this current moment?
2. What challenges and/or struggles have you and/or your family/community experienced under the present sociopolitical context?
3. What are your hopes and dreams for your family/community and/or the future?

The *Testimoniando El Presente* essay assignment is an opportunity for you to actively listen to someone's lived experience, story and voice, especially when some of these voices are often silenced, unheard and/or misrepresented.

Learning objectives

a. To actively and intentionally practice critical reflexivity by engaging *testimonio*.
b. To apply a critical sociopolitical analysis of contemporary social issues to the stories and/or experiences offered by the *testimoniante*.
c. To connect or analyze the *testimonio* in relation to relevant course content, such as theories, perspectives and standpoints from readings, podcasts/multimedia and lectures.
d. To develop a compassionate and critically reflexive understanding of the social conditions associated with COVID-19 and their impact on the *testimoniante* and/or their communities.
e. To describe or imagine possibilities for change, hope and thriving.

Nepantla Moments in Therapy: A Clinical Example with Latinx Immigrants

Pilar Hernandez-Wolfe

ABSTRACT
Therapy can be a site of decolonization in which the traumatic experiences of individuals, couples, families, and communities can be transformed by liberation-based frameworks. In this essay I articulate how key concepts from De Sousa Santos *Epistemologies of the South*, such as the ecologies of temporality, recognition, and productivity, can be integrated within a Mujerista therapy framework to address trauma and resilience. Through a clinical example of a Latinx mother and daughter, I illustrate nepantla moments and the co-construction of *testimonios* involving experiential, narrative, and spiritual levels of experience.

In this case study, I illustrate key aspects of Latinx intergenerational trauma and resilience involving the relationship of Blanca, a marginalized mestiza immigrant from Central America to the USA, and Yesenia, her youngest, U.S.-born daughter. This analysis highlights aspects of the therapeutic process that relocate the concepts of traumatic stress and resilience to a borderland space where they can be addressed and transformed by local experiences and sociohistorical contexts and within an overarching framework of decolonization. My epistemic point of departure recognizes the enduring effects of colonization and coloniality (Mignolo, 2011; Quijano, 2000). and is grounded in De Sousa Santos (2012) *Epistemologies of the South*. This framework acknowledges different ways to understand our existence in this world by attending to our own social locations, histories, conditions, and possibilities. But de Sousa Santos does not claim to have arrived at a new general theory and offers a path for reengaging with the experiences and knowledges of those whose who can no longer be rendered legible by Eurocentric knowledge. From a therapeutic stance, this case analysis is grounded in Mujerista psychology, a relational and multicultural feminist approach that focuses on Latinx lived experiences and pays special attention to immigration, coloniality, place, borderlands, interculturality, language, and spirituality (Comas-Díaz, 2020a, 2020b).

This essay comprises three sections. First, I articulate how key concepts from *Epistemologies of the South* (De Sousa Santos, 2012) and borderland thinking (Anzaldúa, 1999, 2002) offer pathways toward decolonization and expand Western notions of traumatic stress and resilience. Second, I discuss how *testimonios* comprised of somatic, verbal, emotional, and spiritual levels are co-constructed and transformed in the therapeutic space. Third, I discuss a clinical example highlighting parts one and two.

Borderland Thinking: Coloniality, Nepantla, Epistemologies of the South, and the Mujerista Approach

Anibal Quijano (2000) coined the term *coloniality* to refer to the systemic suppression of subordinated cultures and knowledges by the dominant Eurocentric paradigm of modernity and the emergence of knowledges and practices resulting from this experience. However, the emergence of knowledges and practices at the margins has the potential to engender distinct alternatives, thereby fostering a pluriverse of cultural configurations. Mignolo and Walsh (2018) speak of "border thinking" as resulting from the wound of coloniality; that is, experiences and knowledges have emerged from differing and conflicting epistemologies from the South and Eurocentric thought. For Mignolo (2011), border thinking allows us to draw different paths and to enunciate other knowledges after having recognized inequality and accepted the wound inflicted by coloniality. Two interrelated aspects of coloniality are the systemic suppression of local knowledges and the emergence of alternative knowledges resulting from this oppressive experience. It is within this interstice that I locate this case study involving Blanca and Yesenia's relationship and experiences of trauma and resilience. This is a space of exchange and participation in which processes of hybridization occur and where it is possible for the various subcultures to which they belong to be produced and performed without necessary mediation from the center. Gloria Anzaldúa (1999, 2002) calls these interstitial spaces borderlands. They emerge out of coloniality.

According to Anzaldúa (1999, 2000), borderlands are the places in between; the spaces in which border knowledge and border identities are constructed; the gaps, fissures, and silences of hegemonic narratives; and the overlapping border spaces and cultural representations that those who inhabit these spaces negotiate in order to exercise personal and collective agency. The borderland concept is transnational. Furthermore, in *Interviews/entrevistas* (2000), Anzaldúa explained that she began to use the term nepantla to expand the meaning of her original concept of borderlands:

> With the Nepantla paradigm I try to theorize unarticulated dimensions of the experience of Mestizas living in between overlapping and layered spaces of different cultures and social and geographic locations, of events and realities—psychological, sociological, political, spiritual, historical, creative, imagined. (p. 176)

Keating (2006) explained that *nepantla* is a Nahuatl word meaning "in-between space" and involves transformation and "dis-identification from existing beliefs, social structures, and models of identity; by so doing, we are able to transform these existing conditions" (p. 9). Nepantla is a liminal space where transformation can occur.

It is in the interstices or spaces of articulation of cultural difference (where different cultures overlap/displace) where identities are produced, displaced, and negotiated, and hybridity becomes a productive space of enunciation that opens up sites of resistance and potential.

King and Miehls (2008) discussed necessary conditions that coalesce to make possible momentary states of nepantla in psychotherapy. They are regulation, recognition, responsibility, and critical consciousness. They argue that nepantla states occur when there is deactivation of the fight-flight-freeze response. I concur with these authors, as I believe that the work of decolonization integrates body, cognition, and spirit. They add furthermore that there needs to be a good enough "regulation of systems involving hunger, sleep, arousal, social contact, affective states, level of activation or excitation, exploration, attachment and attribution of meanings" (p. 168). Nepantla provides the space for both a cognitive process and an emotional process. Therapy models such as Mujerista, which involves the use of *testimonios* as a main therapeutic tool to help clients articulate their experiences in ways that account for racial, class, gender, and other injustices as a means of healing and empowerment (Comas-Díaz, 2020a, 2020b), are attentive to the emotional impact of social location. The Mujerista approach (Comas-Díaz, 2019) does not treat discrimination, aggressions, and microaggressions as something that can be merely resolved with understanding. Clients need a safe and nurturing therapeutic relationship and interventions that address the somatic and emotional aspects of the everyday and historical wounds of colonization. Clients need emotional regulation to deal with affective intensity. Thus, individual regulation, as well as co-regulation with significant others, allows momentary self-organization and co-regulation.

King and Miehls (2008) describe responsibility as a recognition of the other. They cite Benjamin's conceptualization on the other: the ability "to sustain connectedness to the other's mind while accepting his separateness and difference" (Benjamin, 2004, p. 8). This requires attunement to self, other, and the interaction of the two. Experiential and somatic therapy models (Johnson, 2014; Stavrianopoulos et al., 2014) offer sophisticated and effective ways to safely invite clients to explore connection with another person by taking small risks until they can attune to self, other, and others and take responsibility for what each person contributes to the relationship. Mutual regulation, recognition, and responsibility must be present for critical consciousness to occur in a manner in which clients can listen to, take in, and sit with what each other brings to the conversation.

Conceptually anchored in the work of Paulo Freire (1973/1992), critical consciousness involves the development of a critical awareness of how personal dynamics unfold within social and political contexts. The Mujerista approach attends to the location of clients with regard to colonization, class, gender, ethnicity, and sexual orientation. It fosters awareness within these areas, acknowledging that the causes and/or consequences of some clinical problems reflect political, economic, and psychological oppression and that experiences of oppression require public, institutional, and internal family process solutions (Comas-Díaz, 2019). In therapeutic contexts involving more than one client, the co-construction of testimonios that foster critical consciousness involves mutual regulation and recognition to help clients carry out and flow with transitions of body experience and affect, listen to and accept differences, and, to some degree, feel that we can exist and coexist with what may be beyond our understanding and ability (Bromberg, 1993). King and Miehls (2008,) argue, "It is only when both parties can mutually hold interpersonal tension, that the movement towards third space is possible" (p. 173). When clients are able to sustain uncertainty, contradiction, and difference to a degree, they are better able to tolerate "the tensions associated when one is interacting with others or systems that complicate our own experience" (King & Miehls, 2008, p. 173).

In sum, the concept of coloniality situates my point of departure in therapy within the interstices or borderlands, opens up a dynamic exploration of traumatic stress at a social and personal level, and opens paths to recognition, repair, compassion, wellness, and possibility. Inviting clients to step into momentary states of nepantla involves emotional and cognitive changes that must be weaved in the therapeutic relationship itself and in the process of co-constructing testimonios. Nevertheless, what I have described thus far is not enough. Decolonization in therapy requires that we open our horizons further and invite in other epistemologies, because the world we live in is far from being exhausted by Eurocentric experience or reducible to its terms. De Sousa Santos (2012, 2019), a Portuguese law and sociology scholar, has contributed to social theory by recognizing plural epistemologies, systems, and ways of knowing. I infuse some of the concepts he proposed for an epistemology of the South into my thinking about the potentials of therapy as a decolonization endeavor.

Epistemologies of the South

De Sousa Santos (2012, p. 191) speaks of the sociology of absences *as* an inquiry into that which does not exist and which is furthermore actively produced as nonexistent. He explains that "nonexistence is produced whenever a certain entity is disqualified and rendered invisible, unintelligible, or irreversibly discardable" and that various ways of producing nonexistence are the result of the same rational monoculture. This inquiry into what is absent is an essential aspect of the therapeutic process, as it gives permission to open the doors to the legacies of Indigenous ways of carrying our bodies that we cannot remember due to colonization. Colonization rendered invisible the Indigenous side of our mestizx heritage, but the sociology of absences is a pathway to remember, validate, imagine, adopt, create, and re-create our connections with space, migration, all nonhuman beings, our own bodies, and a spirituality free of the chains of the Christian domination that was brought to the Americas. The five logics of production of the sociology of absences are the monoculture of knowledge, linear time, classification, production, and large scale. I describe the first four, as they are relevant to this case.

The Monoculture of Knowledge

The monoculture of knowledge involves all that is not recognized or legitimated by the Western canon of therapy and is declared outside of what are considered best practices. Nonexistence in this case is akin to what would be considered ignorance. While Western therapy models are very diverse and can offer excellent tools for addressing relief at the levels of symptoms and relational and transpersonal well-being, they generally do not engage with the marginalized knowledges resulting from coloniality—for example, spiritual traditions involving work with the fire, water, and earth that remain in the consciousness and actual practices of mestizx. These practices are marginalized and often categorized as "folk psychology," pushed out of the sphere of acceptable clinical practice, rendered invisible, or seen as something that we do not understand but that "these people do."

The Monoculture of Linear Time

The monoculture of linear time involves the idea that time is linear and that "ahead of time precedes the core countries of the world system" (De Sousa Santos, 2012, p. 95). This is the logic that led to descriptions of humans as "premodern" and "in development." Linearity prevents us from understanding that we are connected to our ancestors past; that time may be circular. It keeps us from discovering the diverse ways in which healing practices have survived and thrived in Latin America and in colonized Latinx communities in the USA. Breaking with the linearity of time in therapy may involve using mindfulness to explore ancestral connections and future lives, dreaming lucidly with alternative lives, inviting conversation with various versions of oneself, and using dream time to explore various locales and settings to retrieve knowledge and objects or to find companion spiritual beings.

The Monocultures of Classification and Production

The monoculture of classification is based in the naturalization of differences, and it is responsible for the racial, gender, and sexual and other hierarchies at the base of structural inequities in the lives of Blanca and Yesenia, the mother and daughter I discuss later. The monoculture of production is about productivity and efficiency, and it produces nonexistence in the form of discardable populations and laziness. Many Latinx and Latina immigrants in the USA take jobs as domestics to earn a living for themselves and for their families abroad. I speculate that their relationships with work impact their social positions in the community and the family and that their perceptions of themselves changes as they are able to enjoy more freedom, recognition, and power. In the case of Blanca, I argue that she experienced a change in her sense of self-worth in the USA and that this was partly the result of her relationship with her occupation. By working hard at cleaning homes and offices, and building her own cleaning business, she gained autonomy, decision-making power, freedom of movement, recognition from her family, and confidence. For her, and many other Latinx immigrants, being valued as cheap labor and the socialization of working until exhaustion began at home as a very young child. Yesenia rebelled against this way of life and found a compromise in her work as a veterinary assistant. The epistemology of absences helps me start therapy with the possibility that mother and daughter can imagine Indigenous and other forms of wisdom that they did not get to learn consciously in the social settings they inhabited.

Being socialized with absences that render most Latinx partially or fully invisible begs the question of what options there are to break with the status quo. De Sousa Santos (2012) proposes that we move from the sociology of absence and its monoculture to ecologies. He proposes ecologies of knowledge, temporality, recognition, productivity, and trans-scale. I discuss the first four, as they are relevant to this case.

Ecologies of Knowledge, Temporality, Recognition, and Productivity

The central idea of the ecology of knowledge is that there is no ignorance or knowledge in general: "All ignorance is ignorant of certain knowledge, and all knowledge is the overcoming of a particular ignorance" (De Sousa Santos, p. 116). Thus, Western therapy models that address relational interactions, meaning, emotion, and somatic levels of experience can be in greater dialogue with spiritual practices that address the here and now of relationships, the past and the future, and interaction, meaning, and emotion from a symbolic perspective. According to De Sousa Santos (2012), the ecology of temporality opens the possibility for autonomous development. In this manner, the healing practices of mestizx curanderx would be contemporaneous with Western therapeutic practices, thus breaking an implicit order in which one is behind the other. They simply become another form of contemporaneity. The ecology of recognition opposes the monoculture of classification and challenges colonial hierarchies such as those of race, gender, and sexual orientation. In his view, this allows for an ecology of differences comprised of mutual recognition. Thus, "the differences that remain when hierarchy vanishes become a powerful denunciation of the differences that hierarchy reclaims in order not to vanish." (De Sousa Santos, 2012, p. 117). The ecology of recognition in therapy allows for a deeper recognition of the complexities in experiences of privilege and lack of privilege in interpersonal relationships. The ecologies of temporality and recognition are especially important in therapy because often the initial traumas and losses resulting from the genocides of colonization are transmitted across generations through such mechanisms as domestic violence and other forms of abuse, whereas colonial suppression of history may make the truth of the original trauma inaccessible to those suffering the wounds of its transmission. Going back and forth in time to imagine relationships before and after colonization, and recognizing multiple possibilities for sharing and organizing relationships based on power, opens up emotional and cognitive channels by which to embrace new possibilities in the here and now.

The ecology of productivity confronts the paradigm of development and infinite economic growth. It affirms alternative systems of production, popular economic organizations, workers' cooperatives, self-managed enterprises, the solidarity economy, and so on. In therapy, this concept opens a path to discussing one's relationship with work beyond satisfaction and growth. It invites themes such as compassion, well-being, solidarity, cooperation, and balance.

I situate the therapeutic endeavor of decolonization within borderlands that open up a dynamic exploration of social and personal aspects of traumatic stress and resilience, where there can be space for recognition, repair, compassion, wellness, and possibility. This work invites clients and therapists to step into momentary states of nepantla that integrate a back-and-forth flow of somatic, emotional, cognitive, temporal, spatial, and spiritual experiences that must be weaved in the therapeutic relationship itself and in the process of co-constructing testimonios (Gil & Inoa Vazquez, 2014). These concepts are consistent with Mujerista psychology, as Mujerismo embraces an interdisciplinary perspective in which inclusion of relevant and consistent concepts and practices is welcomed to serve its own purposes. I believe that the ecologies of knowledge, temporality, recognition, and productivity open up possibilities for us to step into other times, other spaces, other relationships (for example, relationships not confined to humans but including plants, animals, and all other beings), and other spiritualities. This offers a meta-framework that may enrich and is consistent with a Mujerista approach. The realm of spiritual practices that can be weaved into the co-constructions of testimonios offers many possibilities to integrate the symbolic transformation of experience and relationship through connection with the earth, fire, water, and air (Gilmore, 2010), sound (Burns, 2019), dance and movement (Kawano, 2018), ancestral spirits and culturally meaningful divinities, storytelling, household altars, nourishing recipes, and celebrations (Shapiro & Alcántara, 2016), visual art (Hutchings, 2015), and artivism (Shapiro, 2020). An example of a self-determined space of ancestral, traditional, and Indigenous medicine and spiritual practices is the Healing Clinic Collective in Oakland, California. This collective is based in a political orientation for community organizing that offers ancestral, traditional, and Indigenous medicines though which "self-determination 'gets worked out' as health/care and healing" (Aguilar, 2019, p. 2). According to Aguilar (2019), this means that people from populations made vulnerable through racialization and minoritization can experience agency at the levels of the embodied self, the collective body, social structures, and the natural environment.

A Borderlands View of Traumatic Stress and Resilience

I argue that the history of colonialism and the dominant capitalistic ways of production that shape our relationships with the earth and all its inhabitants, other humans, work, our bodies, nutrition, and health also shape the entitlements that people claim; the privileges and lack of privileges they have; their family compositions, life expectations, and traumas and how they make meaning out of these situations; and how they respond to adversity. Coloniality continues to operate in our lives through the promotion of cultural belief systems, definitions of traumatic stress, and treatment approaches that have at their center conceptualizations embracing individualism, medicalization, and the separation of people's experiences of trauma from history and context (Gil & Inoa Vazquez, 2014). Furthermore, the invisibility of our relationship with and impact on the earth and all its beings continues to impact everyone negatively and robs us of possibilities of healing that relationship with the earth and all its beings and elements.

Most Latinx people have a legacy of historical, intergenerational, and community trauma. Traumatic experiences, traumatic stress, and diagnosable conditions such as anxiety, depression, and PTSD may be related to histories of conquest and colonization in Latin America; socioeconomic upheaval; poverty and violence associated with racism, classism, sexism, and homophobia prior to migrating to the USA; and immigration (Cerezo et al., 2020). Often, migration to the USA involves the separation of families and the loss of family, community, and meaningful cultural connection. In the USA, Latinx people face discrimination, lack of access to education and health care, racism, and classism. Like African Americans, they are specially targeted by the police (Rios & Vigil, 2017). However, legacies of historical, intergenerational, and community trauma must be carefully examined to understand the complexities of privilege and oppression for a particular person, couple, or family.

In spite of the many risk factors associated with race, class, gender, ability, age, and sexual orientation for Latinx people, I agree with Chavez-Dueñas et al. (2019) that the impact of traumatic experiences and pathways for resilience can coexist. Adversity can unintentionally yield changes in oneself, others, and the world that may result in adaptive and positive experiences. When experiences of adversity are seen in therapy in social and historical context, it is possible to find interstices with potential for positive change over time. The processes of overcoming adversity are scaffolded. They evolve over time and in the context of learning how to survive, adapt, and thrive (Masten, 2014). Ungar (2006) defined resilience as an individual's capacity to "navigate their way to the psychological, social, cultural, and physical resources that sustain their well-being, and their capacity individually and collectively to negotiate for these resources to be provided in culturally meaningful ways" (p. 225). In their review of current advances in resilience, Ungar and Theron (2020) state that individual resilience involving self-regulation and changes to cognition is "unsustainable unless other co-occurring social and physical systems—such as family, housing, and natural environment—are robust enough to support new regimens of adaptive behaviour" (p. 442). They explain that resilience is multisystemic and accounted for by multiple factors at biological, psychological, social, and natural levels. Individuals who have adequate resources at these levels show more resilience than those who do not. They propose that clinicians assess risk of exposure according to the quantity, type, chronicity, severity, systemic level, and cultural relevance of stressors. Clinicians should address protective factors in regard to stress response, epigenetics, and availability of resources (social, economic, political, and built and natural environments). Furthermore, they stress that context and culture will influence how protective and risk factors are experienced.

Testimonios

According to the Latina Feminist Group (2001), a *testimonio* is a way to create knowledge and theory through personal experiences. In therapy, the process of creating a testimonio is as important as the *testimonio* itself. *Testimonios* document and/or theorize experiences of struggle, survival, and resistance. Testimonios capture the changes of personal identity with political activism and integrate accounts about personal experiences that shape institutional points of view, group or societal transformations, and politics. They are developed in collaboration with others and can build understanding and solidarity.

Testimonios as storytelling in therapy are valid ways for people to express themselves and make sense of their places in the social world. People organize their experiences and memories in the form of narratives. As stories are told and re-created, and as they give voice to what has been silenced, people name and shape the meaning of their relationships. They communicate new meanings to others, generating communication at somatic, emotional, cognitive, and spiritual levels. Perez Huber (2009) states that through identifying micro- and macro-discourses in a story, individuals can develop critical awareness of community and of societal and historical issues, and can engage in personal and/or social action. Testimonios might allow ordinary people to reach a wider audience. They are useful as a collective form of remembering in that they offer a concrete avenue for reconstructing a silenced past.

In therapy, testimonios are co-constructed, weaved in the flow of somatic, experiential, and spiritual work, and they evolve in conversation. Thus, they are not static but are alive in the doing of therapy. In the case study that I analyze in the next section, mother and daughter co-constructed their own testimonios involving the intergenerational themes of trauma and resilience resulting from coloniality. Furthermore, the shifting of language between Spanish and English enriched the co-construction of these testimonios as our therapeutic conversations moved between and across multiple meanings, allowing renewal and reinvention (Polanco, 2019).

Nepantla in Therapy: Mother and Daughter Come to Terms With Their Past and Present

In this case study, I highlight three pivotal moments in a mother–daughter relationship involving states of nepantla and aspects of the therapeutic process in which the experiential, testimonio, and spiritual levels coalesced, illustrating the potential of the ecologies of knowledge, temporality, recognition, and productivity.

Blanca, a 46-year-old, female-identified Latinx from Mexico, was born in a small town and was one of 12 children. Her parents worked the land, and her mother had a double shift involving work outside and inside the home. She was responsible for taking care of the children, cooking, and cleaning, in addition to farming and making artisan sleeping mats for sale. Blanca and her siblings began working at age four. Their duties increased in quantity and complexity as they grew up; they were all expected to contribute inside and outside the household in some way after coming home from school. Blanca completed 10th grade. Her family lived in a small, one-room shack, with no divisions inside. When she was 6 years old, her eldest brother sexually abused her and her sisters. The parents were unprotective. Blanca left her family's home very young and partnered with Martin. While initially positive, the relationship turned conflictive and abusive over the years. Martin took a loan with interest to pay for his migration journey to the USA. When he could not pay it, Blanca was sent to the USA by her family and her husband to work to pay his loan. Her mother took care of her two children for several years. They eventually came to the USA and joined Blanca, Martin, and their youngest sibling, who was born in the USA. Martin was a hands-off father. He provided material security but rarely got involved in his children's activities, set limits, or shared his life with them. In addition, he had an affair with Blanca's sister. Eventually Blanca and Martin divorced.

Blanca's youngest child, Yesenia, was born in the USA. She identified as female and as a queer lesbian and was 24 when they entered therapy. Blanca was most comfortable speaking Spanish, and Yesenia was most comfortable speaking English. However, their knowledge of Spanish and English overlapped enough to allow meaningful conversation without a lot of literal translation. Blanca and Yesenia's relationship was strained due to conflicts over Yesenia's choice of a partner and a legacy of family issues. Yesenia grew up with both of her biological parents until age 10. Like her mother, she suffered sexual trauma; she was assaulted at a party by a peer in college when she was inebriated and could not consent. She attended community college and lived independently with her biracial (African American and white) partner, Jesse. At the time Blanca entered family therapy with Yesenia, Blanca had been in therapy with me for more than a year. Yesenia was in her own individual therapy. They had struggled since Yesenia was a young child because both had *carácteres fuertes*, or strong temperaments, and they clashed. In addition, Yesenia was often caught up in her parents' conflicts due Yesenia's alliance with Martin and challenges around sexual orientation and gender involving Blanca's limited and rigid view of women's roles and nontraditional relationships.

Therapy with Blanca and Yesenia began with the general goal of alleviating ongoing conflicts in communication. As we experientially addressed what these conflicts involved, they evoked memories of past injuries and ruptures that had occurred during Yesenia's childhood and adolescence. From a relational perspective, Yesenia's memories of how she experienced her mother evoked Blanca's memories of how she experienced her own childhood and adolescence.

The first phase of therapy involved co-creating a space safe enough for them to take risks, be vulnerable with each other, and experientially (Johnson, 2021) address emotionally intense arguments by listening and with mutual emotional regulation through emotion-focused therapy (Stavrianopoulos et al., 2014). By responding to the here and now, we explored rigid patterns of interaction and negative affect involving emotional disconnection and the insecure attachment that exacerbated the situation. I encouraged them to acknowledge their fears, and after naming the power differentials in the relationship, I invited them to explore the impact of their actions on each other. This process helped them acknowledge how they were both hurt by parents who could not be emotionally present and who wounded them in ways that were often passed down from their own parents. Yesenia was able to understand, appreciate, and feel compassion for her mother's spousal relationship. That dysfunction involved Martin's under-functioning and Blanca's overinvolvement. Martin's role as a father was mostly focused on covering the family's basic material needs; he was absent from the day-to-day play, feeding, school preparation and follow-up, and friendships. In this context, Blanca, an overly anxious and traumatized mother, felt that she needed to take control over providing the children with structure and discipline. This was an almost impossible task with Martin's frequent and passive undermining of her authority. Blanca became the one responsible for her children, with very little cooperation from Martin. At the same time, Blanca empathized with the pain of her daughter and was able to hear how her authoritarian style hurt Yesenia by creating fear and a lack of trust. Once they started learning to voice their emotional needs and respond to each other with acceptance and compassion, they felt that repair was possible. Next, Blanca and Yesenia worked on sharing their testimonios about their childhoods and adolescences. Blanca chose to speak from her heart using candles of various colors as symbols of her feelings and experiences. Yesenia wrote a letter. We moved back and forth in English and Spanish.

The First Nepantla Moment

The first nepantla moment emerged with the sharing of testimonios in a ritualized manner. A shift in the conversation occurred when Yesenia brought up the historical pain of female-identified people in their family. They felt compassion for these women, who had endured oppression inside and outside of their households. Following up on generating ecologies of temporality, I invited them to bring in these ancestors through imagination and mindfulness. Some of them showed up, along with queer and male-identified people. We held space for them in our sessions and together created a simple fire ceremony to honor their pain and resilience. Blanca consulted with her curandera friends in the USA and Mexico and guided us in making offerings to these ancestors. Yesenia's sisters attended the ritual.

The fire ritual generated more space in which to name and sit with the impact of colonization on their lives. In an open fashion, I invited them to acknowledge anyone who needed to be present in this ritual to create space for potential ecologies of recognition. Yesenia acknowledged the presence of queer people in their extended family and discussed the injuries they suffered as a result of homophobia. Blanca offered rue for her brother Efrain, whom she never talked about.

The Second Nepantla Moment

The second nepantla moment occurred later in session at my office. Yesenia expressed her need to be acknowledged and loved by her mother and other family members as a queer person. The intensity heightened greatly as Blanca and Yesenia discussed how Blanca's sisters and other relatives would respond to Yesenia's identity, as well as their views on homosexuality and queerness. Blanca shared prejudiced beliefs embedded in her Catholic upbringing. Yesenia questioned the roots of those beliefs, asking her mother to consider how "the Bible denies existence of anyone who is not binary and sets Eve up to a path of shame and guilt and inferiority." Blanca shared how fear of god, priests, and hell was instilled in her as a child. Although the emotional temperature rose, they were able to temporarily tolerate it. Blanca shared in tears that her brother Efrain was probably attracted to men and that the family had rejected and isolated him to the point that he left their hometown and never returned. She had lost contact with him. While this conversation stayed at the level of their experience, it helped them to invite connections with social issues involving violence against queer people, raising Blanca's critical consciousness about the contributions of the Catholic Church to colonization in regard to female and queer-identified people. At this time, Blanca was ready to take responsibility for her own homophobia and the ways in which she had hurt Yesenia over the years by making her queerness invisible. Furthermore, they were both able to see and emotionally release the burden of homophobia in their family as a result of the patriarchal order established by colonization. Blanca used herbal baths to cleanse and release this burden. This was both a choice based on understanding and a somatic experience. Yesenia chose to hike to a mountain and make an offering in the form of a bundle of herbs. Yesenia and Blanca achieved momentary states of mutual regulation and understood the other's personal experiences of trauma and how they were tied to violent social forces in different generations of their family.

The Third Nepantla Moment

The third nepantla moment occurred in the relationships that Blanca and Yesenia had with work. As described earlier, Blanca was socialized to labor before she could even speak clearly. Her body grew used to the routine of lots of work and little play. Contemporary neuroscience reminds us that genetic inheritance directs the overall organization of the brain and that experience influences how, when, and which genes will become expressed. As with any other human, Blanca's genes and experiences have contributed to the formation of her brain and mind. Her genetic makeup influences specific connections in the brain. Her experiences, which activate her neurons, shape connections in her brain through the formation of synapses and new neuronal growth. Mental processes shape neural connections, which in turn shape mental processes. Blanca had worked and taken care of others her whole life. This was how she knew how to live and survive. Thus, her relationship with work was deeply ingrained in her cells and offered her many benefits, including emotional release. As an immigrant, she worked very hard to create a small and successful cleaning business, which later allowed her to enjoy a degree of comfort that she never had known before. Yesenia grew up in a home in which her parents worked and she went to school. She got her first job assisting others at a Mexican restaurant at age 16. She held other jobs, including working with her mother, and in all her jobs, she was paid for her labor. She was able to rest and socialize with peers, and she had regular and continued opportunities for play and connection with others within a working-class context.

Given that their relationships with work had evolved in such different ways, it was not surprising that Blanca expected Yesenia to work more and earn more and to contribute to help family members in Mexico. Yesenia had trained as a veterinary assistant and derived a lot of satisfaction from her work at a local veterinary clinic. She loved animals, and she and Jesse had a dog and a cat. Often, she supplemented her income with pet-sitting. Yesenia and Jesse shared their finances and were able to sustain themselves with their incomes. Yesenia had declined her mother's invitations to join her cleaning business and rarely contributed to helping relatives in need. Their arguments around work expectations and productivity were sometimes heated, especially when Blanca needed help.

The therapy process moved to a nepantla state when I asked Blanca and Yesenia to mindfully sit with their work as an entity outside of themselves. Having prepared my office with sage, I invited them to open their senses and smell it. I proceeded to ask them to sit with the smells of their workplaces, and I stimulated a sensual and visual connection with settings and their smells. We then conversed about what various workspaces smelled like and how they experienced them. This brought a rich conversation about the smells of the land versus the smells of offices and about relationships with nonhuman beings, including plants and domestic animals. The emotional temperature flattened when Blanca's testimonio addressed all the caretaking responsibilities that had robbed her of the possibility of play as a child. Her tears had depth, like they were rising from her womb. It seemed as if, for the first time, Yesenia realized how colonization had made her mother useful until she was no longer useful. She articulated out loud how her mother's strength had been exploited by the systems that create poverty and exclusion, by her own family, and by the dominant U.S. culture of productivity and consumerism. At the same time, Blanca appreciated how this strength had helped her survive and had given her children a different life.

In this state of nepantla, mother and daughter listened to each other and discussed their very different relationships with work and productivity. Yesenia invited her mother to experiment with small actions of care for self and enjoyment, and Blanca invited Yesenia to share more in helping her aging grandparents. They discussed differences around familial responsibility, leisure, and the meaning of money. Yesenia acknowledged that she felt embarrassment in regard to her mother's occupation, as it was emblematic of Latinx immigrant work and, in her experience, the target of hostility from peers.

The nepantla space culminated with another fire ceremony, in which they honored ancestors forced into indentured labor and, later, those forced to survive using their children's labor. They hoped for the spiritual release of those who came before them and those who will come after them. They released themselves from the current painful aspects of work and invited a transformation in this relationship. Furthermore, they committed to allow the coexistence of their different views on this relationship for the future.

Nepantla is where neurobiology (Siegel, 2017, 2019), psychology (Bernstein, 2005), social discourse and social practices (Galarza, 2013), and spirituality (Cervantes, 2010; Samuel et al., 2020) connect all at once—where the sum is more than the total of the parts and where something new and different is created. In this case, a key to generating these moments involves a back and forth and a tightening of relationships at the level of the body, emotion, narration, and spirituality.

Conclusion

In this paper, I have articulated how key concepts from *Epistemologies of the South*, such as the ecologies of temporality, recognition, and productivity (De Sousa Santos, 2012), can be integrated with a Mujerista therapy framework in which borderland thinking is emphasized to address trauma and resilience within a context of decolonization. Through the case study of a Latinx mother and daughter, I have illustrated nepantla moments and the co-construction of testimonios involving experiential, narrative, and spiritual levels of experience.

From a Mujerista psychology perspective, Comas-Díaz (2008, p. 15) affirms that "*mujeristas* transform the Latino diaspora, a cultural space inhabited by denizens enmeshed in dynamics of inclusion/exclusion, into a *nepantla* of continuing resistance, reconstruction, and evolution." Thus, therapy can be a site of decolonization in which the traumatic and resilient experiences of individuals, couples, families, and communities are transformed in moments in which readiness and consent at an emotional, cognitive, and spiritual level are present. These moments are achieved in the back-and-forth flow of coherence and lack of coherence that develops in therapy as testimonios get transformed in the telling and retelling and in the emotional and spiritual work of therapy.

References

Aguilar, A. (2019). Envisioning "loving care" in impermanent healing spaces: Sacred and political organizing towards decolonial health/care in Oakland, California. *ISSI Graduate Fellows* Working Paper Series 2018–2019.87.

Anzaldúa, G. (1999). *Borderlands/la frontera: The new Mestiza* (2nd ed.). Aunt Lute Books.

Anzaldúa, G. (2000). *Interviews/entrevistas* (A. L. Keating, Ed.). Routledge.

Anzaldúa, G. E. (2002). Preface. In G. E. Anzaldúa & A. Keating (Eds.), *This bridge we call home: Radical visions for transformation* (pp. 1–5). Routledge.

Benjamin, J. (2004). Beyond doer and done to: An intersubjective view of thirdness. *The Psychoanalytic Quarterly, 73*(1), 5–46. https://doi.org/10.1002/j.2167-4086.2004.tb00151.x

Bernstein, J. (2005). *Living in the borderland: The evolution of consciousness and the challenge of healing trauma*. Routledge.

Bromberg, P. M. (1993). Shadow and substance: A relational perspective on clinical process. *Psychoanalytic Psychology, 10*(2), 147–168. https://doi.org/10.1037/h0079464

Burns, C. E. (2019). Therapeutic uses of the flute within music therapy practice. *Music Therapy Perspectives, 37*(2), 169–175. https://doi.org/10.1093/mtp/miz003

Cerezo, A., Cummings, M., Holmes, M., & Williams, C. (2020). Identity as resistance: Identity formation at the intersection of race, gender identity, and sexual orientation. *Psychology of Women Quarterly, 44*(1), 67–83. https://doi.org/10.1177/0361684319875977

Cervantes, J. M. (2010). Mestizo spirituality: Toward an integrated approach to psychotherapy for Latina/os. *Psychotherapy (Chicago, Ill.), 47*(4), 527–539. https://doi.org/10.1037/a0022078

Chavez-Dueñas, N. Y., Adames, H. Y., Perez-Chavez, J. G., & Salas, S. P. (2019). Healing ethno-racial trauma in Latinx immigrant communities: Cultivating hope, resistance, and action. *The American Psychologist, 74*(1), 49–62. https://doi.org/10.1037/amp0000289

Comas-Díaz, L. (2008). Spirita: Reclaiming womanist sacredness into feminism. *Psychology of Women Quarterly, 32*, 13–21.

Comas-Díaz, L. (2019). Latina adolescent girls at the cultural borderlands. In T. Bryant-Davis (Ed.). *Multicultural feminist therapy* (pp. 155–187). American Psychological Association.

Comas-Díaz, L. (2020a). Journey to psychology: A mujerista testimonio. *Women & Therapy, 43*(1–2), 157–169. https://doi.org/10.1080/02703149.2019.1684676

Comas-Díaz, L. (2020b). Liberation psychotherapy. In L. Comas-Díaz, Lillian & E. Torres Rivera (Eds). *Liberation psychology: Theory, method, practice, and social justice* (pp. 169–185). American Psychological Association. https://doi.org/10.1037/0000198-010

De Sousa Santos, B. (2012). *Una Epistemología del Sur. La reinvención del conocimiento y la emancipación social [An epistemology of the South. The reinvention of knowledge and social emancipation]*. Siglo XXI Editores.

De Sousa Santos, B. (2019). Epistemologies of the South and the future. *From the European South, 1*, 17–29.

Freire, P. (1973/1992). *Education for critical consciousness*. Continuum.

Galarza, J. (2013). Borderland queer: Narrative approaches in clinical work with Latina women who have sex with women (WSW). *Journal of LGBT Issues in Counseling, 7*(3), 274–291. https://doi.org/10.1080/15538605.2013.812931

Gil, R. M., & Inoa Vazquez, C. (2014). *The maría paradox: How Latinas can merge old world traditions with new world self-esteem*. Integrated Media.

Gilmore, L. (2010). *Theater in a crowded fire: Ritual and spirituality at Burning Man*. University of California Press.

Hutchings, J. B. (2015). Symbolic use of color in ritual, tradition and folklore. In A. J. Elliot, M. D. Fairchild, & A. Franklin (Eds.), *Handbook of color psychology* (pp. 340–356). Cambridge University Press.

Johnson, R. (2014). Somatic psychotherapy research: Walking the common ground. *Body, Movement and Dance in Psychotherapy, an International Journal of Theory, Research and Practice, 9*(2), 82–92. https://doi.org/10.1080/17432979.2014.893449

Johnson, S. M. (2021). Attachment principles as a guide to therapeutic change: The example of emotionally focused therapy. In R. A. Thompson, J. A. Simpson, & L. J. Berlin (Eds.), *Attachment: The fundamental questions* (pp. 332–338). Guilford Press.

Kawano, T. (2018). Transmission of the professional identity through an embodied artistic ritual: An investigation of dance/movement therapy welcoming ceremony. *The Arts in Psychotherapy, 57*, 1–10. https://doi.org/10.1016/j.aip.2017.09.001

Keating, A. L. (2006). From borderlands and new Mestizas to nepantlas and nepantleras: Anzaldúan theories for social change. *Journal of the Sociology of Self-Knowledge, 4*, 5–16.

King, E., & Miehls, D. (2008). Third space activities and change processes: An exploration of ideas from social and psychodynamic theories. *Clinical Social Work Journal, 36*(2), 165–175. https://doi.org/10.1007/s10615-007-0117-1

Masten, A. S. (2014). *Ordinary magic: Resilience in development*. Guilford Press.

Mignolo, W. (2011). Geopolitics of sensing and knowing: On (de)coloniality, border thinking and epistemic disobedience. *Postcolonial Studies, 14*(3), 273–285. https://doi.org/10.1080/13688790.2011.613105

Mignolo, W., & Walsh, C. (2018). *On decoloniality*. Duke University Press.

Perez Huber, L. (2009). Disrupting apartheid of knowledge: *testimonio* as methodology in Latina/o critical race research in education. *International Journal of Qualitative Studies in Education, 22*(6), 639–654. https://doi.org/10.1080/09518390903333863

Polanco, M. (2019). En defensa de Spanglish family therapy supervision in the era of English. In L. Charlés & T. Nelson (Eds.), *Family therapy supervision in extraordinary settings: Illustrations of systemic approaches in every day clinical work* (pp. 1–12). Routledge.

Quijano, A. (2000). Coloniality of power. Eurocentrism, and Latin America. *Nepantla, 1*(3), 533–580.

Rios, V. M., & Vigil, J. D. (2017). *Human targets: Schools, police, and the criminalization of Latino youth*. University of Chicago Press.

Samuel, C. A., Mbah, O. M., Elkins, W., Pinheiro, L. C., Szymeczek, M. A., Padilla, N., Walker, J. S., & Corbie-Smith, G. (2020). Calidad de vida: A systematic review of quality of life in Latino cancer survivors in the USA. *Quality of Life Research, 29* (10), 2615–2630. https://doi.org/10.1007/s11136-020-02527-0

Shapiro, E. (2020). Liberation psychology, creativity, and arts-based activism and artivism: Culturally meaningful methods connecting personal development and social change. In L. Comas-Díaz & E. Torres Rivera (Eds.), *Liberation psychology: Theory, method, practice, and social justice* (pp. 247–264). American Psychological Association.

Shapiro, E., & Alcántara, D. (2016). Mujerista creativity: Latin@ sacred arts as life-course developmental resources. In T. Bryant-Davis & L. Comas-Díaz (Eds.), *Womanist and mujerista psychologies: Voices of fire, acts of courage* (pp. 195–216). American Psychological Association. https://doi.org/10.1037/14937-009

Siegel, D. (2017). *Mind: A journey of the heart of being human*. W. W. Norton.

Siegel, D. J. (2019). The mind in psychotherapy: An interpersonal neurobiology framework for understanding and cultivating mental health. *Psychology and Psychotherapy, 92*(2), 224–237. https://doi.org/10.1111/papt.12228

Stavrianopoulos, K., Faller, G., & Furrow, J. L. (2014). Emotionally focused family therapy: Facilitating change within a family system. *Journal of Couple & Relationship Therapy, 13*(1), 25–43. https://doi.org/10.1080/15332691.2014.865976

Ungar, M. (2006). Resilience across cultures. *British Journal of Social Work, 38*(2), 218–235. https://doi.org/10.1093/bjsw/bcl343

Ungar, M., & Theron, L. (2020). Resilience and mental health: How multisystemic processes contribute to positive outcomes. *The Lancet. Psychiatry, 7*(5), 441–448. https://doi.org/10.1016/S2215-0366(19)30434-1

Mujerista Psychology: A Case Study Centering Latinx Empowerment in Psychotherapy

Marlene L. Cabrera and Carrie L. Castañeda-Sound

ABSTRACT
This article uses a case study to illustrate Mujerista tenants for mental health practitioners working with the adult female Latinx population. Reviewed are potential Latinx cultural values, history, traditions, and political movements within the United States. We demonstrate the advantages and limitations of a Mujerista perspective in therapy to offer clinicians exposure to a culturally specific treatment for Latinx women. Further, the case study informs mental health practitioners of the unique issues relevant to some Latinx adult women, such as intergenerational trauma, gender scripts, and spirituality.

Few people were untouched by the COVID-19 pandemic and the resulting loss of life, employment insecurity, and a myriad of stressors that persist with new variants of the disease.

This pandemic unveiled the profound economic, racial, and ethnic disparities such as access to health and mental health care for marginalized communities (Karaye & Horney, 2020; Shim & Starks, 2021). The American Psychological Association reports the United States is in a mental health crisis due to the multiple sources of stress and trauma (American Psychological Association (APA), 2020), with an increasing high demand for mental health service. In the context of this demand and "crisis," clinicians must be careful not to compromise cultural responsiveness and attunement when providing these services. This means less reliance on expert-driven approaches and more on bottom-up approaches (Wessells, 2015). Bottom-up approaches work from grassroots level upward, feature community action, build on existing community strengths, and stimulate collaboration. Thus, using a method that is derived from the environment and cultural values of an individual can be useful for marginalized people.

Liberation psychology empowers marginalized individuals against dehumanizing institutions by exploring strategies to build a genuinely democratic society. The framing of the theory begins with the idea that dehumanization is a historical and current reality and the result of an unjust discrimination toward marginalized communities by the oppressors (Friere, 1970). This focus can be utilized to actively understand the psychology of the oppressed by conceptualizing and directly addressing the repressive sociopolitical structure they actively experience. Liberation psychology argues that although certain groups are oppressed and marginalized, an individual can confront this oppression and reconstruct new values, interests, and needs through the process of *deideologizing and conscientización* [see Comas-Díaz & Torres Rivera, 2020, for more information about Liberation Psychology]. Furthermore, human beings have a capacity to create meaning and make sense of their circumstances, act intentionally, and maintain one's culture, which provides a lens through which to view new encounters (Duran et al., 2008).

Martín-Baró (1994) identified a change in consciousness—transforming one's consciousness and constructing a new reality co-created with their therapist—as a liberating process, while the therapist is also equally and genuinely changed through the relationship (Duran et al., 2008). This framework reflects upon the shared experiences of oppression as experienced by marginalized groups, with an understanding that, from a patriarchal, Eurocentric perspective, the hierarchical category of privilege and power benefits one group over another.

Despite the contributions of Liberation Psychology, it is not without its limitations. The initial formulations developed by Martín-Baró (1994) did not consider the intersectional role of gender, and the marginalization of LGBTQ+ communities was invisible. Much of this is owed to its Christian theological roots and connection to coloniality (Singh et al., 2020); nevertheless, Singh et al. (2020) give voice to applications of liberation psychology to queer and trans communities.

Ada María Isasi Díaz (1996), a theologian who focused on feminist theology, also filled gaps in liberation theology by integrating Latina feminist thought to create Mujerista theology. She highlighted this oversight of gender, ethnicity, and economic oppression and focused on Latina women's experiences. Inspired by Isasi Díaz, Comas-Díaz (2012) initiated Mujerista psychology, which calls for Latinas to develop their inner voice, reconnect with ancestral wisdom, resist oppression, chart their journey, and advocate for social justice. Further, mujeristas fight the established domination that oppresses individuals based on gender, race, class, and sexual orientation. Comas-Díaz (2012) explains that mujeristas go through a metaphorical baptism process where they spiritually give birth to their new self. During their psychospiritual journey, mujeristas acknowledge and give honor to their ancestral legacy, recognize their cultural values, norms, and rituals, while simultaneously recognizing their historical trauma and soul wounds. A mujerista therapist facilitates this concientización by engaging in discourse with the client about their experiences in their environment and the internalization of toxic messages, as well as helping the client reconnect with their spiritual gifts.

In this way, mujeristas reconstruct their perceptions so that they can survive, thrive, and fight their oppression by dispelling colonial, Eurocentric values (Portillo, 2012). During the therapeutic process, the therapist incorporates proverbs, songs, prayers, and testimonies as a way of honoring the Latinx cultural values, rituals, folklore, traditions, creativity, and service to others. This liberates mujeristas from (neo) colonization by deconstructing narratives about mental illness and wellness and the compartmentalization of treatment. Mujersitas focus on holistic healing by incorporating indigenous and spiritual perspectives into treatment. The ultimate honor of the sacredness is actualized through service to humanity that leads to social liberation (Bryant-Davis & Comas-Díaz, 2016). Through social activism, mujeristas are empowered to co-create their environment and reality, fostering further self-realization (Comas-Díaz, 2013).

The Mujerista approach can incorporate spirituality through Catholicism and Christianity, as well as indigenous practices. Although Christianity was imposed on the indigenous people of Latin America, it is not uncommon for their spiritual functionality to work independently from the church. Latinos weaved their pre-conquest traditions into their oppressor's religious sect (Comas-Díaz, 2012). The goal of Mujerista psychology is to provide empowerment to the mujerista by promoting reconnection to her ancestral ties (Isasi-Díaz, 1996). For some clients, this involves the integration of two or more spiritual traditions (e.g., Christianity, Indigenous, Buddhist, secular, etc.), and for others, the ancestral ties are to one practice. This can be a complicated process for clients who have cognitive dissonance about wanting to explore ancestral traditions, but feeling conflicted about what is "allowable," particularly with religions with mandates against this exploration. Ultimately, clients are empowered to choose their path in this journey of exploration.

Mujerista psychology intersects with sociocultural psychology, as it transcends the idea of impacting a single group based on membership alone. When considering Adams and Markus (2001) discussion of the fluidity of patterns, one can understand the affinities in experiences across domains of race, ethnicity, and geographic locations of women globally. Comas-Díaz (2013) confirms this fluidity in patterns across various ethnic backgrounds of women by stating that Mujerista psychology can be useful for women of various ethnic backgrounds. Thus, the spirit of the Mujerista applies to the culture of women as a whole, embodying strength, power, and resilience.

This then weaves Mujerista psychology into an anti-racist, intersectional feminist theoretical frame.

Components of Mujerista Psychology

In *Womanist and Mujerista Psychologies: Voice of Fire, Acts of Courage,* Bryant-Davis and Comas-Díaz (2016) introduce the psychological pillars of Womanism and Mujerismo. In the edited book, Mujerismo is described as an inclusive method to feminism and liberation psychology. The components of Mujerismo—Reauthoring the Life Story; Living out the *Patrón*; Envisioning Transformation; Psycho-spirituality, *La Lucha* (social justice)—are described in the following section and then demonstrated through the case study of a client.

Reauthoring the Life Story

In order to develop *concientización*, or critical consciousness, one must recognize and name a history of oppression and use the memory to move forward (Martín-Baró, 1998). By helping a client recognize how oppression and marginalization in her personal and collective identities have served as obstacles, she can begin to better understand her cultural identity(ies), decolonize internalized notions of deficiency, and in turn (re)establish improved psychological, spiritual, and social functioning. This gives the client the opportunity to critically think about her past in relation to her ancestors and decide how she chooses to move forward with the goals she has established for her future. This should not just be at the individual level, but also should include relational and collective movement. The shifting between the past, present, and future, particularly with regard to collective trauma, will be demonstrated in the case example.

The mechanism and transmission of intergenerational trauma is present within communities (e.g., Native Americans, African Americans, and Holocaust survivors) that experience traumatic events (Henderson et al., 2021; Ortega-Williams et al., 2021). These events don't just target an individual, they target a collective community. The trauma is held personally and can be transmitted over generations. Even family members who do not have a direct experience of the trauma itself can feel the effects generations later (Evans-Campbell, 2008).

Ancestors have mechanisms for healing, too. Reconnecting people to the vibrant strengths of their ancestry and culture (e.g., art, dance, spirituality, ceremonies), helping people process the grief of past traumas, centering testimonios, and creating critically conscious historical narratives can have healing effects for those experiencing historical trauma.

While scholarly literature on historical trauma has mostly focused on indigenous peoples of North America and descendants of enslaved peoples from Africa, research has shown that colonialism in Latin America is another source of intergenerational trauma (Comas-Díaz, 2006). According to Sabin et al. (2003), Guatemalan refugees who experienced multiple traumatic effects due to human rights violations were found to have a high prevalence of depressive and anxiety symptoms twenty years after the conflict. Also, colonialism has been shown to affect the identities of Latin American colonized populations (Varas-Díaz & Serrano-García, 2003). The colonized population is perceived as inferior, and the history and culture of the colonized group is devalued (Chavez, 2011; Chavez-Dueñas et al., 2014; Varas-Díaz & Serrano-García, 2003). The dominant group imposes its own culture and defines what is normal (Chavez, 2011, Chavez-Dueñas et al., 2014; Varas-Díaz & Serrano-García, 2003), and deviations from the dominant culture lead to negative self-perceptions (Varas-Díaz & Serrano-Garcia, 2003). In a study of the effects of colonization on the identities of Puerto Rican youth, the authors found shame and anger were associated with perceived lack of collective identity, and reports showed a desire to emulate the dominant culture (Varas-Díaz & Serrano-García, 2003). The authors surmised that the internalization of inferiority is conveyed through self-hate and distorted self-image (Varas-Díaz & Serrano-García, 2003). Equally harmful was the colonizer's imposed value of deeming women as inferior to men (Bryant-Davis & Comas-Díaz, 2016).

Living out the Patrón (Blueprint)

Creating a *patrón* can help clients define what is most important (i.e., their values) and take effective action guided by those values (Bryant-Davis & Comas-Díaz, 2016; Gloria & Castellanos, 2016). These values often act as a compass or blueprint in the direction of intentional and effective behavior. The Mujerista therapist will generally employ a variety of exercises to help the client identify values. For example, exploring painful emotions may interfere with a client's ability to choose purposeful and values-guided action. Exploring the connections of these emotions to intergenerational trauma and coloniality is a step toward critical consciousness and liberation. Thus, the individual will begin to act with intent to manifest or engage change.

Envision Transformation

In order to transform one's life, an individual must first envision their rebirth. Trusting that transformation is not only feasible and that the client can take on a liberated role or manifest change is central to the revelation.

This is not about wishing that things were different for oneself, family, or their community at large. Rather, it is the realization that change is needed or desired for progress while engaging the process of recognizing how change can be achieved (Bryant-Davis & Comas-Díaz, 2016, p. 102.)

It is both insight and faith that ignites one's strength and is critical to establishing one's patrón.

Through this process, the client will envision how learning to use her voice and creating her blueprint of cultural values could allow her to help herself, her family, and her community in the future. By accessing the same familial vision for change and focused strengths of her ancestors, the client can manifest her transformation. The clinician is not trying to pull her away from her social support system, but instead encouraging her to locate sources of strength in her family and community and to find her voice.

Psychospirituality

While Roman Catholicism plays a significant role in providing for Latina well-being (Falicov, 1998), Comas-Díaz (2012) notes that *espiritismo, curanderismo,* and *Santería* are other forms of indigenous practice utilized as a healing method. In the practice of espiritismo, personal challenges that the client endures are viewed as spiritual development. The goal of espiritismo is to assist the individual with positively reframing events in their lives. *Espiritismo* (or spiritism) is a common syncretistic religion practiced most often in Puerto Rico, Cuba, and Santo Domingo, although it is also practiced in other Latin American countries. It incorporates 19th-century spiritualism imported from Northern Europe into Catholic and Taino traditions (Laria & Lewis-Fernández, 2006). Falicov (1998) defines *espiritismo* as a spiritual practice based on:

> ... an invisible world of good and evil spirits that can attach themselves to human beings, thus influencing behavior. Beliefs in the existence of benevolent and malevolent spirits are embedded deep in the history and living traditions of indigenous peoples in the Americas (p. 162).

In modern society, it is also common for Puerto Rican women, in particular, to draw on Taino tradition to hold close to the spiritual presence of a loved one even after death (Falicov, 1998). Falicov stated that many Puerto Ricans and some Cubans, mainly those who reside in the eastern region of the island, rely on the services of *espiritistas* (spiritualists or mediums), who can communicate with the spirits and who have healing powers. For Latina women and within Latinx cultures generally, issues related to health and well-being involve a multifaceted interaction between physical, psychological, social, and spiritual factors (Falicov, 1998). She also noted that although it is difficult to tease out or separate the causation between psychological and somatic disorders and between naturalistic and spiritual elements, these elements combine and affect each other. Furthermore, Santería has relevance to feminist psychological practice because it includes several powerful goddesses, highlighting the divine feminine (Asikiwe, 2021), thus offering powerful models to females. Santería was described by Laria and Lewis-Fernández (2006) as:

> ... a fusion of Catholic saints and African gods among some Latino cultures. [It is] the most common of Latino syncretistic religions, most frequently practiced in Cuba, Puerto Rico, Argentina, Brazil, Colombia, Mexico, and Venezuela. Santería is a syncretism of African, primarily Yoruban, traditions and Catholicism. It involves an elaborate pantheon of deities called orishas or Santos (saints) who exert influence over all elements of life. Most frequently, orishas are called on to intervene in matters related to health, wealth, and social relations, especially those of a romantic nature (p. 138).

It is important to note that colonization involves the dehumanization of people and their communities, as well as an attempt to erase religious and spiritual practices. Clients may be hesitant to share their spiritual beliefs because of a fear of rejection or being pathologized. Therapists unfamiliar with these religious practices should also be careful about exoticizing the client's spiritual beliefs and/or asking intrusive questions about sacred ceremonies and practices.

La Lucha and Social Justice

Major influences on Mujerista psychology have stemmed from Latina feminist scholars who approach mental health care by promoting human development and the common good by addressing issues related to both the individual and distributive justice. Latina feminist psychology includes empowerment of the individual to actively confront injustice and inequality in society because they affect the client as well as those in their systemic contexts (Castañeda-Sound et al., 2016; Crethar et al., 2008). A Latina feminist psychological intervention results in clients identifying areas of their life where they have power to make change (see Power Analysis by Brown, 2009) and navigating the interpersonal skills to collaborate with allies to address structural obstacles affecting well-being (Crethar et al., 2008). As clients develop awareness and skills in these areas, they become increasingly capable of standing up to the injustices that they face in their lives. Within the Mujerista treatment, the therapist and client engage in discussions that humanize the dehumanized. Through discussing the myths and realities of immigration and acculturation, stereotyping and discrimination in educational and employment settings, and housing insecurity, engagement in social justice can heal the client's community, and empowerment is further facilitated.

Case Study

This de-identified case study illustrates Mujerista approaches to psychotherapy conducted in a community counseling clinic. Sofia, a 24-year-old, cisgender, heterosexual woman, lived in a low-income neighborhood of a metropolitan area of Los Angeles, California. She identified as a bilingual Latina and was born in a Central American country. She was reared in a Catholic household, and she frequently consulted local *Curanderas* (spiritual advisors) for spiritual advice, a practice in which her family members regularly engaged in. This case study is unique in that it reflects psychotherapy as imperfect and non-linear and is shared from the perspective of the primary therapist (Marlene).

Sofia's Reasons for Seeking Psychotherapy

Sofia sought psychotherapy for help with her anxiety, but she also endorsed significant and persistent low mood, difficulty making decisions, and low self-esteem. She shared that she often feels lonely and depressed when alone and typically cries when others are not around. Sofia also reported that she believes herself to be "unattractive and overweight" and that she eats excessively to cope with low mood, family tensions, and relationship distress. Sofia denied ever having thoughts of suicide or of harming herself.

Sofia was in a long-term, monogamous relationship with a man of Asian descent, but added that she has been having an "affair" with another man for a year prior to seeking therapy. She met her "lover" during her graduate program, and she was initially attracted to him because he was intelligent, confident, and Latino. This caused significant distress, and she had difficulty concentrating due to the worry that her affair would be discovered. Additionally, upon the Curandera's discovery of Sofia's affair via omens during a ritual session, she began to experience increased anxious distress as the Curandera informed her that the affair will "weaken her soul." Regarding her current long-term relationship, Sofia disclosed that she was no longer in love with her partner, but that the thought of breaking his heart caused her further emotional distress.

Sofia understood her struggle with making decisions as stemming from her upbringing. She and her younger sister were raised to follow their family's instructions, including what clothing to wear, music to listen to, and the "right" people to associate with. Sofia further stated that her parents closely monitored her choice of friends and that they discouraged her from associating with people from Mexico or African Americans because they were considered "inferior."

Sofia reported that her relationship with her father was an additional source of significant distress. Sofia described her father as a strict disciplinarian who was both controlling and domineering. He used fear tactics to control her behavior, such as telling her not to go to the beach because she will drown. Additionally, Sofia expressed fears of defying her parent's instructions, feeling her father might retaliate by putting a spiritual hex on her. Sofia reported that the idea of letting her father down particularly exacerbated her anxious distress.

Sofia described herself as "shy and introverted" and having difficulty communicating throughout her life. She struggled with low self-esteem when she was in middle school when she realized that she was different from her fellow classmates, specifically because she identified herself as one of the "poor kids."

Sofia moved away to attend college, and while she enjoyed her time away from her parents, she still longed for her family. Sofia explained she was "extremely" attached to her parents and calls them multiple times a day. She reported having conflict with her parents regarding attending social events without them, causing her to feel isolated from her peers and harbor resentment toward her parents. Due to her traditional upbringing congruent with her cultural background, she was not able to express her frustration toward her parents. She further noted that her daily decision-making skills were impacted by her parents' expectations that she communicate each decision with them first. She imagined their scrutiny when engaging in any decision-making, which was often debilitating and resulted in rumination and indecisiveness. After she graduated from a local university, Sofia's father became "cold" and regularly reminded her that she was not better than him. She did not feel comfortable discussing her feelings with her parents for fear that she would insult them.

Early Phase of Therapy - Lessons Learned

I (Marlene) initially selected a cognitive behavioral approach to help Sofia manage her feelings of depression related to her romantic relationships and her low self-esteem. Sofia presented as aloof in sessions, often spoke with a fairly low tone, and responded with "Yeah, I understand" with no follow up statements. Most sessions revolved around her intensifying feelings for her lover and the need to terminate her relationship with her boyfriend. She primarily discussed her fear of disappointing her family because of her belief that they were counting on her boyfriend's financial support in the future. Additionally, as the suspicion of her affair grew amongst her family, her parents began checking in on her more. Her mother called every hour to ensure that she was with her boyfriend, at home, or at school. Her father arrived at her apartment unannounced to visit and "keep tabs."

Sofia began to miss sessions often and at one point did not return to treatment for almost a month. Sofia informed me that she did not feel a "connection with the treatment." I offered the option of changing to a new approach to psychotherapy, a Mujerista Psychology framework. Sofia agreed, and the therapeutic relationship shifted after this session when Sofia had more space to contribute to the direction of the sessions.

A New Beginning - Therapeutic Alliance as Comadres

I incorporated a Comadre approach (Comas-Díaz, 2013) to the therapeutic relationship. The term comadre is utilized in Latinx cultures and means co-mother and midwife. Comadre represents the intimate relationship between a mother and her child's Godmother. It also represents a best friend who can be called upon at any time, which is how I utilized the approach. As a comadre, I assisted the client in reconnecting to her gendered cultural identity. It promoted decolonization and supported empowerment by reconnecting Sofia to her power and gifts as a woman, including intuition, prophetic abilities, and healing. It also promoted a feminist therapeutic relationship that resembles an intimate friendship, while encouraging transformation. Similar to an intimate friendship, where a close female friend listens and witnesses her friend's stories, the feminist therapist bears witness to her client's story of distress. Through this process, I helped Sofia to recover her voice and to re-author her life stories (Comas-Díaz & Weiner, 2013).

Reauthoring Her Story

In order to develop concientización, one must recognize a collective history of oppression and use the memory to move forward (Sloan, 2002), rather than internalize pain and suffering as a personal deficit. By providing Sofia a culturally-specific and safe space, she was able to process how historical events have played a major role in her adult life, contributing to her healing. Sofia stated in session that when she is in public, she typically scans the room in hopes of identifying other people of color. She provided an example of a situation where she was the only woman of color in a public space and that she immediately felt as if she had to be on her best behavior for fear that she would make a mistake. She explained that she was anxious and afraid of furthering any negative stereotypes of the Latino community. While this experience can be understood at the individual level, it also can be conceptualized as the lingering and continued effects of oppression across generations.

Working with this historical trauma involves identifying her *patrón* (blueprint), so she can become better able to make room for values-based actions that support well-being (Bryant-Davis & Comas-Díaz, 2016; Gloria & Castellanos, 2016). I employed a variety of exercises to help her identify chosen values that can act as a compass or blueprint in the direction of intentional and effective behavior. She identified her family as being the most important part of her life, including the arts and community service. When it came to assessing factors that were more aligned with individuality (i.e., power, wealth, success), she identified them as being lower in her value system.

Intertwined with the development of the patrón was *envisioning transformation*. Having faith that transformation is attainable and it is an individual's right to take on different roles or manifest change is central to the vision. This is not about wishing that things were different for oneself, family, or their community at large. Rather, it is the realization that change is needed or desired for progress while engaging the process of recognizing how change can be achieved. Through this process, Sofia envisioned how learning to use her own voice and creating her own blueprint of cultural values could allow her to help her family and her community in the future. By accessing the same familial vision for change and focused strengths of her parents, grandparents, and ancestors, Sofia found a way to manifest her own transformation. As Sofia realized that the clinician was not trying to pull her away from her family, while encouraging her to find her voice, she felt comfortable in voicing her needs and concerns. As she gained more trust in the process, Sofia became increasingly more open to exploring what and how her transformation would unfold.

Middle-to-Late Phase of Therapy

During the middle-to-late phase of our therapeutic work together, Sofia made significant changes in her life. Sofia decided to end her relationship with her boyfriend and marry her lover, despite her parent's disapproval. She disclosed that the decision was difficult for her and that she experienced guilt and shame for proceeding with the relationship in the manner that she had. Furthermore, she decided to move with her new husband to a city two hours away from her family. She reported that she had been anxious about informing her father about her decision, so she sought out her curandera for protection. Sofia disclosed that her father and mother accused her of abandoning the family when she informed them of the elopement; nevertheless, she initiated a collaboration with her father on how to best utilize her financial support to the family household. Sofia continued to financially support her family; however, she began to make firm decisions on where the resources were best allocated. This was met with some resistance from her father, as it was perceived as a significant shift in the power dynamics of their respective familial roles; however, after she communicated that her active participation was solely for the betterment of the family, he reluctantly agreed.

Psychospirituality

Much of our therapeutic work incorporated spirituality in the sessions, as well as discussions about the intersectionality of culture, power, and oppression and how it impacts her identity, emotions, and behavior. Sofia spoke about feeling connected to the spirit world by participating in curanderismo and that she believed that it provided her with strength in the "outside" world. Spiritually, the Black Madonna was a figure she perceived as a protector and healer of all. The Black Madonna was used during guided visualization activities, specifically at times when she discussed interpersonal conflict with her family. For our sessions, Sofia brought a small statue of the Black Madonna that was strategically placed in the room. The Black Madonna was utilized as a focus for strength and empowerment. At one point, she brought a sage spray to use in the therapeutic room when she accidentally overheard a clerk describe the room as the "spooky" one. She used the spray to cleanse the space of any negative energy. Also, when Sofia knew she wanted to introduce a topic that was difficult for her, she brought a small cup of water to capture any negative energy that may have been created when her experiences were verbalized.

Late Phase of Therapy- Critical Consciousness and Engaging in La Lucha

At this point in treatment, I began to actively implement guided imagery, including body scanning techniques, and further incorporate psychospirituality into treatment. Sofia and I had already utilized concept mapping, bibliotherapy, and other forms of narration to explore the multiple intersections of her identity, the various oppressive messages she had received about appropriate expressions of emotion, and how she had internalized different messages she had received at a familial, institutional, and social level. From this emerged her discussion of society and the reality that women of color are marginalized. The political tides had turned in the U.S., and it was difficult for Sofia to escape the negative messages regarding her culture. She reported that she was inspired to work closer with other Latinx women who struggled with self-esteem and creatively write about the "beauty" of Latinas.

We often spoke about different figures in religion and history who she admired. For some sessions, she was invited to research an important historical Latina figure to be discussed during following sessions. She brought up the story of La Malinche and the Black Madonna. I was embarrassed to inform her that I was unaware of who La Malinche was and what she represented in history. My ignorance may have served treatment, as this allowed Sofia to teach me something about our culture. She went on to describe La Malinche as a woman who is accused of betraying the Native Americans for the conquistadores. She explained, "But if you think about it, La Malinche was full of street smarts, a total bad-ass. She was no longer a slave but a power player with these foreign and dangerous men." This was a jumping off point for a comparison with her own life, identity, and navigation of colonial oppression.

Our discussions about systemic oppression had the theme of humanizing the dehumanized. Her empowerment was facilitated through naming how engagement in social justice could heal Sofia's community. We discussed the myths and realities of immigration, stereotyping and discrimination, acculturation, education, and public policy implications. Sofia was not foreign to this concept; she herself stated that her need to work with the Latinx population was a motivating force to pursue her academic career. She reported that she had a calling of sorts, to inspire and cultivate a strong Latino pride for generations to come.

Conclusion

A mujerista orientation can be understood as a "sensibility or approach to power, knowledge, and relationships rooted in convictions for community uplift" (Bernal et al., 2006, p. 7). This sensibility is born out of navigating marginality both within and outside Latinx communities. Bryant-Davis and Comas-Díaz (2016) write that Latinas must advocate for themselves not just in communities where they are marginalized because of their gendered-coded ethnicity and race, but also marginalized solely because of their gender. "Latinas must navigate cultural scripts and balance gender expectations" (Bryant-Davis & Comas-Díaz, 2016, p. 98). This experience of battling oppression based on gender, race, and ethnicity (and other identities) is intersectional oppression (Chavez-Dueñas et al., 2019), and these identities should not be parceled out in our clinical conceptualizations and interventions.

The Mujerista case study presented in this paper illustrates the importance of addressing intersectionality of the client, as well as of the important people in her life. Sofia's parents held racists views that impacted their views of who she could have as friends and romantic partners. Yet, their own lives were wrought with oppression. Upon arriving to the U.S., Sofia's parents were often recipients of hostile attitudes, discrimination, and rejection. As a result of their low socioeconomic status in their country of origin, Sofia identified that her parents' inability to speak English and lack of social capital exacerbated their sense of alienation in the U.S. and strengthened the family's collectivistic values. Thus, it is important to conceptualize Sofia not just as an individual but also as part of a family system. For Sofia, familismo is considered one of the most important culture-specific values. It was critical that the mujerista therapist not challenge this cultural value in a way that was threatening to Sofia, but instead maintain a stance of cultural humility and radical empathy (Comas-Díaz, 2020). Radical empathy compels therapists to deconstruct their mindset that an individual has no power in their situation. By inviting the client to actively participate in their treatment allows individuals to be the expert of their experiences and the creator of their empowerment. This approach breaks top-down approaches of communication practiced in more traditional treatment modalities that derive from a medical model. It also provides a constant discovery of reality because both the client and therapist provide expertise of their experiences (Mehra et al., 2004).

Disclosure Statement

No potential conflict of interest was reported by the author(s).

References

Adams, G., & Markus, H. (2001). Culture as patterns: An alternative approach to the problem of reification. *Culture & Psychology*, 7(3), 283–296. https://doi.org/10.1177/1354067X0173002

American Psychological Association (APA). (2020). *Stress in America^{TM} 2020: A national mental health crisis.* Author.

Asikiwe, J. (2021). The ancient Orichas: Yoruba traditions, sacred rituals, the divine feminine, and spiritual enlightenment of African culture and wisdom.

Bernal, D. D., Elenes, E. A., Godinez, F. E., & Villenas, S. A. (2006). *Chicana/Latina Education in everyday life: Feminista perspectives on pedagogy and epistemology.* State University of New York Press.

Brown, L. S. (2009). *Feminist therapy.* American Psychological Association.

Bryant-Davis, T. E., & Comas-Díaz, L. (2016). (Eds.). *Womanist and mujerista psychologies: Voices of fire, acts of courage.* American Psychological Association.

Castañeda-Sound, C. L., Martinez, S., & Duran, J. E. (2016). Mujeristas and social justice: La lucha es la vida. In T. Bryant-Davis and L. Comas-Diaz, *Womanist and Mujerista Psychologies: Voices of fire, acts of courage* (pp. 237–259). APA Press.

Chavez-Dueñas, N. Y., Adames, H. Y., & Organista, K. C. (2014). Skin-color prejudice and within-group racial discrimination: Historical and current impact on Latino/a populations. *Hispanic Journal of Behavioral Sciences, 36*(1), 3–26. https://doi.org/10.1177/0739986313511306

Chavez-Dueñas, N. Y., Adames, H. Y., Perez-Chavez, J. G., & Salas, S. P. (2019). Healing ethno-racial trauma in Latinx immigrant communities: Cultivating hope, resistance, and action. *The American Psychologist, 74*(1), 49–62. https://doi.org/10.1037/amp0000289

Chavez, J. (2011). Aliens in their native lands: The persistence of internal colonial theory. *Journal of World History, 22*(4), 785–809. http://www.jstor.org/stable/41508018

Comas-Díaz, L. (2006). Latino healing: The integration of ethnic psychology into psychotherapy. *Psychotherapy, 43*(4), 436–453. https://doi.org/10.1037/0033-3204.43.4.436

Comas-Díaz, L. (2012). *Multicultural care: A clinician's guide to cultural competence.* American Psychological Association.

Comas-Díaz, L. (2013). Comadres: The healing power of a female bond. *Women & Therapy, 36*(1–2), 62–75.

Comas-Díaz, L., & Torres Rivera, E. (Eds.). (2020). *Liberation psychology: Theory, method, practice, and social justice.* American Psychological Association.

Comas-Díaz, L. (2020). Liberation psychotherapy. *Liberation psychology: Theory, method, practice, and social justice* (pp. 169–185). American Psychological Association. https://doi.org/10.1037/0000198-010

Comas-Díaz, L., & Weiner, M. B. (2013). Sisters of the heart: How women's friendships heal. *Women & Therapy, 36*(1–2), 1–10. https://doi.org/10.1080/02703149.2012.720199

Crethar, H. C., Rivera, E. T., & Nash, S. (2008). In search of common threads: Linking multicultural, feminist, and social justice counseling paradigms. *Journal of Counseling & Development, 86*(3), 269–278. https://doi.org/10.1002/j.1556-6678.2008.tb00509.x

Duran, E., Firehammer, J., & Gonzalez, J. (2008). Liberation psychology as the path toward healing cultural soul wounds. *Journal of Counseling & Development, 86*(3), 288–295. https://doi.org/10.1002/j.1556-6678.2008.tb00511.x

Evans-Campbell, T. (2008). Historical trauma in American Indian/Native Alaska communities: A multilevel framework for exploring impacts on individuals, families, and communities. *Journal of Interpersonal Violence, 23*(3), 316–338. https://doi.org/10.1177/0886260507312290

Falicov, C. J. (1998). Latino families in therapy: A guide to multicultural practice. *Adolescence, 34,* 640–640.

Friere, P. (1970). *The pedagogy of the oppressed.* Continuum Publishing Group.

Gloria, A. M., & Castellanos, J. (2016). Latinas poderosas: Shaping mujerismo to manifest sacred spaces for healing and transformation. In T. Bryant-Davis & L. Comas-Díaz (Eds.), *Womanist and mujerista psychologies: Voices of fire, acts of courage* (pp. 93–119). American Psychological Association. https://doi.org/10.1037/14937-005

Henderson, Z. R., Stephens, T. N., Ortega-Williams, A., & Walton, Q. L. (2021). Conceptualizing healing through the African American experience of historical trauma. *The American Journal of Orthopsychiatry, 91*(6), 763–775. https://doi.org/10.1037/ort0000578

Isasi-Díaz, A. M. (1996). *Mujerista theology: A theology for the twenty-first century.* Orbis Books.

Karaye, I. M., & Horney, J. A. (2020). The impact of social vulnerability on COVID-19 in the U.S.: An analysis of spatially varying relationships. *American Journal of Preventive Medicine, 59*(3), 317–325. https://doi.org/10.1016/j.amepre.2020.06.006

Laria, A. J., & Lewis-Fernández, R. (2006). Latino Patients. In R. F. Lim (Ed.), *Clinical manual of cultural psychiatry* (p. 119–173). American Psychiatric Publishing, Inc.

Martín-Baró, I. (1998). Imágenes sociales en El Salvador = Social images in El Salvador. *Revista de Psicología General y Aplicada, 51*(3–4), 387–396.

Martín-Baró, I. (1994). *Writings for a liberation psychology.* Harvard University Press.

Mehra, B., Merkel, C., & Bishop, A. P. (2004). The internet for empowerment of minority and marginalized users. *New Media & Society, 6*(6), 781–802. https://doi.org/10.1177/146144804047513

Ortega-Williams, A., Beltrán, R., Schultz, K., Ru-Glo Henderson, Z., Colón, L., & Teyra, C. (2021). An integrated historical trauma and posttraumatic growth framework: A cross-cultural exploration. *Journal of Trauma & Dissociation, 22*(2), 220–240. https://doi.org/10.1080/15299732.2020.1869106

Portillo, N. (2012). The life of Ignacio Martín-Baró: A narrative account of a personal biographical journey. *Peace and Conflict, 18*(1), 77–87. https://doi.org/10.1037/a0027066

Sabin, M., Lopes Cardozo, B., Nackerud, L., Kaiser, R., & Varese, L. (2003). Factors associated with poor mental health among Guatemalan refugees living in Mexico 20 years after civil conflict. *JAMA, 290*(5), 635–642.

Shim, R. S., & Starks, S. M. (2021). Covid-19, structural racism, and mental health inequities: Policy implications for an emerging syndemic. *Psychiatric Services, 72*(10), 1193–1198. https://doi.org/10.1176/appi.ps.202000725

Singh, A. A., Parker, B., Aqil, A. R., & Thacker, F. (2020). Liberation psychology and LGBTQ. + communities: Naming colonization, uplifting resilience, and reclaiming ancient his-stories, her-stories, and T-stories. *Liberation Psychology, 2020*, 207–224. https://doi.org/10.1037/0000198-012

Sloan, T. (2002). Psicologia de la Liberacion: Ignacio Martín-Baró. *Revista Interamericana de Psicologia/Interamerican Journal of Psychology, 36*(1 & 2), 353–357. https://doi.org/10.30849/rip/ijp.v36i1 & 2.421

Varas-Díaz, N., & Serrano-García, I. (2003). The challenge of a positive self-image in a colonial context: A psychology of liberation for the Puerto Rican experience. *American Journal of Community Psychology, 31*(1–2), 103–115. https://doi.org/10.1023/A:1023078721414

Wessells, M. G. (2015). Bottom-up approaches to strengthening child protection systems: Placing children, families, and communities at the center. *Child Abuse & Neglect, 43*, 8–21. https://doi.org/10.1016/j.chiabu.2015.04.006

Anti-Colonial Futures: Indigenous Latinx Women Healing from the Wounds of Racial-Gendered Colonialism

Nayeli Y. Chavez-Dueñas ⓘ, Hector Y. Adames ⓘ, and Jessica G. Perez-Chavez

ABSTRACT
Indigenous Latina women experience simultaneous forms of oppression, including racism, sexism, and colonialism, which we describe as *racial-gendered colonialism*. To promote epistemic diversity in responding to *racial-gendered colonialism* in psychotherapy, we propose three practical clinical guidance grounded in (a) Maya cosmology and (b) the *Intersectionality Awakening Model of Womanista Treatment Approach* (I AM Womanista) developed by Chavez-Dueñas & Adames. The article provides a path for psychotherapists to integrate the past, present, and future as they accompany Indigenous Latina women in their healing. To accomplish this goal, we present an overview of Indigenous Latina women's collective history, their present 21st-century gendered-racial realities, and ways to support this group in envisioning and working toward anti-colonial futures—that is, a future of liberation that goes beyond *racial-gendered colonialism*.

Latinidad often conjures erroneous notions of a homogeneous group—one race, same culture, agender, and indistinguishable narratives. This concept of Latinidad minimizes, silences, and often ignores how women are uniquely oppressed both within and outside the borders of Latinidad (Adames et al., 2021; Chavez-Dueñas et al., 2014; Chavez-Dueñas & Adames et al., 2021). When a gendered lens is used to depict Latinidad, it often fails to consider the racialized experiences of Latina women (Adames et al., 2016; Castañeda-Sound et al., 2016; Comas-Díaz, 1996). This stubborn notion of Latinidad erases, invalidates, and actively discounts the unique realities of Indigenous Latinas, AfroLatinas, and AfroIndigenous Latinas (Adames et al., 2021; Chavez-Dueñas & Adames et al., 2021).

Consequently, how gender-based ethno-racial systems of oppression interact to dehumanize, denigrate, and dismiss Indigenous Latinas, AfroLatinas, and AfroIndigenous Latinas go unchallenged. This article focuses on the narratives and lived realities of Latinas of Indigenous descent.

Making sense of the dehumanization of Indigenous Latinas can be deeply painful, but it can also ignite our curiosity about what we can do as therapists. For instance, what actions can we take in therapy to honor and validate the gendered ethno-racial realities of Indigenous Latinas? What preparation do we need to be effective in our work with members of this community? How do we navigate the perplexing and often disorienting nature of colonialism and its contemporary manifestations (e.g., racism, sexism, cissexism, gendered-racism, heterosexism) in the lives of Indigenous Latinas? What about in our practice as therapists? Sitting with these questions may evoke an array of complex emotions. Some of us may feel hopeless. Perhaps we may be fueled by what Brittney Cooper (2018) describes as *eloquent rage*—that is, righteous rage. We may also move into action by creating ways to structurally and therapeutically address all the superimposed systemic wounds that so many Indigenous Latinas experience simply for being Indigenous, women, Latinas, and *Indigenous Latina Women* all at once.

In 2020, Chavez-Dueñas and Adames introduced and described the *Intersectionality Awakening Model of Womanista Treatment Approach* (I AM Womanista), which provides a strength-based counter-narrative on Black, Indigenous, and other Women of Color (WOC). The model describes WOC as brilliant, revolutionary, and self-determined beings. *I AM Womanista* also acknowledges and calls for clinicians to co-create therapeutic spaces where gendered-racism's burden and emotional toll are examined and addressed. Three assumptions guide the *I AM Womanista* therapeutic approach and include:

> (a) understanding Latinas from the inside out (e.g., considering multiple social identities) is important in therapy; however, it is equally vital to integrate how systemic forces impact Latinas from the outside in (e.g., sexism, racism, homonegativity); (b) knowledge of history is essential for mental health providers to contextualize the unique experiences of Latinas, and (c) providers assisting Latinas in connecting or reconnecting with their collective history and their ancestral roots. (Chavez-Dueñas & Adames et al., 2021, p. 86)

This paper builds on the *I AM Womanista* clinical stance by focusing on Indigenous Latinas and addressing the importance of assisting clients in envisioning a future of liberation. To this end, this article aims to help psychotherapists working with Indigenous Latinas identify, acknowledge, and respond to the clinical implications of gendered ethno-racial oppression. To achieve this goal, we discuss (a) the collective history of Indigenous women in Latin America, (b) the racial-gendered realities that Indigenous Latinas face in the 21st century, and (c) the imagining of a future beyond racial-gendered colonialism. We offer practical clinical guidance grounded in Maya cosmology. The four Indigenous Maya Energies is a call to action centered on "work to defend mother earth, the rights of women, nature and all that is sacred and grounded in a matriarchal culture" (Mayan League, 2020, para. 5). Developed by the Mayan League (2020), the four energies include:

1. Ancestral knowledge as the basis of all actions,
2. Work for justice and human rights not only for Indigenous people but also for Mother Earth,
3. Collective work as a family, community, and nations to defend our People and Mother Earth, and
4. Build a path for justice and dignity with our people.

The Past: Collective History

The past is key to the future. Our past has the wisdom that can help us build a future ... by looking toward, the past, toward those who were the first inhabitants, to those who first had wisdom, who first made us (Marcos, 2002, p. 84).

Women in Traditional Indigenous Cultures

Before colonization, Indigenous women were valued, respected, and seen as powerful sacred beings in traditional Indigenous cultures throughout the Americas. They were honored for their role in creating life and passing down Indigenous culture to the new generations. All in all, their existence and role in Indigenous society were esteemed and treated with dignity. Moreover, women in the Americas were ensured access to wealth and power before colonization (see Adames & Chavez-Dueñas, 2017; Chavez-Dueñas & Adames et al., 2021; Kellogg, 1988; Silverblatt, 1987). However, there was variability in how women across the different Indigenous cultures effectuated wealth and power. For instance, in some cultures (e.g., Aztec civilization), parallel transmission of rights was utilized to ensure that women had full access to economic resources (Kellogg, 1988; Silverblatt, 1987).

Indigenous women also held independent rights over all acquired and inherited goods and property regardless of marital status. Women were given the right to participate in a variety of leadership positions, with some cultures granting women the power to declare war, distribute wealth in their community, and make decisions about membership in their nations (The Canadian Research Institute for the Advancement of Women—2016; Silverblatt, 1987). In the realm of religion, women had influence and were respected. Many deities were portrayed as feminine, including the gods of sustenance, dedicated to maize (i.e., Xilonen, Chicomecoatl) and running water (i.e., Chalchiuhtlicue; Kellogg, 1988). Put succinctly, women across different Indigenous cultures were socialized to view themselves as powerful sacred beings.

Racial-Gendered Colonialism

The conquest of the Americas marked by destruction, violence, and cruelty forever changed the role of Indigenous women in society. The bloody conquest led to the oppressive colonization system that seized control over Indigenous lands and people. Patriarchy, or the social system of domination based on the ideology that gender is binary—and that within the binary—men are superior, consequently holding primary power and predominate in positions of leadership and authority, was imported and imposed in the Americas through colonization (see Tickner, 2001; Unger, 1979). Colonialism and patriarchy impacted Indigenous women in powerful ways. To illustrate, Nina Cordell (2016), an Indigenous Woman from Thompson, Manitoba, stated,

> We've gone from sacred, to scared, to scarred. Before contact, women were respected as sacred beings. Contact with settlers introduced a new way of life where people were scared by the changes imposed on them and that they had to adapt to. Today we are scarred by the legacy of colonialism, the residential schools, the Sixties Scoop. Those scars will always be there, but they don't define us. It's a scar; it's not an open wound. We're in transition. Now we want to learn and relearn, accept the traditions and ceremonies, and feel the beauty of the culture again. And be ready to welcome people back, be ready to help them connect back with being sacred again. (p. 4)

Racism, or the interpersonal, cultural, or institutional oppression of groups of people based on White racial superiority (Helms & Cook, 1999; Jones, 1997; 2000), was also imported to the Americas through colonization (Adames & Chavez-Dueñas, 2017). Racism was inflicted through a system of racial stratification based on the social interpretation of how people look (e.g., skin color, facial features). This system strategically placed White people (Europeans) at the top and Black (enslaved Africans) and Indigenous people (Natives) at the bottom of the racial stratification, hence impacting who had access to power and resources (Adames & Chavez-Dueñas, 2017; Chavez-Dueñas et al., 2014; Soler Castillo & Pardo Abril, 2009). White supremacy had a calamitous impact on Indigenous people, resulting in decimating of their cultures and the annihilation of millions of Native People

(Chavez-Dueñas & Adames et al., 2021; Livi-Bacci, 2008; Soler Castillo & Pardo Abril, 2009). Overall colonization led to denied opportunities, exclusion, and erasure of Indigenous history and culture in the educational system. For Indigenous women, the interlocking impact of three forms of oppression—racism, sexism, and colonialism, what we are calling *racial-gendered colonialism*, uniquely shaped their realities.

Our description of racial-gendered colonialism builds on the traditions and scholarly contributions of Black women. Essed (1991) theorized and coined the term *gendered-racism* to describe the unique way gender and race are weaponized and used against Black women (see also Lewis et al., 2017). Today, the framing of gendered-racism is applied to help understand the experiences of non-Black Women of Color (see Chavez-Dueñas & Adames et al., 2021; Keum et al., 2018). However, since women from Latin America can be of any race (e.g., White, Black, Indigenous, Mix), we intentionally choose to place the construct of "racial" first to underscore the unique ways Black and Indigenous Latinas are oppressed by colonialism (see Adames et al., 2021; Chavez-Dueñas et al., 2014).

When using a racial-gendered colonialism lens to understand Indigenous women in Latin America, we begin to see how they are robbed of political, religious, and economic power (Kellogg, 2005). For instance, across Latin America, gendered-racist beliefs were institutionalized by enacting laws that took away the rights of Indigenous women to continue owning property by classifying married women as legal minors. Chavez-Dueñas and Adames et al. (2021) describe that:

> This law required women to seek authorization from their husbands before engaging in any legally based transaction. In other words, Indigenous women could not freely dispose of their property and other assets without their husband's permission. These misogynistic laws further eroded the power and authority that Indigenous women once had, leading to the loss of opportunities for them to fill positions of autonomous authority in their communities (Vitale, 1997). Hence, Indigenous women lost the right to their material possessions and their bodies. They were frequently victims of sexual abuse, exploitation, and torture and were often forced into concubinage with Spaniard men (Kellogg, 2005; Silverblatt, 1987). (p. 90)

Through colonization, which utilized White supremacy and patriarchy, Indigenous women lost their previously held power and influence. To illustrate, Indigenous women went from being influential members of society with the structural power to make decisions about their bodies, communities, and futures to becoming mere economic and sexual commodities exploited by the colonizers (Kellogg, 2005; Silverblatt, 1987). Part of colonization included erasing Indigenous women's history and inculcating them into submissiveness and obedience. To illustrate, marianismo, or the gender-role ideology that expects women to model their behaviors after the Virgin Mary, supported this colonial gendered-racial socialization. Marianismo expected Indigenous women to be humble, self-sacrifice, and passively take the abuse that came in the form of racial-gendered colonialism (Comas-Díaz, 1988, Ginorio et al., 1995, Gil & Vasquez, 1996). However, marianismo was not always successful. Many examples of Indigenous women resisting their racial gender oppression exist despite these stories frequently excluded from history books (Chavez-Dueñas & Adames et al., 2021; Reeves, 2018). As a result, today's Indigenous women must learn and internalize their history as influential, self-sufficient, respected, dignified warriors who fought to protect themselves, their families, and communities against the evils of hate. Unearthing the past is the key to the future and how Indigenous women heal in the present.

Working with Indigenous Latinas requires therapists to understand the unique history and culture of Indigenous Latinxs and how colonization and patriarchy operate in people's lives. It is vital for therapists who know Indigenous history and culture to recognize that it is impossible to know everything about the rich diversity among Indigenous communities—and that intellectual knowledge is insufficient. We also need to seek consultation from members of the Indigenous community and therapists who may have a nuanced understanding of the particular group to which the client belongs.

Practical Guidance 1: History Matters, and It Liberates—Integrate Ancestral Knowledge in Therapy

We invite therapists working with Indigenous Latinas to integrate ancestral knowledge throughout the therapeutic process. As a prerequisite to achieving this therapeutic goal, they need first to assess what they know about the history of Indigenous Latinas. In turn, therapists may realize that they need to expand their knowledge base in this area. Table 1 provides key resources for building therapists' knowledge of Indigenous history and culture. Developing knowledge about Indigenous Latina women can better equip therapists to listen and help clients process content that spontaneously emerges in therapy.

Assessing and Using Ancestral Knowledge in Therapy

In therapy, it may be fruitful for Indigenous Latinas to explore ways to connect, reconnect, or strengthen their relationship with their community and consider traditional forms of healing (e.g., herbal remedies, ointments, massages, rituals, prayer, dance, art). For example, Indigenous people have used medicinal herbs to treat illness (e.g., the arnica plant used to treat pain and injuries) for many centuries. Therapists can assist clients in

Table 1. Essential resources to build knowledge regarding Indigenous Latina women.

Resources	Descriptions
Adames & Chavez-Dueñas (2017)	This book addresses the racial and ethnic diversity within the Latinx population. The book offers a comprehensive history of Indigenous women in Latin America through an interdisciplinary lens.
Anton (1973)	This book describes some of the earliest civilizations of the Americas, including the Aztec, Maya, and the Inca. The volume describes the role of women in these civilizations.
APA Division 45 Warrior's Path Presidential Task Force (2020)	The Society for the Psychological Study of Culture, Ethnicity, and Race commissioned the report to discuss and identify ways to oppose colonial and neocolonial praxis that contribute to the psychological damage of Indigenous People.
Hall (2012)	The article outlines some of the significant challenges experienced by Indigenous Latinas due to racial, gender, and socio-economic discrimination.
Kellogg (2005)	The book offers a comprehensive history of Indigenous women in Latin America through an interdisciplinary lens.
Sieder & Sierra (2010)	The report addresses the specific challenges faced by Indigenous women in Latin America seeking justice. The report explicitly addresses the difficulties related to discrimination due to ethnicity, gender, and social class.
Stephen (2002)	This article provides an ethnographic description of the diversity in sexualities and genders within the Zapotecs in Oaxaca. The author connects contemporary elements of gender and sexuality to Indigenous Zapotec roots.
The Mayan League (2020)	This organization's goal is to "promote, preserve, and transmit the cosmovision and worldview, culture, history, and contributions" guided by the teaching of Maya elders. It provides various resources for people to understand the Maya cosmovision and the challenges faced by their descendants.

thinking of such healing practices as derived from ancestral knowledge passed down from generation to generation.

Working with Clients Who Lack Ancestral Knowledge

As discussed earlier in this article, the history of colonization and information about Indigenous communities is often missing from formal education and training in mental health. When included, it is usually from the perspective of the colonizers. The omission and distortion of history may lead Indigenous Latinas to develop various degrees of knowledge about their collective existence and connection to their culture (i.e., ethno-racial identity development). Clinically, we recommend that therapists listen to the ways Indigenous Latina clients speak or fail to speak about their community and culture. Therapists are encouraged to create opportunities for clients to discuss their connection or disconnection to their Indigeneity. Therapists can also assist clients in developing critical consciousness, which will help them understand the importance of gaining ancestral knowledge—for instance, assisting clients in connecting current challenges in their life to historical events (e.g., colonization). Once clients become curious about their history, therapists can facilitate this process by identifying resources (e.g., books, connecting with people from the community who can transmit knowledge through the oral tradition) to help clients gain or expand ancestral knowledge. Therapy can also be a place for clients to process their emotional reactions that may surface as they learn about their cultural history and begin to identify patterns on how they connect to the challenges that brought them into treatment. Indigenous clients who identify as queer or two-spirit can benefit from knowing that people who do not fit into the binary ways in which society is structured have always existed (e.g., Zapotec *muxe/muxhe* from Oaxaca Mexico, see Adames & Chavez-Dueñas, 2021 and Stephen, 2002). Learning how Indigenous Latinx cultures valued and respected non-binary people can be healing and liberating. It can also serve as a source of affirmation and validation of their humanity.

Working with Clients Who Have Ancestral Knowledge

We argue that history matters and liberates, but knowing history alone does not necessarily promote growth and healing. Liberation requires work, and psychotherapy can be a place to do some of that labor. Therapists can assist their Indigenous Latina clients in engaging in this process by creating space in therapy for unearthing history. For instance, as Indigenous clients begin to discuss how their history shows up in their lives, therapists can help them process and grieve the many ways in which the history of colonization and racial-gendered oppression has harmed them, their communities, and Mother Earth. This process can also be a source of self-affirmation for clients. To illustrate, clients can contextualize their experiences by recognizing historical patterns of racial-gendered oppression that are still alive today and continue to impact Indigenous clients in subtle and overt ways. Our Indigenous client's collective past is present in the here and now.

The Present: The Realities of Racial-Gendered Colonialism

> We are not myths of the past, ruins in the jungle or zoos. We are people, and we want to be respected, not to be victims of intolerance and racism. (Menchu, 1989, para 1)

People often describe Indigenous communities throughout Latin America as belonging to a "prehistoric era whose evidence can be observed in museums. That part of our history, patiently rescued by archaeology, is made into a set of exotic objects from remote times that have no link with the present. Thus, its protagonists are considered to be people who lived on the margins of history, in myth or in legend" (Correa, 1992, p. 52). Despite this depiction, millions of Indigenous people are alive today. They survived colonization, genocide, and the many ways Latin American countries uphold White supremacy culture, which attempts to eradicate their presence and contributions to society. Today, about 42 million Indigenous

People live in Latin America, making up nearly 8% of the total population (World Bank Group, 2015). Mexico, Guatemala, Peru, and Bolivia have the largest populations, with more than 80% of the regional total, or 34 million Indigenous people residing in these four countries (World Bank Group, 2015).

While millions of Native People are alive today throughout Latin America, the impact of colonization and White supremacy culture continues to reverberate. To illustrate, being born Indigenous in Latin America increases the probability of being raised in economic hardship. Such poverty impacts 43% of the Indigenous population, a proportion more than twice the rate of non-Indigenous (21%) people who live in poverty (World Bank Group, 2015). In addition, Indigenous people have less access to sanitation (18%) and electricity (15%) than the non-Indigenous population in Latin America. There is also a wage gap between Indigenous and non-Indigenous Latinx Americans. For example, regardless of educational level, gender, age, and residence, Indigenous people earn about 12% less than non-Indigenous people in urban Mexico (World Bank Group, 2015).

Racial gendered disparities between Indigenous and non-Indigenous women are alarming. For instance, Indigenous women in Bolivia earn approximately 60% less than non-Indigenous women for the same positions (World Bank Group, 2015). Indigenous women are also less likely to complete secondary school than non-Indigenous women (World Bank Group, 2015). Their academic performance level is lower than non-Indigenous Latin American women, leading to high illiteracy rates (Hall, 2012).

Wars and internal political conflict also disproportionately impact Indigenous women. For instance, during the civil war in Guatemala, of the women who were sexually abused 88.7% were Indigenous women of compared to 10.3% of Mestiza women (Álvarez et al., 2017). While women in Latin America are vulnerable to gender-based violence, Indigenous women are uniquely impacted by the combination of gendered-racism, anti-Indigeneity, lower education rates, and higher poverty rates (Hall, 2012; World Bank Group, 2015). Data on Latina women in the U.S. are typically reported by nationality or ethnic origin, failing to capture the unique ways racism impacts Indigenous Latinas (Adames et al., 2021). However, we argue that the unique challenges they face in the U.S. mirror Indigenous women in Latin America.

Practical Guidance 2: Resist Racial-Gendered Colonialism by Working Collectively for Social Justice, Human Rights, and Mother Earth

The foundation of human rights is to do no harm—a tenet of our professional ethics as health care providers (APA, 2017; National Association of

Social Workers, 2017; Pope et al., 2021). To this end, as therapists, we need to learn, acknowledge, and understand the current oppressive realities of Indigenous Latinas both during the evaluation and the treatment process. These realities include the effect of racial-gendered colonialism.

Naming and Addressing Racial-Gendered Colonialism in Therapy

"Those of us on Mother Earth will continue to stand for justice, for truth, and for our right to live our sacred teachings. We are the living representation of our ancestors and our millennial traditions" (Oxe' Choj, 2020, para. 10). Indigenous women have not been silent about the injustices they face. From organizing to protect their land, children, and Mother Earth to creating pathways to practice their traditional rituals, Indigenous women have disrupted and resisted structures designed to oppress and silence them in multiple ways (Chavez-Dueñas & Adames et al., 2021). For centuries Indigenous women have been creating, connecting, and building community in the face of compounding forms of dehumanization. Organizing and resisting have shaped the lives of Indigenous women and have been instrumental in how they heal from the wounds of racial-gendered colonialism—this too must be central to the therapeutic process.

Therapy can be a place where clinicians and clients can co-create a space where oppression can be named, discussed, and challenged. To facilitate this process, we encourage clinicians to integrate therapeutic approaches—such as *Liberation Psychotherapy* (Comas-Díaz, 2020), *Intersectionality in Psychotherapy* (Adames et al., 2021), *Healing Ethno-Racial Trauma* (HEART; Chavez-Dueñas et al., 2019), and *Radical Healing in Psychotherapy* (Adames et al., 2022 and see also French et al., 2020). These liberatory and anti-colonial treatment approaches are designed to help BIPOC clients develop and nurture a social justice orientation that helps them resist internalizing the poison of oppression.

Nurturing a social justice and human rights orientation begins with caring for oneself. Therapists can assist Indigenous Latina clients in identifying barriers preventing them from engaging in actions that contribute to wellness. Discussions can explore and identify ways to engage in self-care, including joy, pleasure, and rest, grounded in the client's cultural practices. Therapists need to help clients name how barriers to self-care may be connected to gendered-racism—this will serve as a buffer for clients to not self-blame. Clinicians can also listen for moments in therapy when Indigenous Latina clients share experiences of challenging oppression or defying unjust rules. Moments can be as subtle as a client saying, "What happened to my sister was just wrong," to a more overt statement such as "All women deserve respect and dignity." These moments should be validated, normalized, and expanded upon in therapy. For instance, invite the client to emotionally process what it was like to speak up in these instances, what challenges they experienced, and how they felt afterward. Engaging with clients in conversations about resisting oppression and embracing a social justice orientation that extends to the protection of Mother Earth may allow clients to expand their critical consciousness and cognitively and emotionally connect their actions to individual, collective, and environmental justice. To borrow from Joan Phillip, "we just want to be alive. It's a fight that's holistic. It's about loving ourselves, loving our land, loving the people" (Phillip, n.d.). According to research, collectively organizing for social justice can be therapeutic and improve oppressed communities' overall wellness (Han et al., 2015; Ortega-Williams et al., 2020). Together, this process may create opportunities for clients and therapists to explore the importance of building community, resisting together, and envisioning a future of collective liberation for people, groups, and respect for Mother Earth.

The Future: Building an Anti-Colonial Existence

> Let there be freedom for the Indigenous People, wherever they may be in the American Continent or elsewhere in the world because while we are alive, a glow of hope will be alive as well as a true concept of life. (Menchu, 1992, para. 17)

While colonialism and gendered racism violently tries to rob Indigenous women of envisioning, uniting, and building a collective destiny of liberation, it has not always been successful. To illustrate, Indigenous women have defied their dehumanization by coming together to organize and stand up for their freedom throughout history (see Chavez-Dueñas & Adames et al., 2021; Kellogg, 2005; Reeves, 2018). Anchored in their traditional culture, many Indigenous women had an unwavering belief that they deserved to live a life of dignity, respect, and equity. This liberatory ideology empowered Indigenous women to envision anti-colonial futures igniting and fueling acts of resistance which undoubtedly contributed to systemic change. Actively imagining and working toward anti colonial futures has allowed Indigenous women to experience a sense of autonomy, joy, collective fulfillment, and determination to do what is necessary to protect and heal Mother Earth and her natural resources.

Envisioning an existence free of oppression while working toward anti-colonial futures is a way for Indigenous Latinas to heal and for their community to thrive (Adames et al., 2022; Comas-Díaz & Torres Rivera, 2020; French et al., 2020; Mosley, 2020). Therapy can be one of many spaces where Indigenous Latinas can begin or continue envisioning and working for a future of collective liberation and healing.

Practical Guidance 3: Envision and Work toward an Existence beyond Colonization, Patriarchy, and Racial-Gendered Colonialism

The future matters, and it matters today. Supporting Indigenous Latinas to envision a future of liberation and self-determination is one way to honor and recover their traditional cultural heritage lost to colonization. This approach can be healing.

We encourage therapists to listen for moments when the client shares wishes, fantasies, and hopes about the future to accomplish this goal. During these instances, therapists can welcome the client to stay with their desire and help clients imagine a future where they reclaim and reestablish equilibrium among all genders, including two-spirit people destroyed by colonization. Therapists can also assist clients in considering ways to ensure that their vision of liberation reflects their traditional Indigenous culture and not the oppressors'. Part of this vision for Indigenous women includes a re-affirmation or nurturing of an idea of a future grounded in peaceful and harmonious coexistence with others and with Mother Earth. As clients engage in envisioning, therapists can encourage them to process their emotions and share what it is like to imagine a future where they experience a sense of belongingness, safety, and joy. Suppose the client seems hopeless or does not bring up wishes or spontaneously imagine their future. In that case, the therapist can plan how best to create opportunities in therapy for the client to talk about a better future. For instance, they can ask clients to imagine a future where they are autonomous, treated with dignity, and where Mother Earth is respected and protected. How would their life, the lives of other Indigenous women, and their People be different? How would their environment be in contrast to today's? Then the therapist can help clients process their emotional reactions to these questions. Through this process, Indigenous Latinas may experience a sense of motivation which may help them build a path toward doing what they can to make that vision a reality for themselves and future generations.

Conclusion

Echoing the Guatemalan human rights Indigenous activist and feminist Rigoberta Menchú, "The revival of hope for the oppressed Indigenous peoples demands that we reassert our existence to the world and the value of our cultural identity. It demands that we endeavor to actively participate in the decisions that concern our destiny" (1992, para. 28). This article discussed the importance of considering the unique history and current challenges experienced by Indigenous Latinas due to colonization and gendered-racism. We describe how the psychotherapeutic process can be a healing space that elicits insight and encourages expansive ways for

Indigenous women to navigate oppression. Addressing racial-gendered colonialism in psychotherapy requires that Indigenous Latinas honor their past to move forward into the future while resisting and creating joy in the present. Therapy is also a way for clinicians to invite and support our clients to resist internalizing how they and their community are subjugated. In turn, the process may enhance clients' hope and motivation to work toward their liberation, the liberation of all Indigenous people, and the protection of Mother Earth. We affirm that together we can build anti-colonial futures for all.

ORCID

Nayeli Y. Chavez-Dueñas http://orcid.org/0000-0002-3721-3937
Hector Y. Adames http://orcid.org/0000-0003-2169-1165

References

Adames, H. Y., & Chavez-Dueñas, N. Y. (2017). *Cultural foundations and interventions in Latino/a mental health: History, theory, and within-group differences.* Routledge Press.

Adames, H. Y., & Chavez-Dueñas, N. Y. (2021). Reclaiming all of me: The racial queer identity framework. In K. L. Nadal & M. Scharron del Rio (Eds.), *Queer psychology: Intersectional perspectives* (pp. 59–79). Springer.

Adames, H. Y., Chavez-Dueñas, N. Y., & Jernigan, M. M. (2021). The fallacy of a raceless Latinidad: Action guidelines for centering Blackness in Latinx psychology. *Journal of Latinx Psychology, 9*(1), 26–44. https://psycnet.apa.org/record/2020-69785-001

Adames, H. Y., Chavez-Dueñas, N. Y., Lewis, J. A., Neville, H. A., French, B. H., Chen, G. A., & Mosley, D. V. (2022). Radical healing in psychotherapy: Addressing the wounds of racism-related stress and trauma. *Psychotherapy* (Advance online publication). https://doi.org/10.1037/pst0000435.

Adames, H. Y., Chavez-Dueñas, N. Y., & Organista, K. C. (2016). Skin-color matters in Latino/a communities: Identifying, understanding, and addressing Mestizaje racial ideologies in clinical practice. *Professional Psychology: Research and Practice, 47*(1), 46–55. http://dx.doi.org/10.1037/pro0000062.

Álvarez, B. C., Valey, H., Castellanos, P. P., Martinez Velázquez, P. M., Patal, M. T., Xico, D. E. Y., & Navarro, S. (2017). *Changing the face of justice: Keys to the strategic litigation of the Sepur Zarco Case.* https://static.wixstatic.com/ugd/f3f989_2e09bd4a929e40328a-b0a330a7115f65.pdf

American Psychological Association (2017). *Ethical principles of psychologists and code of conduct* (2002, amended effective June 1, 2010, and January 1, 2017). https://www.apa.org/ethics/code/

Anton, F. (1973). *Woman in pre-Columbian America.* Abner Schram Publishing.

APA Division 45 Warrior's Path Presidential Task Force. (2020). *Protecting and defending our people: Nakni tushka anowa [The warrior's path] report.* American Psychological Association Division 45 Society for the Psychological Study of Culture, Ethnicity and Race.

Castañeda-Sound, C. L., Martinez, S., & Durán, J. E. (2016). Mujeristas and social justice: La lucha es la vida. In T. Bryant-Davis, & L. Comas-Díaz (Eds.), *Womanist and mujerista psychologies: Voices of fire, acts of courage* (pp. 237–259). American Psychological Association.

Chavez-Dueñas, N. Y., & Adames, H. Y. (2021). Intersectionality awakening model of Womanista: A transnational treatment approach for Latinx women. *Women & Therapy*, 44(1–2), 83–100. https://doi.org/10.1080/02703149.2020.1775022.

Chavez-Dueñas, N. Y., Adames, H. Y., & Organista, K. C. (2014). Skin-color prejudice and within-group racial discrimination: Historical and current impact on Latino/a populations. *Hispanic Journal of Behavioral Sciences*, 36(1), 3–26. https://doi.org/10.1177/0739986313511306.

Chavez-Dueñas, N. Y., Adames, H. Y., Perez-Chavez, J. G., & Salas, S. P. (2019). Healing ethno-racial trauma in Latinx immigrant communities: Cultivating hope, resistance, and action. *American Psychologist*, 74(1), 49–62. https://doi.org/10.1037/amp0000289.

Choj, O. (2020). *Justice for Tata Domingo! No more killings of our spiritual leaders*. Mayan League.

Comas-Díaz, L. (1988). Feminist therapy with Hispanic/Latina women: Myth or reality? *Women & Therapy*, 6(4), 39–61. https://doi.org/10.1300/J015V06N04_06.

Comas-Díaz, L. (1996). LatiNegra: Mental health issues of African Latinas. In M. P. Root (Ed.), *The multiracial experience: Racial borders as the new frontier* (pp. 167–190). Sage.

Comas-Díaz, L., & Torres Rivera, E. (Eds.). (2020). *Liberation psychology: Theory, method, practice, and social justice*. American Psychological Association. https://doi.org/10.1037/0000198-000.

Cooper, B. (2018). *Eloquent rage: A Black feminist discovers her superpower*. St. Martin's Press.

Cordell, N. (2016). How colonialism affects women. Resource development in northern communities; local women matter. *Fem North Net*. https://www.criaw-icref.ca/wp-content/uploads/2021/04/Local-Women-Matter-4-How-Colonialism-Affects-Women.pdf

Correa, F. (1992). Imagen de lo "indio" en el Desarrollo y la identidad nacional. In L. Cespedes (Ed.), *Diversidad es riqueza. Ensayos sobre la realidad colombiana*. Instituto Colombiano de antropología, consejería presidencial para los derechos humanos.

Essed, P. (1991). *Understanding everyday racism: An interdisciplinary theory*. Sage Publications.

French, B. H., Lewis, J. A., Mosley, D. V., Adames, H. Y., Chavez-Dueñas, N. Y., Chen, G. A., & Neville, H. A. (2020). Toward a psychological framework of radical healing in communities of color. *The Counseling Psychologist*, 48(1), 14–46. https://doi.org/10.1177/0011000019843506.

Gil, R. M., & Vasquez, C. I. (1996). *The Maria paradox*. Perigee.

Ginorio, A., Guttierrez, L., Cauce, A. M., & Acosta, M. (1995). The psychology of Latinas. In C. Travis (Ed.), *Feminist perspectives on the psychology of women* (pp. 89–108). American Psychological Association.

Hall, C. (2012). Latin America's Indigenous women. *Human Rights and Human Welfare: Minority Digest*, 13(1), 39–50. https://www.du.edu/korbel/hrhw/researchdigest/minority/Indigenous.pdf.

Han, H., Nicholas, A., Aimer, M., & Gray, J. (2015). An innovative community organizing campaign to improve mental health and wellbeing among Pacific Island youth in South Auckland, New Zealand. *Australasian Psychiatry: Bulletin of Royal Australian and New Zealand College of Psychiatrists*, 23(6), 670–674. https://doi.org/10.1177/1039856215597539.

Helms, J. E., & Cook, D. A. (1999). *Using race and culture in counseling and psychotherapy: Theory and process*. Allyn & Bacon.

Jones, C. P. (2000). Levels of racism: A theoretic framework and a gardener's tale. *American Journal of Public Health*, 90(8), 1212–1215. https://doi.org/10.2105/AJPH.90.8.1212.

Jones, J. M. (1997). *Prejudice and racism* (2nd ed.). McGraw-Hill.

Kellogg, S., Josserand, J. K., & Dakin, K. (1988). Cognatic kinship and religion: Women in Aztec society. In J. K. Josserand & K. Dakin (Eds.), *Smoke and mist: Mesoamerican studies in memory of Thelma D. Sullivan* (pp. 666–681). British Archaeological Reports Press.

Kellogg, S. (2005). *Weaving the past: A history of Latin America's indigenous women from the prehispanic period to the present*. Oxford University Press.

Keum, B. T., Brady, J. L., Sharma, R., Lu, Y., Kim, Y. H., & Thai, C. J. (2018). Gendered racial microaggressions scale for Asian American women: Development and initial validation. *Journal of Counseling Psychology*, 65(5), 571–585. https://doi.org/10.1037/cou0000305.

Lewis, J. A., Williams, M. G., Peppers, E. J., & Gadson, C. A. (2017). Applying intersectionality to explore the relations between gendered racism and health among Black women. *Journal of Counseling Psychology*, 64(5), 475–486. https://doi.org/10.1037/cou0000231.

Livi-Bacci, M. (2008). *Conquest: The destruction of the American Indios*. Polity Press.

Mayan League. (2020). *Maya cosmovision*. Mayan League.

Menchu, R. (1992). *Acceptance and Nobel lecture* [Speech transcript and translation]. Brown University.

Menchu, R. (1989). *Convention 169 and International Day of the world's indigenous people*. https://www.ilo.org/century/history/iloandyou/WCMS_190269/lang–en/index.htm.

Mosley, D., Neville, H. A., Chavez-Dueñas, N. Y., Adames, H. Y., Lewis, J. A., & French, B. H. (2020). Radical hope in revolting times: Proposing a culturally-relevant psychological framework. *Social and Personality Psychology Compass*, 14(1), 1–12. https://doi.org/10.1111/spc3.12512

National Association of Social Workers. (2017). *Code of ethics of the National Association of Social Workers*. https://www.socialworkers.org/About/Ethics/Code-of-Ethics.

Ortega-Williams, A., Wernick, L. J., DeBower, J., & Brathwaite, B. (2020). Finding relief in action: The intersection of youth-led community organizing and mental health in Brooklyn, New York City. *Youth & Society*, 52(4), 618–638. https://doi.org/10.1177/0044118X18758542.

Phillip, J.[@NahidAhmed16], (2021, January 7). [Tweet] *We just want to be alive. It's a fight that's holistic. It's about loving ourselves, loving our land, loving the people*. https://twitter.com/NahidAhmed16/status/1347221566501826560?s=20&t=SqzHbm7dPfkLl85_lgKUVw

Reeves, A. (2018). Transforming gender roles in the colonial Andes: Native Andean female resistance to colonial Spanish constructs of gender hierarchy. In *Margins II: A journal of exploratory research and analysis* (pp.1–11). Retrieved from https://www.csustan.edu/sites/default/files/groups/University%20Honors%20Program/Journals/transforminggenderrolesinthecolonialandesareeves.pdf.

Sieder, R., & Sierra, M. T. (2010). *Indigenous women's access to justice in Latin America*. CHR Michelsen Institute. https://www.cmi.no/publications/file/3880-indigenous-womens-access-to-justice-in-latin.pdf.

Silverblatt, I. M. (1987). *Moon, sun, and witches: Gender ideologies and class in Inca and colonial Peru*. Princeton University Press.

Soler Castillo, S., & Pardo Abril, N. G. (2009). Discourse and racism in Colombia: Five centuries of invisibility and exclusion. In T. A. Van Dijk (Ed.), *Racism and discourse in Latin America* (pp. 131–170). Lexington Books.

Stephen, L. (2002). Sexualities and genders in Zapotec Oaxaca. *Latin American Perspectives*, *123*(29), 41–59.

Tickner, A. J. (2001). Patriarchy. In R. J. Barry Jones (Ed.), *Routledge encyclopedia of international political economy: Entries P–Z* (pp. 1197–1198). Taylor & Francis.

Unger, R. K. (1979). Toward a redefinition of sex and gender. *American Psychologist*, *34*(11), 1085–1094. https://doi.org/10.1037/0003-066X.34.11.1085.

Vitale, L. (1997). *Historia social de los pueblos de América Latina: Pueblos originarios y colonia*. Talleres de Impresos Atali.

World Bank Group (2015). *Indigenous Latin-America in the twenty-first century: The first decade*. World Bank Group. http://documents1.worldbank.org/curated/en/145891467991974540/pdf/Indigenous-Latin-America-in-the-twenty-first-century-the-firstdecade.pdf

Abolitionist Feminism, Liberation Psychology, and Latinx Migrant Womxn

Daniela Domínguez

ABSTRACT
The increased presence of Latinx migrant womxn in immigration detention centers reflects the colonial, racialized, gendered, and capitalist nature of the punishing business in the United States. For Latinx migrant womxn, trauma from painful encounters with immigration detention may compound with suffering related to colonialism, imperialism, militarism, and racial capitalism. Grounded in the emancipatory frameworks of abolition feminism and liberation psychology, this article offers multi-level critical reflection strategies to support therapists in their efforts to resist the violent and oppressive nature of the immigration industrial complex and prison industrial complex.

Background: The Immigration Industrial Complex

Since its founding, the United States (U.S.) government has forcefully displaced and removed Black, Indigenous, and migrants of Color within the United States and across international borders (Goodman, 2020; Hernandez, 2019). Beginning in the late 19th century and due to increased migration to the United States from certain parts of Asia and Europe (i.e., Southern and Eastern Europe), members of the U.S government, led by cisgender White men, began to draw xenophobic connections between criminality and immigration (see number 1 in Figure 1; Domínguez et al., 2021; Goodman, 2020). These conflated connections had little to do with official crime rates, and more to do with the social dynamics of a stratified "modern/colonial/capitalist world-system" that prioritizes the *economic*, *military*, and *symbolic* interests of White and wealthy U.S. citizens (e.g., Chinese Exclusion; Gilmore, 2007; Grosfoguel, 2003, p. 49; Richie & Martensen, 2020). These interests work to maintain the hegemony of the United States in today's capitalist world-economy.

The world-system logics of capital accumulation, military expansion, symbolic strategies of prestige and honor, and ethnoracial, gender, and

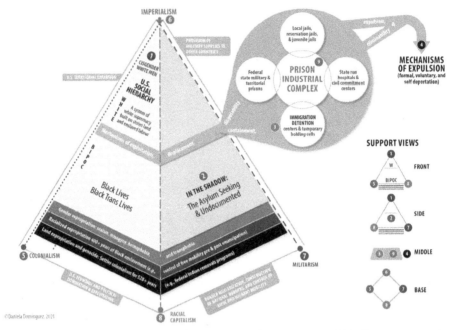

Figure 1. Prison industrial complex and immigration detention. *Note.* This figure presents how colonialism (5), imperialism (6), militarism (7), and racial capitalism (8) shape and reinforce the current social structure in the United States, which advantages White groups, marginalizes BIPOC, and maintains immigrants in the shadow (2); how the immigration industrial complex amplifies the size and power of the prison industrial complex (3); and how through mechanisms of exploitation, displacement, disposability, containment, expulsion, and eliminability, individuals end up incarcerated or deported (4). This figure is a visual representation of earlier abolition scholarship (Davis, 2003; Gruber, 2020; Richie & Martensen, 2020; Story, 2019; Thuma, 2019).

sexual hierarchies (Grosfoguel, 2003, p. 49) have shaped and reinforced the *immigration industrial complex* (e.g., see Secure Communities Program; Domínguez et al., 2021; Goodman, 2020). The immigration industrial complex (IIC), a term introduced by immigration activists and scholars, is used to reference the racist ideologies and profit interests, public and private, that drive legislators and leaders to design immigration policies and infrastructure that solidify the borders and hegemony of White and wealthy Americans in a modern/colonial world (see number 3 in Figure 1; Domínguez et al., 2021; Golash-Boza, 2009; Hernandez, 2019). The IIC represents the "racist, colonial culture and global capitalist system we are living in today" (Grosfoguel, 2002, p. 210). In it, migrants become colonial "others."

The economic, military, and symbolic interests of the U.S. were represented in the formation of the U.S. Bureau of Immigration in the 1890s, the exponential militaristic expansion of the Department of Homeland Security (DHS) in the aftermath of September 11, 2001 and recent efforts to construct a wall that would extend across the U.S. two thousand mile-length southern border (Gonzalez, 2011; Goodman, 2020; Hernandez, 2019). The construction of the border wall symbolizes the idea that "Americans" (i.e., us) are deserving and in need of protection, and immigrants or asylum seekers (i.e., them) are potential criminals who must be controlled (Domínguez et al., 2021). These colonial ideologies have contributed to the deportation of 57 million people since 1882 and the continued suffering of migrants, their families, and entire communities (Domínguez et al., 2021; Hernandez-Arriaga & Domínguez, 2020).

Among those impacted by the global racial, ethnic, gender, and sexual hierarchies of the "modern/colonial/capitalist world-system" are Latinx migrant womxn (Grosfoguel, 2003). Latinx migrant womxn are defined in this article as adult Latinx asylum seekers and undocumented womxn, a marginalized group in the colonial imaginary of the U.S. I focus specifically on adult Latinx migrant womxn in U.S. immigration detention, the fastest-growing form of incarceration (Hernandez, 2019). I use the term womxn in an expansive manner and the term Latinx in intersectional ways (Adames et al., 2021).

The Present Article

Scholars with a special interest in migration, immigration, and Latinx mental health have contributed to our understanding of pre-migration, during migration, and post-migration processes (Foster, 2001). Their psychological research has shed light on the unique experiences of (im)migrants (Chavez-Dueñas et al., 2019; Perreira & Ornelas, 2013), their interlocking systems of oppression (Comas-Díaz, 2021; Domínguez et al., 2012), as well as the sociopolitical stressors impacting their families (Domínguez et al., 2018). Liberation psychologists and abolition feminists have also contributed to immigration, abolition, and psychological literature with their analysis of immigration detention and incarceration from the prism of structural violence and entangled structuring logics (Davis, 2003; Gilmore, 2007; Kaba, 2021).

Although abolition feminists (Davis, 2003; Gilmore, 2007) and liberation psychologists (Martín-Baró, 1994; Montero, 2007) have made significant contributions to social justice movements and scholarship, there continues to be an underrepresentation of their impressive work, including their analysis of mass incarceration, in psychology journals and related fields. This underrepresentation may be because psychology and therapy journals often prioritize scholarship that focuses on traditional or modern psychological models, rather than liberatory models that confront oppressive environmental conditions (Comas-Díaz & Rivera, 2020; Domínguez et al., 2021). This preference for modern psychological models may be because of the

Table 1. Overview of two emancipatory frameworks.

	Abolition feminism	Liberation psychology
Scholars and leaders	Angela Davis, Beth Richie, Ruth Wilson Gilmore, Gina Dent, Mariame Kaba, Rose Braz, anti-prison and political activists, artists	Ignacio Martín-Baró, Maritza Montero, Lillian Comas-Diaz, Mary Watkins, Helene Shulman
Roots and contributing streams of thought	Interdisciplinary foundation: Gender, sexual, Queer, and Black liberation movements; anti-racist queer feminist activism; prisoners' and psychiatric patients' rights struggles; anti-violence and anti-capitalist politics; prison; participatory and critical research	Interdisciplinary foundation: Liberation theology; indigenous psychologies; feminism; collaborative arts; dynamic depth psychologies; critical, community, and peace psychology; (post)colonial studies; Queer theory; participatory and critical research
Groups and Campaigns	Critical Resistance–INCITE; Survived and Punished; Project NIA; Love and Protect	Association of Maya Ixil Women; The Green Belt Movement
Analysis	Requires a critical and emancipatory analysis of oppressive power relations and forces, including those within feminist movements (e.g., carceral feminism)	Requires a critical and emancipatory analysis of oppressive power relations and oppressive forces, including those within psychology (e.g., Eurocentric and positivist approaches)
Focus, values, and, strategies	Acknowledge the disinvestment, dispossession, exploitation, and wounding that oppressive structures have inflicted on marginalized communities Resist authoritarian regimes, repressive government discourse, and neoliberal ideologies that promote individual responsibility Center and privilege those on the margins of society Connect people and their struggles to form new social relations in a free and democratic world (i.e., a world free of prisons, state and interpersonal violence) Access and rely on radical imagination; critical consciousness and an ongoing examination of power imbalances; communal traditions; collective memory and responsibility; coalition building, mutual aid, and solidarity; community organizing; participatory projects, and anti-racist and distributive justice practices	

Note. Separate columns indicate differences. Merged columns indicate similarities. This table is not meant to be comprehensive. It is meant to provide only some examples.

dominant "Western/masculinist idea that we can produce knowledges that are unpositioned, unlocated, neutral, and universalistic" (Grosfoguel, 2002, p. 209). Abolition feminists and liberation psychologists are critical of hegemonic perspectives and attempt to move beyond the dominant colonial imaginary.

This article grounds itself in the emancipatory frameworks of abolition feminism and liberation psychology (Table 1). First, I provide an overview of these two frameworks. Second, I propose that the increased presence of Latinx migrant womxn in immigration detention reflects the gendered, capitalist, colonial, and racialized nature of the punishing business in the U.S; a punishing business situated within a multidimensional capitalist world-system (Grosfoguel, 2003). Third, I offer multi-level reflection strategies to help spark dialogue among therapists about prison abolition and liberation. These strategies do not provide comprehensive solutions. They are shared to generate honest exchanges and to facilitate *freedom dreaming* beyond the possibilities of a modern/colonial/capitalist world-system. My hope is that these reflections will catalyze new reflections identified by the community itself. Robyn Kelley (2002) defined freedom dreaming as the belief that to create a better world, we must first imagine it.

Abolition Feminism

Most feminist schools share the basic premise that a person who identifies as "woman" (e.g., Latinx migrant womxn) is vulnerable to unique discrimination and violence in a patriarchal world that must be eradicated (Gruber, 2020). Although they share this basic premise, feminists have emerged from different sociocultural backgrounds, political contexts, and ideologies (Bryant-Davis & Comas-Díaz, 2016; Castañeda-Sound et al., 2016). First wave feminists often focused on suffrage initiatives while they simultaneously excluded Black Indigenous Womxn of Color (BIWOC) from feminist spaces. Second wave feminists often included BIWOC in their movement, but focused on gender issues and not racism, ethnocentrism, and poverty. Queer BIWOC such as "Audre Lorde, Barbara Smith, Cherrie Moraga, Merle Woo, Paula Gunn Allen, and Gloria Anzaldua faced head-on the profound racism and heterosexism" of second wave feminists (Mohanty, 2003, p. 4). In response to white feminism's exclusion of BIWOC and their struggles, third-wave feminists focused on collective liberation, womxn's experiences with multiple forms of oppression and coined concepts like intersectionality (Crenshaw, 1989), womanism (Walker, 1983), and mujerismo (i.e., Spanish for womanism; Isasi-Díaz, 1994).

In the 1980s and 1990s, at around the same time that intersectionality and womanism were introduced (read *Womanist and Mujerista Psychologies* by Thema Bryant-Davis and Lillian Comas-Diaz for more information), other powerful feminist groups showed their commitment to law and order in an effort to end gender-based discrimination and violence (Gruber, 2020). These feminist groups' support for punitive policies and prosecution contributed to the creation of a "prison nation" that today renders BIWOC vulnerable to violence, criminalization, and incarceration (Story, 2019). Their adoption of an incarceration-centric perspective re-created patriarchal systems of abuse that continue to push Queer, working-class, and migrant BIWOC further into the margins of society (Davis, 2003; Gruber, 2020; Richie & Martensen, 2020; Thuma, 2019). Sociologist Elizabeth Bernstein (2010) referred to their feminist practice as *carceral feminism*.

Unlike carceral feminism, abolition feminism resists and counteracts the idea that incarceration is necessary to end gender-based violence and crime. In fact, abolition feminists argue that incarceration perpetuates violence against womxn, especially BIWOC. An example of prisons' violent nature, they explain, is the prevalent, unacknowledged, and "habitual" presence of sexual assault during incarceration (e.g., strip and body cavity searches; Davis, 2003, p. 81).

Abolition feminism is rooted in gender, sexual, Queer, and Black liberation movements, and it centers criminalized, incarcerated, marginalized womxn, and transgender folx (Davis, 2003). Rather than conceptualizing prisons as buildings, abolition feminists view prisons as a set of gendered, racial, and class relationships across and beyond the *carceral space* (Gruber, 2020; Story, 2019; Thuma, 2019). The carceral space constitutes the "relationships and geographic practices through which the state's capacities of containment, displacement, and dispossession are put to work for *racial capitalism*" (see number 8 in Figure 1; Story, 2019 p. 6). Racial capitalism is the process of extracting social and economic value from the racial identity of an individual (Robinson, 2021). Immigrant detention "is part of a carceral landscape in the United States that includes more than two million citizens behind bars" (see number 3 in Figure 1). The carceral space protects the existing structures and global political-economic processes of racial capitalism that dispossess BIWOC, submit them to forced forms of labor, and profit the white elite. In this carceral space, BIWOC remain in disadvantaged and subjugated positions within the global, racial, and ethnic hierarchies of coloniality.

For migrant BIWOC who often experience violence inside and outside of prison, treatment from the *prison industrial complex* (PIC) can be particularly destructive because they often find themselves at the intersection of sexism, racism, nativism, and classism (Davis, 2003). The PIC is a term used by scholars to analyze "the overlapping interests of government and industry that use surveillance, policing, and imprisonment as solutions to economic, social and political problems" (see number 9 Figure 1; Critical Resistance, 2021, paragraph 1). The PIC has grown exponentially, especially as prisons are increasingly being used for immigration detention. Between 1980 and 2019, the number of incarcerated womxn has increased by more than 700 percent from a total of 26,378 in 1980 to 222,455 in 2019 (The Sentencing Project, 2019).

The majority of incarcerated womxn are BIWOC, the "colonial others" (Grosfoguel, 2002, p. 207). The increased and longer incarceration of "colonial others" means higher profits for private corporations and the maintenance of the capitalist world-economy. In the modern/colonial world-system, capitalist accumulation has shaped, dominated, and persuaded other logics, including state military security and symbolic strategies of prestige and honor (Grosfoguel, 2003, p. 49). The capitalist world economy is clearly visible in the cost of detention, deportation, and reported annual revenues of detention conglomerates. In 2015, the cost of DHS's detention and deportation operations involved $9 million per day (Domínguez et al., 2021; Goodman, 2020). In 2016, private detention companies such as CoreCivic and GEO Group reported annual revenues of $1.85 billion and $2.18 billion, respectively (Domínguez et al., 2021; Goodman, 2020). The capitalist economy provides an understanding for the need to control prisons and BIWOC; it results in capital accumulation and the political success of those who benefit from it (Grosfoguel, 2003). The coloniality of power is visible in the IIC and PIC.

Abolition feminism opposes gendered, racialized, and carceral violence, pursues the abolition of all forms of incarceration, advocates for investment in social programs rather than imprisonment, and struggles for a free world without borders. For abolitionists, it is not just about tearing down and divesting resources from the carceral state. It is about building a new world that nurtures relationships, health, and the environment (Kaba, 2021). Like other theories and practices of feminism, abolition feminism "has shaped and has been shaped by the penal state" (Gruber, 2020, p. 17). There are other emancipatory frameworks that envision a new democratic world besides abolition feminism. One of them is liberation psychology.

Liberation Psychology

Founded by Ignacio Martín-Baró (Martín-Baró 1991) in the 1980s in El Salvador, liberation psychology emerged in reaction to modern psychological models that primarily focus on intrapsychic processes rather than the collective injustices caused by colonialism, imperialism, militarism, and racial capitalism (Burton & Guzzo, 2020). Martín-Baró, a U.S. trained psychologist and Jesuit priest, observed the social conditions that contributed to the suffering, exclusion, and hunger of the impoverished communities of El Salvador (Lykes & Sibley, 2014). As a result, he expressed a desire for a new psychology that would address violence, trauma, poverty, war, and abuses by elite groups. In this pursuit, he called on psychologists to surrender their expert stance, to break out of bystanding postures that strengthen oppressors, and to center the interests of the marginalized (see number 2 Figure 2; Torres Rivera, 2020).

Following the path paved by Martín-Baró, liberation psychologists commit to ongoing and recursive *conscientization, acompañamiento*, and social action (Norsworthy & Khuankaew, 2020). Conscientization involves genuine engagement in active emotional and cognitive processes to learn more about the systems of domination that disadvantaged communities encounter (Freire, 1973). Through critical reflection, they work to uncover and counter taken-for-granted beliefs that devalue the cultural wealth, knowledge, and experiences of the poor and excluded (Montero, 2007). They also promote *acompañamiento* ["mutual vulnerability and struggle"] between members of oppressed and privileged groups (Siham Fernandez, 2020, p. 91). Through acompañamiento, liberation psychologists' social action seeks to amplify the cultural assets and strengths of disadvantaged communities. Liberation psychology pursues freedom from hegemonic systems through conscientization, acompañamiento, and social action (Martín-Baró, 1994; Norsworthy & Khuankaew, 2020). In this process, it aims to disrupt the modern/colonial/capitalist world-system (Grosfoguel, 2003).

Therapists' integration of liberation psychology and abolition feminism may be particularly suitable for Latinx womxn in immigration detention. Therapists can learn resistance and advocacy strategies to support criminalized and incarcerated womxn from abolition feminism. They can also benefit from liberation psychology's analysis on the psychological effects of violence, poverty, and trauma within Latin American communities. Through their integration, therapists may be in a better position to understand and confront the ways in which the IIC maintains the oppressive influences of today's modern/colonial/capitalist world-system.

Latinx Migrant Womxn in U.S. Immigration Detention

Before Detention

Latin American nation-states continue to "live today under the regime of global coloniality imposed by the United States" (Grosfoguel, 2002, p. 205). Under this regime, the United States' economic, military, and symbolic interests have forced the migration of millions of peripheral migrants from Latin America to the United States. These interests are conceptualized by Ramon Grosfoguel (2003) as "a single multidimensional capitalist world-system with multiple structuring logics" (p. 49). Throughout history, some of these logics have dominated over the others in an entangled and dialectic relationship.

Examples of these multiple entangled interests include U.S. foreign policy interests (e.g., the U.S.'s installment of unpopular Latin American leaders), capital accumulation (e.g., U.S. sales of weapons to Latin American governments and paramilitary groups), and U.S. labor objectives that determine when and which migrants are valuable or disposable (Gonzalez, 2011). For example, the lower value awarded to peripheral transmigrants from Latin America compared to middle class White migrants from Europe is due to their positionality within the existing class and racial hierarchies. Grosfoguel (2003) explains that in today's modern/colonial world-system, the capitalist accumulation logic dominates and influences other logics. For example, in this capitalist economy, a Latin American executive living in

Mexico has a higher status and more resources to mobilize transnationally than a Latinx labor migrant from the same country. He states that "the status of transmigrants as well as their cultural/symbolic and social capital are conditioned by their relational location along the axes of the modern/colonial/capitalist world-system" (p. 31). These structural logics have endangered and impoverished many peripheral Latinxs and are the underlying reason for their overwhelming migration.

The presence of gender-based violence, sexism, misogyny, heterosexism, and transphobia in Latin America has also forced the migration of Latinx migrant womxn to the U.S. (Chavez-Dueñas et al., 2019; Foster, 2001; Perreira & Ornelas, 2013). During their migration, Latinx migrant womxn often encounter treacherous migration journeys that involve traveling across dangerous oceans and rivers, boarding trains and buses, crossing the desert, or other hazardous conditions (Young, 2021). The impact of these during-migration experiences (i.e., in-transit trauma) may compound with the effects of pre-migration trauma (Foster, 2001; Hernandez-Arriaga & Domínguez, 2020). Their migration may be particularly dangerous because they are often situated at the intersection of sexism, racism, nativism, and classism. In the modern/colonial/capitalist world system, BIWOC "still have in general a lower status and class position than 'white' European/Euro-American males" (Grosfoguel, 2002, p. 31).

For some Latinx migrant womxn, trauma often continues once they arrive in the U.S. (i.e., post-migration trauma; Foster, 2001). Their conditional and often unwanted entry to the U.S. is related to their subordinate status in the modern/colonial/capitalist world-system. Their apprehension by Customs and Border Protection (CBP) or Immigration Customs Enforcement (CBP) is evidence of the dominant/subordinate relations within a world system dominated by white cisgender men (see number 1 in Figure 1; Domínguez et al., 2021).

Apprehension

When [and if] Latinx migrant womxn arrive in the U.S., they often turn themselves over to U.S. authorities or cross the border without U.S. authorization (Domínguez, 2019). Thousands of them are apprehended at U.S ports of entry by CBP or in the interior of the U.S. by ICE every year. In 2019 alone, more than half a million immigrants were apprehended and detained (Young, 2021). Those apprehended at the border are often detained in temporary holding cells (Domínguez, Hernandez-Arriaga et al., 2020). After they spend hours or days in temporary cells, they are either transferred to an immigration detention facility or are expelled from the U.S. through expedited removals (see number 4 in Figure 1). Those apprehended in the U.S. interior may be taken to federal prisons, local jails, privately-run detention centers, juvenile detention centers, or family immigration prisons (see number 3 in Figure 1; Goodman, 2020; Hernandez, 2019). Whether apprehended near the border or in the U.S. interior, Latinx migrant womxn often end up incarccrated with the general population of prisoners in local and state incarceration facilities. Their poor treatment in hazardous detention facilities and prisons is an indicator of the peripheral zones of the modern/colonial/capitalist world-system they come from (Grosfoguel, 2003).

Detention

Five percent of the total 10.5 million undocumented immigrant population is detained or deported each year, the majority are from Latin America (Young, 2021). The average length of detention for migrants has nearly doubled to 39.4 days between 2015 and 2018 (Department of Homeland Security, 2020). Some detainees are pregnant, and others are incarcerated with infants, toddlers, and young children. According to a 2019 report from the ACLU (American Civil Liberties Union, 2019), from October 2017 through August 2018, ICE detained 1,655 pregnant womxn; 28 of them had miscarriages in ICE custody. The same report indicated that between 2009 and 2016, the number of women in ICE custody increased by 60 percent, up to 14.5 percent. Latinx womxn who are apprehended by CBP tend to have lower lengths of stay due to expedited removals, whereas womxn with U.S. interior criminal cases are typically detained for longer periods of time (Department of Homeland Security, 2020).

Reports indicated that the detention facilities in which they are detained are undergoing congressional investigations of human rights violations for their alleged neglect and abuse against Latinx womxn. Allegations were reported in the areas of maternal health (Rayasam, 2019), reproductive autonomy (e.g., being pressured into mass hysterectomies; Rose, 2020), physical health (e.g., exposure to COVID-19 virus; Congress of the United States, 2020), sexual abuse (Gonzalez, 2019; Kriel, 2020), medical racism against Black migrant womxn in detention (RAICES, 2021), and the abuse and death of transgender womxn (Gutíerrez & Portillo, 2018). A 2018 report indicated that LGBTQ people in ICE detention were 97 times more likely to be victims of sexual abuse than non-LGBTQ people (Gruberg, 2018). BIPOC womxn, especially transgender womxn, continue to have a lower status and class position in the modern/colonial/capitalist world-system (see pyramid structure in Figure 1; Grosfoguel, 2003).

Although there is significant evidence of the adverse health consequences of immigration detention, facilities continue to fail to provide adequate standards of care (von Werthern et al., 2018). For example, only 21 of 230 ICE facilities offer face to face mental health services (Rayasam, 2019). This is problematic because there is a higher rate of mental health concerns among detained immigrants than the general population (von Werthern et al., 2018). With the former in mind, therapists must demonstrate the political will to advocate on behalf of Latinx migrant womxn in detention. To do so effectively, they must first examine their positionality within the modern/colonial/capitalist world-system, the institutions they belong to, and their relationship to the IIC and PIC. I offer the following multi-level reflection strategies for support.

Multi-Level Reflection Strategies

Abolition feminists and liberation psychologists practice on multiple fronts and in multi-level ways. They emphasize that for liberation from punitive and repressive systems to be accomplished, profound transformations of self, community, and societal structures are required. Grounded in both frameworks, the next section outlines reflection strategies at the individual, mutual aid, institutional, and policy levels. These reflection strategies, which are meant to be liberation-based *entry* points (not solutions), can be used by those who are already participating in the struggle for prison abolition, as well as those who are in the process of learning about it. These strategies, which are also meant to be used on an ongoing basis, invite therapists to examine our role in prison construction and or abolition and to imagine a new psychology that contributes to a free society in a democratic world; a free society that values, sees, hears, and celebrates Latinx migrant womxn. The questions included under the "individual level" section are meant to be answered privately. The rest of the questions are meant to be answered in collaboration with loved ones, community members, colleagues, and leaders.

Individual Level

Abolition feminism and liberation psychology encourage us to engage in critical reflection to transform ourselves. Through critical reflection, we can explore our beliefs regarding gender, violence, immigration, and incarceration (Gruber, 2020). Critical reflection can be accessed through writing, oral accounts, art, and other approaches that can serve as anti-oppressive tools that facilitate conscientization. Personal reflection is important because the modern/colonial world is embedded not only in relations of exploitation and "domination, but in the production of subjectivities and knowledges" (Grosfoguel, 2003, p. 208). The next questions can be used for personal reflection.

1. What do abolition and liberation mean [and look like] to me? Why do they matter?
2. What would a world without human cages and borders look like? How come?
3. How are my beliefs/knowledges about punishment and criminalization aligned with feminist, antiracist, anti-capitalist, and anti-imperialist struggles? How do they differ?
4. How do I benefit from the IIC, PIC, and/or the systems that sustain them?
5. How do I respond to dominant narratives or attacks that depict BIPOC, including Latinx migrant womxn, as criminals or potential security threats to the United States?
6. How is the liberation of Latinx migrant womxn and incarcerated communities tied or connected to my own liberation? How come?

These questions at the individual level may help anchor us in the values of abolition feminism and liberation psychology (Table 1 to understand these values). When reflecting on these questions, we might wonder—Can we actually abolish prisons and immigration detention centers? According to abolitionist Mariame Kaba (2021), "We can, We must. We are" (p. 2).

Mutual Aid Level

Abolition feminism and liberation psychology are rooted in the mutual aid "principles of anti-capitalism, anti-imperialism, racial justice, gender justice, and disability justice" (Spade, 2019, see chart on website). Mutual aid exists outside of the bureaucracy and politics of local, state, and national health and psychological associations, and it involves taking responsibility for others by building new community relationships that are more survivable (Spade, 2019). Through membership in mutual aid groups that oppose gendered, racialized, and carceral violence, therapists can address some of the physio-psycho-socioeconomic needs of Latinx migrant womxn in a non-professionalized volunteer role (e.g., letter writing to incarcerated individuals, monetary support). The following questions are meant to catalyze conversations at the mutual aid level:

1. How do prisons and detention centers protect or harm our community's survival?
2. How can we be in solidarity with Latinx migrant womxn outside and inside of prisons?
3. What tactics can we use together to counteract the mechanisms of exploitation, displacement, disposability, and expulsion that impact those living in human cages?

4. How is our participation in mutual aid (outside of the profession) elevating the values of abolition feminism and liberation psychology?
5. How can therapists use their specific skills and training, in a de-professionalized way, to support incarcerated communities (e.g., sharing with community members information about the psychological distress and trauma associated with prisons and incarceration)?

There are several mutual aid groups with the political will and steadfast commitment to change the national discourse on immigration and incarceration. One example is the Bay Area Border Relief (BABR), which is composed of a group of volunteers who support migrants and asylum seekers at the U.S. Mexico Border. BABR's initiatives include working with immigration attorneys to represent and advocate on behalf of migrants and asylum seekers in detention. Members of BABR include, but are not limited to, social workers, psychologists, and other therapists who work as volunteers. Two other examples include Survived & Punished (S&P) and Project Nia, which are a coalition of grassroots groups committed to eradicating the criminalization of violence survivors. S&P volunteers include community organizers, survivor advocates, legal experts, policy advocates, and currently and formerly incarcerated survivors.

When reflecting on the former questions, we might also wonder—Where can I find mutual aid groups? As abolitionist Mariame Kaba explains, "Start where you are. Connect with others doing the work. Experiment" (Kaba, 2021, xix). To learn more about local mutual aid groups, visit the Town Hall Project's Mutual Aid Hub (2020) for more information.

Institutional Level

Liberation psychology and abolition feminism offer therapists a road map to move beyond an emphasis on individual wellness to focus on the ways in which institutions and systems perpetuate colonialism, imperialism, militarism, and racial capitalism. This broader emphasis is critical because psychologists have produced research that shows that oppression operates on the individual and interpersonal levels within a larger institutional or structural system (Neville et al., 2012; Pieterse et al., 2012). Therefore, the role of our institutions in prison construction or abolition must be examined. It may be helpful to answer the following questions with colleagues from institutions and divisions in which we hold professional memberships (e.g., American Psychological Association, Society for the Psychology of Women, National Latinx Psychological Association, etc.):

1. How do detention centers and prisons protect or harm our institution and therapeutic treatment?
2. What resources and education are our institutions offering to help us understand the PIC, the IIC, and the unique experiences of Latinx migrant womxn in detention?
3. How does the PIC and IIC hinder the development of therapeutic approaches that contribute to a free society?
4. How is our institution collaborating, consciously or implicitly, in the exploitation of incarcerated communities, including Latinx migrant womxn in detention (e.g., history of Office of Refugee Resettlement sharing youth's psychotherapy notes with ICE)?
5. How is our institution investing or divesting in resources for carceral systems?

National psychological, health, and therapy associations, for example, are in a unique position to energize a united and interdisciplinary coalition of providers to examine their role in prison construction and or abolition.

Policy Level

Abolition feminists and liberation psychologists actively believe in the process of social transformation through radical imagination and hope. Abolition feminism, for example, teaches us that tearing down the PIC and IIC is not only urgently needed, but also possible. Holding on to the possibility of social change involves commitment to freedom dreaming. Kaba (2021) explains that hope is a discipline that must be cultivated. One way of cultivating hope is by celebrating small victories with others who are in the struggle for liberation. Small victories can take place in the form of policy changes in the direction of PIC and IIC abolition. The following are questions to help facilitate hope:

1. What policies or initiatives exist that suggest that PIC and IIC abolition are possible (e.g., learn about cities like Oakland which removed law enforcement from schools)?
2. What anti-violence policies, within our reach, can we advocate for that move beyond prison reform and toward PIC and IIC abolition (e.g., defund the police)?
3. How can therapists reach out to policymakers to demand full divestment from prisons and investment in social programs, including those that contribute to the mental health of Latinx migrant womxn?
4. What are some concrete ways in which a broad coalition of health associations, health professionals, and therapists can come together to lobby

for anti-violence and pro-migrant policies? Who is already doing it (e.g., learn about Psychologists for Social Responsibility and their efforts to abolish ICE)?
5. If policies were passed to divest from the PIC and IIC, which programs and services would therapists want the government and community to invest in?

Policymakers would benefit from accessing the expertise of abolition feminists and liberation psychologists to formulate a more radical policy agenda. Similarly, to make prison abolition a reality, abolition feminists and liberation psychologists may benefit from collaboration with scholars and policymakers with successful policymaking records (Crowley et al., 2019). Together, prison abolition is possible.

Conclusion

In this article, I highlighted the impressive and revolutionary work that abolition feminists and liberation psychologists have shared with society and promoted the integration of liberation psychology and abolition feminism to support Latinx migrant womxn in immigration detention. These two liberatory frameworks can help us have a clearer understanding of the impact of colonialism, imperialism, militarism, and racial capitalism in the lives of those around us (Burton & Guzzo, 2020; Domínguez, 2019). In particular, abolition feminism is well suited to help therapists understand the ways in which the PIC exploits, dispossesses, and abuses incarcerated communities, especially BIWOC who are vulnerable to multiple forms of oppression including sexism, racism, nativism, and classism (Davis, 2003).

Abolition feminism, liberation psychology, and the "modern/colonial/capitalist world-system" remind us that Latinx migration is the result of the "United States' global geopolitical symbolic/ideological strategies and its colonial/racist [and sexist] social imaginary" (Grosfoguel, 2003, p. 204). They also remind us that the liberation of Latinx migrant womxn will not be possible unless the existing colonial/racial/gendered/and sexual hierarchies are dismantled. If therapists do not have a clear understanding of these hierarchies and oppressive forces, we may end up recreating patriarchal and punishing behaviors that push BIWOC further into the margins of society (Davis, 2003; Gruber, 2020; Richie & Martensen, 2020; Thuma, 2019).

In this article, I also offered reflection strategies in the form of open questions to help bring people together to discuss prison abolition and liberation. These conversations are critical and urgent because the PIC has grown exponentially with the increased presence of immigration detainees, many of them Latinx migrant womxn. While questions at the individual level are meant to be reflected privately, the rest are meant to enhance social connection and critical consciousness, both important values in liberation psychology and abolition feminism. The questions included in this article are meant to elicit and facilitate radical imagination and solidarity between and with people from different backgrounds and disciplines. As Dr. Anneliese Singh (2020) has explained, it is important to set "accountability networks that hold us and help us retrain, relearn, lean in, support, and engage in the most challenging conversations we can have about liberation" (Singh, 2020, p. 1125). Therapists can participate in prison abolition and support the liberation of Latinx migrant womxn.

Acknowledgments

Gratitude to Leni Sánchez for helping with the technical and visual aspects of Figure 1.

Disclosure statement

No potential conflict of interest was reported by the author(s).

ORCID

Daniela Domínguez http://orcid.org/0000-0001-9410-1002

References

Adames, H. Y., Chavez-Dueñas, N. Y., & Jernigan, M. M. (2021). The fallacy of a raceless Latinidad: Action guidelines for centering Blackness in Latinx psychology. *Journal of Latinx Psychology*, 9(1), 26–44. https://doi.org/10.1037/lat0000179

American Civil Liberties Union. (2019). Still worse than second-class: Solitary confinement of women in the United States. Retrieved on March 28, 2021 from https://www.aclu.org/sites/default/files/field_document/062419-sj-solitaryreportcov-er.pdf.

Bernstein, E. (2010). Militarized humanitarianism meets carceral feminism: The politics of sex, rights, and freedom in contemporary antitrafficking campaigns. *Signs*, 36(1), 45–71. https://doi.org/10.1086/652918.

Bryant-Davis, T., & Comas-Díaz, L. (Eds.). (2016). *Psychology of women book series. Womanist and mujerista psychologies: Voices of fire, acts of courage.* American Psychological Association.

Burton, M., & Guzzo, R. (2020). Liberation psychology: Origins and development. In L. Comas-Díaz, & E. Torres Rivera (Eds.), *Liberation psychology: Theory, method, practice, and social justice* (pp. 133–147). American Psychological Association.

Castañeda-Sound, C. L., Martinez, S., & Durán, J. E. (2016). Mujeristas and social justice: La lucha es la vida. In T. Bryant-Davis & L. Comas-Díaz (Eds.), *Psychology of women book series. Womanist and mujerista psychologies: Voices of fire, acts of courage* (p. 237–259). American Psychological Association.

Chavez-Dueñas, N. Y., Adames, H. Y., Perez-Chavez, J. G., & Salas, S. P. (2019). Healing ethno-racial trauma in Latinx immigrant communities: Cultivating hope, resistance, and action. *The American Psychologist, 74*(1), 49–62. https://doi.org/10.1037/amp000028.

Congress of the United States. (2020, September 15). Re: Lack of medical care, unsafe work practices, and absence of adequate protection against COVID-19 for detained immigrants and employees alike at the Irwin County Detention Center. Retrieved on November 10 from http://jayapal.house.gov/wp-content/uploads/2020/09/DHS-IG-Letter-9.15.pdf.

Comas-Díaz, L. (2021). Sociopolitical trauma: Ethnicity, race, and migration. In P. Tummala-Narra (Ed.), *Cultural, racial, and ethnic psychology. Trauma and racial minority immigrants: Turmoil, uncertainty, and resistance* (p. 127–146). American Psychological Association. https://doi.org/10.1037/0000214-008

Comas-Díaz, L., & Rivera, E. T. (2020). Liberation psychology-crossing borders into new frontiers. In L. Comas-Díaz, & E. Torres Rivera (Eds.), *Liberation psychology: Theory, method, practice, and social justice* (pp. 133–147). American Psychological Association.

Crenshaw, K. W. (1989). Demarginalizing the intersection of race and sex: Black feminist critique of antidiscrimination doctrine, feminist theory and antiracist politics. *University of Chicago Legal Forum, 140*, 139–167. https://chicagounbound.uchicago.edu/uclf/vol1989/iss1/8.

Critical Resistance. (2021). The prison industrial complex. Retrieved from https://criticalresistance.org/mission-vision/notso-common-language/#:~:text=The%20prison%20industrial%20complex%20(PIC,economic%2C%20social%20and%20political%20problems.

Crowley, M., Supplee, L., Scott, T., & Brooks-Gunn, J. (2019). The role of psychology in evidence-based policymaking: Mapping opportunities for strategic investment in poverty reduction. *The American Psychologist, 74*(6), 685–697. https://doi.org/10.1037/amp0000466.

Davis, A. (2003). *Are prisons obsolete?* NY: Seven Stories Press.

Department of Homeland Security. (2020). *U.S. immigration and customs enforcement budget overview.* Retrieved on March 29, 2021 https://www.dhs.gov/sites/default/files/publications/19_0318_MGMT_CBJ-ImmigrationCustoms-Enforcement_0.pdf.

Domínguez, D. G., Coppock, J., & Polanco, m. (2018). Immigrant and binational individuals and couples: Risk factors for relationship dissatisfaction, conflict, and divorce. In Abbie Goldberg and Adam P. Romero (Eds.). *LGBTQ divorce and relationship dissolution: Psychological and legal perspectives and implications for practice.* Oxford University Press.

Domínguez, D. G., García, D., Martínez, D. A., & Hernandez-Arriaga, B. (2020). Leveraging the power of mutual aid, coalitions, leadership, and advocacy during COVID-19. *The American Psychologist, 75*(7), 909–918. https://doi.org/10.1037/amp0000693.

Domínguez, D. G., Hernandez-Arriaga, B., Noriega, M., García, D., & Martínez, D. A. (2021). They treat us like we are not human:" Asylum seekers and "la migra's" violence *Psychology of Violence.*

Domínguez, D. G., Hernandez-Arriaga, B., & Paul, K. S. (2020). Cruzando Fronteras: Liberation psychology in a counseling psychology immersion course. *Journal of Latinx Psychology, 8*(3), 250–264. https://doi.org/10.1037/lat0000148.

Domínguez, D. G., Solórzano, B., & Peña, E. (2012). Non-heterosexual bi-national families: resilient victims of sexual prejudice and discriminatory immigration policies. *Journal of GLBT Family Studies, 8*(5), 496–508. https://doi.org/10.1080/1550428x.2012.729954

Foster, R. P. (2001). When immigration is trauma: Guidelines for the individual and family clinician. *The American Journal of Orthopsychiatry, 71*(2), 153–170. https://doi.org/10.1037/0002-9432.71.2.153.

Freire, P. (1973). *Education for critical consciousness.* Seabury Press.

Gilmore, R. W. (2007). *Golden gulag: Prisons, surplus, crisis, and opposition in globalizing California* (Vol. 21). Univ of California Press.

Golash-Boza, T. (2009). The immigration industrial complex: Why we enforce immigration policies destined to fail. *Sociology Compass, 3*(2), 295-309. https://doi.org/10.1111/j.1751-9020.2008.00193.x

Gonzalez, R. (2019, February 26). *Sexual assault of detained migrant children reported in the thousands since 2015*. National Public Radio.

Goodman, A. (2020). *The deportation machine: America's long history of expelling immigrants*. Princeton University Press.

Gonzalez, J. (2011). *Harvest of empire: A history of Latinos in America*. Penguin Group USA.

Grosfoguel, R. (2002). Colonial difference, geopolitics of knowledge, and global coloniality in the modern/colonial capitalist world-system. *Review, 25*(3), 203-224. http://www.jstor.org/stable/40241548

Grosfoguel, R. (2003). *Colonial subjects: Puerto Ricans in a global perspective*. Univ of California Press.

Gruber, A. (2020). *The feminist war on crime: The unexpected role of women's liberation in mass incarceration*. University of California Press.

Gruberg, S. (2018, May 30). *ICE's rejection of its own rules is placing LGBT Immigrants at severe risk of sexual abuse*. Center for American Progress.

Gutíerrez, J., & Portillo, S. (2018). Trans (formation) of a movement: Roxsana Hernández, an immigrant transgender woman from Honduras, died in ICE detention earlier this year. LGBTI activists refuse to let her death be in vain. *NACLA Report on the Americas, 50*(4), 392-394. https://doi.org/10.1080/10714839.2018.1550983.

Hernandez, D. M. (2019). Carceral shadows. Entangled lineages and technologies of migrant detention. In R. T. Chase (Ed.), *Caging borders and carceral states: Incarcerations, immigration detentions, and resistance*. UNC Press Books.

Hernandez-Arriaga, & Domínguez, D. G. (2020). Dibujando en tent city: Art by asylum seeking children in the U.S.-Mexico border. *Latinx Psychology Today Bulletin, 7*(1). https://www.nlpa.ws/assets/docs/newsletters/FALL2020.pdf

Isasi-Díaz, A. M. (1994). Mujeristas: A name of our own. In N. B. Lewis (Ed.), *Sisters struggling in the spirit: A women of color theological anthology* (pp. 126-138). Women's Ministries Program, Presbyterian Church (USA).

Kaba, M. (2021). *We do this 'til we free us: Abolitionist organizing and transforming justice*. Haymarket Books.

Kelley, R. D. (2002). *Freedom dreams: The black radical imagination*. Beacon Press.

Kriel, L. (2020, August 14). *ICE guards "systematically" sexually assault detainees in an El Paso detention center, lawyers say*. Texas Tribune.

Lykes, M. B., & Sibley, E. (2014). Liberation psychology and pragmatic solidarity: North-South collaborations through the Ignacio Martín-Baró fund. *Peace and Conflict: Journal of Peace Psychology, 20*(3), 209-226. https://doi.org/10.1037/pac0000045

Martín-Baró, I. (1991). Developing a critical consciousness through the university curriculum. In J. Hasset & H. Lacey (Eds.), *Towards a society that serves its people: The intellectual contributions of El Salvador's murdered Jesuits* (pp. 220-244). Georgetown University Press.

Martín-Baró, I. (1994). *Writings for a liberation psychology*. (A. Aron & S. Corne, Trans. & Eds.). Harvard University Press.

Mohanty, C. T. (2003). *Feminism without borders: Decolonizing theory, practicing solidarity*. Duke University Press.

Mutual Aid Hub. (2020). *Mutual aid network*. Town Hall Project.

Montero, M. (2007). The political psychology of liberation: From politics to ethics and back. *Political Psychology, 28*(5), 517–533. https://www.jstor.org/stable/20447068.

Neville, H. A., Spanierman, L. B., & Lewis, J. A. (2012). The expanded psychosocial model of racism: A new model for understanding and disrupting racism and white privilege. In N. A. Fouad, J. A. Carter, & L. M. Subich (Eds.), *APA handbook of counseling psychology, Vol. 2: Practice, interventions, and applications* (pp. 333–360). American Psychological Association.

Norsworthy K., & Khuankaew, L. (2020). Transnational feminist liberation psychology. In L. Comas-Díaz, & E. Torres Rivera (Eds.), *Liberation psychology: Theory, method, practice, and social justice* (pp. 133–147). American Psychological Association.

Perreira, K. M., & Ornelas, I. (2013). Painful passages: Traumatic experiences and post-traumatic stress among US immigrant Latino adolescents and their primary caregivers. *International Migration Review, 47*(4), 976–1005. https://doi.org/10.1111/imre.12050.

Pieterse, A. L., Todd, N. R., Neville, H. A., & Carter, R. T. (2012). Perceived racism and mental health among Black American adults: A meta-analytic review. *Journal of Counseling Psychology, 59*(1), 1–9. https://doi.org/10.1037/a0026208.

RAICES. (2021, March 3). *Black, pregnant, detained*. Retrieved on March 29, 2021 from https://www.raicestexas.org/2021/03/04/pregnant-and-detained/

Rayasam. (2019, July 21). *Migrant mental health crisis spirals in ICE detention facilities*. Politico. https://www.politico.com/story/2019/07/21/migrant-health-detention-border-camps-1424114

Richie, B. E., & Martensen, K. M. (2020). Resisting carcerality, embracing abolition: Implications for feminist social work practice. *Affilia, 35*(1), 12–16. https://doi.org/10.1177/0886109919897576.

Robinson, C. J. (2021). Black Marxism: The making of the Black radical tradition.

Rose, J. (2020, September 16). *ICE almost deported immigrant woman who says she got unwanted surgery while detained*. National Public Radio.

Sands. (2020, September 24). Immigrants in US custody died after 'inadequate' medical care, congressional investigation finds. *CNN*. Retrieved on November 13, 2020 from https://www.cnn.com/2020/09/24/politics/immigrants-ice-inadequate-medical-care/index.html.

Siham Fernandez, J. (2020). Liberation psychology of and for transformative justice: Centering acompañamiento in participatory action research. In L. Comas-Díaz, & E. Torres Rivera (Eds.), *Liberation psychology: Theory, method, practice, and social justice* (pp. 133–147). American Psychological Association.

Singh, A. (2020). Building a counseling psychology of liberation: The path behind us, under us, and before us. *The Counseling Psychologist, 48*(8), 1109–1130. https://doi.org/10.1177/0011000020959007.

Spade, D. (2019). *Mutual aid chart*. http://www.deanspade.net/2019/12/04/mutual-aid-chart/.

Story, B. (2019). *Prison land: Mapping carceral power across neoliberal America*. University of Minnesota Press.

The Sentencing Project. (2019). Incarcerated women and girls. Retrieved from https://www.sentencingproject.org/publications/incarcerated-women-and-girls/

Torres Rivera, E. T. (2020). Concepts of liberation psychology. In L. Comas-Díaz, & E. Torres Rivera (Eds.), *Liberation psychology: Theory, method, practice, and social justice* (pp. 133–147). American Psychological Association.

von Werthern, M., Robjant, K., Chui, Z., Schon, R., Ottisova, L., Mason, C., & Katona, C. (2018). The impact of immigration detention on mental health: A systematic review. *BMC Psychiatry, 18*(1), 1–19. https://doi.org/10.1186/s12888-018-1945-y.

Walker, A. (1983). *In search of our mothers' gardens: Womanist prose*. Harcourt.

The Connectivity Bridge – A Clinical Understanding: Postcolonial Therapy with Latinx Women Living in the United States

Carmen Inoa Vazquez

ABSTRACT
The negative effects brought by intergenerational trauma affecting Latinx women that transmits across generations has not received the appropriate attention that recognizes the cumulative emotional and psychological wounding brought by the experience of migration associated with the legacies of colonialism, political violence, and related stressors. Intergenerational trauma can be recognized and ameliorated with the application of postcolonial psychotherapy modalities that endorse the relevance of cultural representation, identity, and location, with specific reference to migration, gender, race, and ethnicity that focus on promoting liberation and healing. This article will address the interconnections (The Connectivity Bridge) between gender specific cultural values and/or national narratives that perpetuate the colonial thinking of superiority vs inferiority, based on gender and/or ethnicity, and the creation of negative self-identifications evidenced by many Latinx women. A clinical application will briefly illustrate the existing relationship between postcolonialism, ancestry, feminism, and the migration experience that can affect Latinx women living in the United States. Four cultural expectations of gender specific behaviors with ties to colonialism endorsed by Latinxs will be discussed, namely machismo, marianismo, attitudinal *familismo* or the feeling of support one expects from family, and *simpatia*, a cultural relational script that also carries gender specific behavioral expectations. An application of a liberation/decolonization healing approach will also illustrate and challenge the assumptions that gender specific expectations of behavior are antiquated and no longer relevant to modern Latinx women with a history of migration, born or residing in the United States who continue being affected by a continuation of the traumatic effects of the previously suffered oppression in the country of origin for many Latinx women and their descendants.

Different Faces of Oppression Endured by Latinx Women

The awareness that clinical work geared to healing Latinx women as a group can be applied uniformly is not only challenging, but illusory at best, and nearly impossible at worst due to the existing differences based on personality factors and countries of origin. On the other hand, the difficulties brought by migration associated with colonization and the intersectional descriptors that define Latinx women, albeit not applicable to all Latinx women, seem to hold formidable power in their emotions and definition of self. The difficulties brought by the migration experience have been amply documented (Cerdeña et al., 2021; Dreyer, 2019), reinforced by the statistics showing that over one-third of Latinxs in the United States are foreign-born. Although this number varies according to the country of origin and there has been a decline in the growth of the migrant population from Latin American-Caribbean, the region is still a large source of migrants (Noe-Bustamante & Lopez, 2019).

Latinxs and their descendants who have migrated from Latin America and the Caribbean to the United States or Canada have been found to be particularly vulnerable to intergenerational trauma due to legacies of colonialism, political violence, and migration-related stressors. The trauma experienced in the country of origin by those who have migrated to the United States does not seem to disappear upon arrival to the new country; on the contrary, it often is exacerbated by prejudice brought by racism and marginalization associated to racial identity, language, cultural values, histories of colonization, dispossession, and political violence and continues to affect even those that have not physically migrated (Cerdeña et al., 2021; Dreyer, 2019). The effects of intergenerational trauma can be better understood when viewed from the lenses of the oppression felt in the country of origin and continued in the host culture often combining historical, socioeconomic, and geopolitical causes. It is this combination of stressors defining the entire experience of oppression that differs from the known symptomatology included in the definition of PTSD associated with specific horrendous risks and exposures during the process of migration, including violence. The continuation of the effects of trauma previously experienced by those families that have migrated to a new country, ranging from separation from loved ones and the confrontation of challenges related to language difficulties and/or adaptation to new cultural values, have been recognized to cause a continuous experience of trauma that has been defined as "oppression trauma." That is, oppression originating in historical, socioeconomic, and geopolitical experiences can result in significant and continuous suffering (Comas-Díaz et al., 2019).

The concept of generational trauma or the trauma that can affect different generations in a continuum was first recognized as a syndrome by

Vivian M. Rakoff, M.D., and colleagues in 1966 and associated to traumatic experiences brought by the Holocaust in the Jewish population. These observations prompted other studies that have reported a 300% increase in psychiatric referrals that included high representation of prolonged stress (Nir, 2018). The syndrome has also included other groups, including the Indigenous and Blacks populations, but there needs to be a better recognition of the legacy of the effects of intergenerational trauma caused by migration and colonial oppression that have been suffered by Latinxs (Phipps, 2014).

The focus of this article will address a postmodernist perspective that incorporates the psychological importance of cultural values, identity, migration, and the intersectional components of Latinx women residing in the United States, specifically the relevance of sharing a history of migration experienced directly on their flesh or through their ancestors. The intersectional descriptors or intersectionality, a concept coined by Kimberly Crenshaw in 1989, could be applied to this group by including diversity in terms of race, class, place of origin, and marginalization.

Although the description of my clinical work within this article refers to cisgender heterosexual professional or entrepreneurial Latinx women, the information presented within has relevance to the broader Latinx community, including lesbian, gay, bisexual, and queer identities (Comas-Díaz & Vazquez, 2018; Sharron-del Rio & Aja, 2015). My observations over three decades of clinical work with Latinx women have noted the negative experiences of migration that seem closely related to transgenerational trauma, a fact that has also been supported in the literature (Dreyer, 2019; Haverluk, 1997), including scoping reviews that incorporate many studies and research efforts where findings indicate that "Latinxs-individuals who have migrated from Latin America to the United States or Canada and their descendant-are particularly vulnerable to intergenerational trauma due to legacies of colonialism, political violence, and migration-related stressors" (Cerdeña et al., 2021, p. 1).

The specific focus on career women was deemed important to illustrate the continuous feelings of dissatisfaction with self that included perceived failures with their achievements regardless of the real level of success attained and level of resilience to move forward with their lives. The dynamics revolving around feelings of lack of success, psychological disempowerment, high levels of anxiety, and stress connect with the experience of migration. The connection or "The Connectivity Bridge" is closely related to the national narratives held within the culture of origin (Latinx) that strongly values the importance of hard work as a mean of attaining power, self-sufficiency, freedom, and recognition. However, the associations to the definition of success for many migrants and their descendants also requires achieving psychological "safety" or the perception they belong and not to be perceived as "the other." It also seems that to justify the sacrifices brought by migration, the attainment of career or monetary success is not always enough to mitigate the negative effects and stressors brought by this experience. According to the narratives of many Latinx women, choosing a better place to live, or being able to place the children in competitive schools, and other practices that can be on par with the attainment of success does not translate to feeling psychologically empowered. These narratives show that a sense of failure or disenchantment that could include feelings of "being the other" or "not having a sense of belonging" do not dissipate by the attainment of career success, in particular when intersectional definers, including class, ethnicity, language, or age, are continuously producing negative experiences, including those affecting family members. Rather than blaming the system, the blame is on the self for not "protecting" those family members that have suffered the stressors brought by migration.

The emphasis on career women does not exclude other Latinx women who are not professionals and who struggle with intergenerational trauma that creates difficult daily stressors. Latinx women who have migrated to the United States and suffer intergenerational trauma related to migration and their struggles with poverty, discrimination, and the legacy of colonialism are very real (Alcántara et al., 2013; Cuevas et al., 2016; Fortuna et al., 2008, 2019). What has been evident within a clinical context is that career women who have attained success and show resilience facing obstacles in their lives express feelings that define low self-esteem and poor sense of worth. It can be challenging for clinicians to connect these negative components with the negative experience of the migration of self and or their ancestors, while at the same time appearing to be resilient and successful in their careers. The importance relies on being mindful and to consider any existing stressors brought by migration trauma to self or to ancestors. These explorations do not provide a priori knowledge to the clinician to determine whether the psychological disempowerment narrated by Latinx women is brought by migration trauma alone or is exacerbated by the negative experience. Exploring personality traits such as self-sacrifice, self-control, loyalty, or the ability to be self-aware is an important component in the assessment of Latinx women who have a history of migration, but it is also very important not to neglect the exploration of the history of migration and neglect the transnational reality brought by the negative experience of migration. It could be equally damaging to assume that the presenting distress in a Latinx woman is due solely to transnational trauma as it would be to neglect the exploration and consideration of existing personality traits, level of acculturation, or rearing patterns that brought the presenting distress.

My application of a postmodernism approach in my psychotherapy practice recognizes the importance of fostering a narrative in the Latinx woman seeking psychological help that incorporates the knowledge or truth within the therapeutic dialogue. This dialogue will benefit from considering a possible negative trauma that has been found to be passed across generations and does not assume that level of support or evidence of resilience can be automatic buffers from the continuation of trauma in many Latinx women. In particular, within forced migration, there may be relevant interconnections of the historical processes of colonization, postcolonial development, political dynamics, and cultural manifestations that could exacerbate the experience of trauma brought by migration.

Postcolonial Psychotherapy with Latinx Women: Connecting Manifestations and Expressions of Migration Trauma within a Cultural Context

The practice of postcolonial psychotherapy recognizes the importance of the interconnections of the historical processes of colonization, postcolonial development, political, and cultural manifestations. It draws on early writings of the psychology of colonization, notably those of Frantz Fanon (1963) and Albert Memmi (1967), on the contributions of indigenous writers (Anzaldúa, 2002, 1987; Comas-Díaz & Torres Rivera, 2020; Katz, 2017), and on an array of contemporary writings in critical social, literary theory, and cultural studies (O'Mahony & Donnelly, 2010). These works provided a foundation for an understanding of postcolonial thinking that focused on structures of power and specific psychological approaches that brought an understanding of postcolonialism that were later advanced by a postmodernist perspective that included cultural representation, identity, and location, with reference to migration, gender, race, and ethnicity (Comas-Díaz & Vazquez, 2018) and specifically addressing migrant women mental health (Diaz-Granados et al., 2006: O'Mahony, 2010).

A challenging view for clinicians working with intergenerational trauma experienced by Latinx women is the assumption that certain stressors brought by migration could also be based on personalities or different levels of cultural adaptations and other variations and definers. In this regard, the question asked is how can clinicians differentiate intergenerational trauma from other stressors unrelated to negative migration? While the answer to this question cannot be unequivocal, the idea is to present another dimension that needs to be addressed with those Latinx women that seek psychological help and have a history of migration. It must be recognized that negative self-assigned definitions that surface in the narratives of Latinx women intricately connect to cultural values that embrace both national and cultural levels of identification and thinking and evidence important effects of intergenerational trauma that continue to be an important component of Latinx women self-identification and sense of competence.

The transformative impact of migration on contemporary and future societies involves not only people, but cultures and religions. Both cultural and national narratives have been associated with the attainment of well-being and often intertwine with cultural values in societies, as such exert collective power in the identification of self that determine a person's worth according to achievements based on ideals and core values of a society, whose members are expected to adhere and maintain this way of thinking (Billing, 1995; Eason et al., 2021).

Relevant Cultural Values

According to Hofstede (1980, 1991), cultures can be defined as a collectively shared social knowledge and understanding by members of a society, including values, beliefs, and habitual social norms within a group of individuals. What poses significant relevance to this definition is that different cultural groups have different preferences for dealing with similar sets of problems and apply different weight to the application and reinforcement of the maintenance and adherence to these values. Societies and human beings are heterogeneous, not every member of a culture adhere to these definitions and observations. Yet, the understanding and application of cultural guidelines that could determine behavioral functioning in any society is an important factor to consider when working with a diverse population in a clinical setting. Attention to the history of migration of Latinx women and their relatives is a key element of the dynamics of intergenerational trauma.

Behavioral expectations and their applications are not only passed from generation to generation in a variety of ways, but can serve as guideposts for identification and self-definition that can create psychological conflicts that affect self-esteem, self-worth, and the achievement of well-being or support self-validations. They hold expectations that carry psychological power that can enhance a level of belonginess to a group based on adherence and serve to maintain cultural identification that carry power for many individuals who have migrated and find themselves psychologically missing previous support, difficulties with the attainment of a new language, and adaptational pressures to a new culture or acculturation.

Although cultural values are only a fraction of what defines a woman's identity, they can serve as a powerful force in her view of the world. They can simultaneously provide anchoring and solace but can also create inner turmoil and disconnect, as evidenced in their narratives in the clinical setting. These societal/cultural identifiers can be out of awareness for a number of women and can be brought into consciousness through the application of a Latina Feminist Psychology, a modality that started nearly four decades ago to recognize the relevance of Latinx culture and history (Comas-Díaz, 2020; Russo & Vaz 2001). When the dynamics defined by society are internalized by Latinx women to translate as "being the other," not belonging, not having made it to be part of the main cultural group, covert aggressions that relate to migration or other prejudicial definers, the level of well-being is diminished. These negative effects can place Latinxs on a quandary like race craft, a term coined by Barbara Fields, a historian who together with her sister, the sociologist Karen Fields (2012), state that the concept of race is like witchcraft, where the perpetrator and victim see the negative attributes as "real." Borrowing from this concept, it can be extrapolated that many Latinx women can be affected by negative identifications that include the thinking of groups, institutions, and cultural dimensions that hold strong negative stereotypical beliefs that are accepted as truisms and pose threats to the attainment of positive self-worth, psychological empowerment, and overall health behaviors.

The attainment of good health and well-being has been addressed across several epidemiological studies that have reported findings of women experiencing nearly twice the rate of depression and other mental health problems than men (Courtenay, 2000; Nuñez et al., 2016). Similar results of my clinical observations of Latinx women have also concurred with these findings, specifically when related to the sociocultural scripts of machismo and marianismo, both gender specific determinants of female and male role socialization, even after adjusting for sociodemographic covariates that further an understanding of the importance of these social constructs. My clinical observations have also corroborated that these feelings are often out of awareness, paired up with high levels of anxiety, dissatisfaction with self or the feeling of not "being good enough," and other mental health problems, brought by clashing cultural values (e.g., decision on parenting or upbringing of their children and deciding on what would be the best method to apply that would bridge ancestry values with "modern" values).

This thinking becomes an existential quandary when daily life decisions may include solutions that involve different cultural expectations and may clash with each other. For example, the need to choose between a collectivistic behavioral response, such as: where the "us" takes precedence over the "I," an important concept in the Latinx culture, versus taking an individualistic way of thinking, a valued behavior in the United States, where the "I" comes before the "us" (Vazquez, 2004). These tensions gain momentum when faced with having to make a decision that affects the family.

The importance of the family or the different expectations based on gender are not solely in the ownership of Latinxs, given that other cultural groups also adhere and practice them, but are very present within Latinx cultural beliefs and values, and seem to offer positive reinforcement to the members of the culture, particularly for those with a migration experience. These concepts do not manifest in sequence nor are represented in all the narratives portraying Latinx women, but are salient enough to be considered important clinically and can offer another dimension necessary to achieve psychological empowerment. That is to recognize that to attain a positive identification with valued cultural beliefs, a "rewriting" that provides an accurate identification of the negative definers of gender definition with ties to colonialism must occur. This "rewriting" can be attained through the application of a Latina Feminist psychology modality that can bring into awareness the connections (The Connectivity Bridge) between intergenerational trauma and the need to mitigate the anxiety that result from self-blame for not being able to fix the "wrongs" that are brought by society. This application aims to help Latinx women reconnect and recognize the effect of past traumas suffered by self or their ancestors and the connections with negative self-definitions that bring feelings of guilt and poor self-worth, while attaining a new understanding of their cultural values that enhances both their cultural identifications and self-worth. It is a bridge that connects the culture of the ancestors with new cultural values, while discarding the negative identifications that are brought by both cultural belief systems. By understanding the source of the narratives that can erroneously define self as dysfunctional, Latinx women attain a liberating level of self-definition.

The following descriptions of gender specific behavioral expectation concepts are not without critics because their definitions have been considered to carry prejudice and to perpetuate negative myths with emotional overtones that also can carry a prejudicial association solely applicable to Latinxs (Gil & Vazquez, 1997; Morales, 2015). The intent in discussing them is to show how they can also exert psychological pressures that are the basis of personal identity and self-understanding and prompt an answer to the question: "who am I" (Neisser, 1994). Let us start with marianismo and machismo.

Marianismo and Machismo

Marianismo and machismo are strong gender identifiers practiced by Latinxs. Both concepts have been associated with superiority/inferiority according to gender and have been overgeneralized in the public parlance termed to be old world, not applicable to today's Latinxs, lacking relevance and holding negative stereotype descriptors for Latinxs. These concepts hold positive and negative power within the Latinx culture within the migration experience. For example, the assumption that some of the gains exemplified in the potential and opportunities for women to become presidents, vice presidents, and corporate CEOs is an indication that these concepts are irrelevant in the attainment of psychological empowerment and well-being can be deceiving. Even when considering that there have been women presidents in Latin America, the reality is that there are also significant limitations for women's rights that require an exploration into the effects and psychological presence of gender specific descriptors that are considered important components in the upbringing of many Latinx women.

Marianismo, in essence, is the female counterpart to machismo and holds associations to colonialism. Although not clear whether it was conceptualized in the time of the Spanish conquest, it carries cultural beliefs that in a nutshell expect women to behave in a specific manner, such as to be more "respectful of the man of the house," ideologically to be sexually pure, obedient, and kind. The cultural concept of marianismo first proposed in the academic literature in 1973 by Evelyn Steven as a set of values that not only are associated with being a woman in Latin American culture but can also be seen as the other face of machismo (Arredondo, 2018; Cano, 2003; Gil & Vazquez, 1997).

A look at the definition of machismo points to disagreements as to whether the concept was even real or propelled by the wind of prejudice for Latinxs. There is even controversy as to the origin being connected to Andalusia or even to the "Latin cultures" going back to the Romans. In any definition one adheres to, it is a colonial concept with an association of male supremacy that had ties to maintaining private property and fortunes for males, including being the owners of women and keeping his wife under lock and key in order to protect his fortune and line of descends. This practice was the male assurance that the child who inherited his money was his own (Morales, 2015). Sociologist Alfredo Mirandé (1997) pointed to a discrepancy in centering machismo within the Latinx culture in a negative manner, particularly when used widely to describe rock stars, entertainers, athletes, or other "superstars" who are not Latinx in a positive manner; yet within the Latinx culture, males were attributed negatively to dominance, patriarchy, authoritarianism, and spousal abuse.

The consideration of the effects of marianismo and machismo within a clinical context that focuses on decolonization, psychological empowerment, and social justice is to advance an understanding of both the presence and power these concepts may still exert in Latinx women's functioning and self-definition. That is, the manner these beliefs determine interactions with institutions of power and other relevant sources.

Attitudinal Familismo

The third cultural value, significantly prevalent during self-narratives of Latinx women, not necessarily in that order, is attitudinal familismo or the expectation of support from one's family. This concept differs from familism, or the importance of the family, a value that has been described as a potential factor protecting mental health in Latinxs, in particular as it refers to depression, suicide, substance abuse, internalizing, and externalizing behaviors in the Latino or Hispanic population within the United States. Although, the protective view of familism has also been found in the empirical literature as conflicting at times (Valdivieso-Mora et al., 2016).

The importance that Latinx women place on respecting and supporting the family (familism) can explain the impact of their identification with the negative stressors suffered by their ancestors (Fuligni & Pedersen, 2002). This sense of obligation becomes a connectivity bridge, merging the experiences of the two worlds, including an unconscious pressure to maintain those valued cultural beliefs, where there are very specifics guidelines as to what constitutes a good woman or the respect that must be afforded to the man of the house. Similarly, these beliefs integrate a script on how to be "simpática," "bien educada, or polite," all attributes valued by both culture and family. They are remnants of the past, but simultaneously a continuation of cultural values that are expected to be reinforced in the new place where family members are expected to provide and be provided with support. These carry an obligation that requires the caring and protection of one's family, including when making decisions about the self (Davila et al., 2011; Parsai et al., 2009).

There are important differences to consider between the definitions of attitudinal familism and familismo or the "expectation" of support from one's family. Attitudinal familism has been implicated by many as a protective variable against mental health problems and fosters the growth and development of children (Calzada et al., 2013; Valdivieso-Mora, 2016; Zeiders et al., 2013), while familism needs to be understood from the different definitions that can produce different experiences in individuals. That is, structural familism refers to the physical proximity to family members, while behavioral familism refers to the family's values and expectations, and attitudinal familism refers to the expectations from family members. These different definitions can provide a clearer understanding on how thoughts and feelings might relate to expectations of level of support from and to family and the degree of closeness that is expected from each other. The term "obligatory familism" is a belief that can be dimensional and salient in the narratives of Latinx women with a history of migration that consider: (a) the extent to which an individual believes the family has a responsibility to provide support (economic, social, or emotional) to other family members and (b) referent familism which carries the expectations of the adherence and maintenance of certain behaviors that are representative of the family values and expectations (Marsiglia et al., 2009; Sabogal et al., 1987).

The study and understanding of familism has presented contradictory findings that are deemed to be the result of the differences among Latinxs, but also brought by the specific descriptors or definitions of familism that can have different interpretations, as well as applications. That is, some studies have only found familism to ameliorate stress, particularly acculturative stress of no significance in reducing the effects of discrimination and economic hardship (Umaña-Taylor et al., 2011). Similarly, studies trying to determine whether familism has a positive effect on some mental health problems such as depression are inconsistent throughout the literature, where some studies reported no interaction between the two, while others reported more depression related to higher level of adherence to familism (Zeiders et al., 2013): and others reported that familism can have a protective effect on depression (Ornelas & Perreira, 2011).

The inconsistencies that define familism can pose confusion among clinicians on how to best help Latinx women to rewrite the "scripts" embedded within their intergenerational trauma. This rewriting can be achieved through the application of Latina Feminist psychology that incorporate aspects of the colonization and the inner tension brought by the immigration experience.

Orgullo and Simpatía

These two concepts will be briefly described and presented in a case vignette that will illustrate their application. Trying to define these concepts can be challenging due to the possible interpretations of their definitions among Latinxs. For example, a definition of orgullo can be positive and negative and can fluctuate between feeling good or guilty of an act, deed, or oneself. The application of orgullo within a Latina Feminine psychology could be applied to enhance one's self-worth, such as being proud of achievements, but clinicians should be mindful that it can also surface negatively intertwined with feelings of sacrifice, endorsed within marianismo, and the taking of responsibilities or stressors in a stoic, but potentially unhealthy posture.

The adverse effects of orgullo can include a sense of superiority that leads to rejection, like being considered selfish, self-centered, or narcissistic. At the same time, when applied in a positive manner, it can carry significant psychological self-empowerment for the Latinx woman (e.g., when applied to self, ancestors, and their migrant history). As exemplified in the response of a sixth-generation Mexican American man to the question: "how are you able to maintain so many traditional aspects of the Mexican culture? He responded Orgullo de Raza" (pride in my heritage), (Vazquez, 2004, p. 9).

The concept of orgullo surfaces in the narratives of Latinx women by presenting behaviors that can be unrealistic to maintain without affecting physical and mental health. The application of this concept during a Latina Feminist therapy aims to provide a new practical and positive position that will serve as an enhancement or self-motivator to boost self-esteem. It can be applied to provide positive feelings while rewriting the "script" that would understand and place the negative effects as defined by society, not the individual (e.g., processing feelings of shame because an ancestor is not educated or cognizant of the United States culture, practices indigenous healing cures or rituals, or when encountering the postcolonial position that views poor countries and their inhabitants as inferior).

Orgullo can be a protector factor in resolving intergenerational trauma by helping in the resolution of feelings of powerlessness despite having achieved career success (e.g., by sorting out the misconceptions that being a good mother requires her to be present on a regular basis). These feelings can be powerful and exert significant pressure, particularly if looking at the other side of the motivation brought by the intergenerational trauma that has left scars that many Latinx women do not want to repeat with their children. The conflict fluctuates between not wanting to repeat the migration sufferings, but at the same time wanting to attain success in careers. In these occasions, orgullo can be applied to highlight the attainment of their present success and at the same time validate the sacrifices made by the ancestors who may have made the success of the descendants possible. Orgullo can also be used as a positive force when the discussion of intersectional components refers to issues of race, ethnicity, language, or age.

The definition and understanding of simpatía can also present some challenges clinically, but again can be a protective factor. It will be briefly described and then illustrated in the case vignette that follows. Simpatía is quite prevalent in the narratives of Latinx women who tend to confuse politeness and proper manners with self-deprecation, followed by anger that they describe as detrimental to feeling psychologically empowered. When simpatía is practiced as a gender expectation of behavior that demands conformity, the psychological work should explore the role models that may have fostered this way of thinking and their connections to a colonial thinking in the upbringing. This awareness can help Latinx women gain insight on how the attainment of being assertive is concomitant with the attainment of psychological empowerment.

There is no equivalent translation of simpatía in English, but it is close to good manners and common courtesy. It is understood as a "cultural script" (Triandis 1984), a specific model of how to appropriately relate, and is highly valued among the many Latinx women that I have helped. This cultural script also provides guidance on self-actualization with the collectivistic view of Latinxs.

Clinical Applications—Case Illustration

This case illustrates a narrative that portrays the effects of the gender specific behavioral components of marianismo, machismo, familismo, orgullo, and simpatía within the framework of transgenerational trauma in a professional Latinx woman. Similar narratives have been amply represented and addressed within the Latina Feminist psychology clinical modality.

Marina (not her real name, every precaution was taken to respect the privacy of this narrative) sought help because as she stated, "I have reached the limits of my tolerance at an emotional/spiritual level. I don't like the way I am feeling, which is anxious all the time, unable to sleep and I need help." Marina attained an education that afforded her a high position in her place of work, so she was not experiencing monetary deprivation. In fact, she said, "I should be grateful and not complain but am afraid I cannot be of help to my family or be functional at work."

At the time Marina sought help, she was in the middle of an exceedingly difficult court procedure dealing with custody issues for her 3-year-old daughter, Isabel. She was divorcing a Latinx man, Marco, who was born and raised in a country in Latin America, where up until 1998, men oversaw managing the home and marital assets.

Marina had previously left an important position in NY to follow her husband when he returned to his country of birth where she encountered powerful remnants of colonial thinking that determined different modes of behaviors for both men and women (machismo, marianismo). Her husband's parents, who owned a company in that country, made her feel that she was a bad wife because she did not allow her husband to be the good provider, "*como Dios manda*" or as ordained by God, particularly when they were not facing any monetary problems that required her to work. She disregarded these criticisms and opted to continue working, hoping to move ahead in her career. Despite the commitments announced in that country to reduce inequality, the reality was different. She encountered disapproval and discrimination in terms of salary and advancement. Experiencing these inequalities made her feel upset and prompted the decision to return to New York to move ahead in her career. To her surprise, Marco followed, and after settling in their new home, she became pregnant and had a daughter, whom she named Isabel. Soon after Isabel's birth, the couple filed for divorce.

The court decided to divide the custody of their daughter fifty/fifty, a decision that created great pain for Marina and made her feel like a failure. During this process, the couple had to deal with a mediator to resolve custody issues. Marina felt that her wishes regarding issues that involved school choices, vacation trips, and other child routines were disregarded by the mediator, whom she felt was not understanding her parenting concerns as a Latinx mother. She felt the mediator was siding with her husband when he told her that their interaction was difficult and toxic. She perceived this statement as directed specifically to her and sent her into a state of panic and self-reproach where she blamed herself for acting inappropriately and angry rather than acting calmly like Marco. These interactions created a great deal of anxiety for Marina and revived painful memories relating to earlier years of the migration experience she lived as a child. Even after decades have passed, these memories brought debilitating feelings for Marina, vivid reminders of the early years of the migration experience, where as a child, she felt inadequate, confused, and ashamed. She narrated the experiences of having to be her mother's interpreter, having to babysit for her sisters, and cook. She said: "it was deja vu again, and this successful business-woman is again falling apart." She could not rationally deal with the stressors brought by court procedures that made her feel "powerless and incompetent." She was reexperiencing marianista and machista thinking, where men have power and women suffer. These painful memories rendered her paralyzed in the sense that she allowed the mediator and her husband to silence her because she was feeling very frightened and afraid to be termed an angry Latinx woman.

Marina said that she could not understand why she became so confused with fears and feelings of failure during the process of navigating the courts, dealing with custody issues, and reexperiencing these humiliations in her own flesh that despite defining herself as a very resilient women, very successful in her career, she was still facing discrimination and prejudices based on gender, language issues, and physical appearance. Marco felt entitled to call her a bad mother, according to Marina; he took every opportunity to belittle her and reinforce the thinking that she brought this upon herself because she could have stayed home to take care of their daughter. The countries where both Marco and Marina grew up still support the requirements for women to stay at home with their children, a main reason that Marina waited until she was in her late thirties to become pregnant and have her beautiful little girl, Isabel.

Marina, who fought with tenacity to move up the corporate ladder, acknowledged she was smart and talented, had high energy to work long hours, but had no voice when in the presence of a judge or the mediator, who were both men and powerful. These representations of oppression and machismo in Marina's mind enhanced the unresolved fear that Marina's corporate success was not able to liberate without understanding the psychological pressure exerted by the traumatic memories that she had suffered whether personally or through her mother's narratives. The court's representatives were painful reminders of those authority figures who had represented colonial powers. She also felt that Marco was more eloquent and capable than she was (not true). This self-deprecation made it very difficult to express her valid opinion and disagreements with Marcos to inform her female lawyer with accurate facts in her favor.

The history of Marina's migration is relevant to gain a better understanding of her narrative. She was brought to the United Stated by her mother at age of 12 together with her siblings, Magda and Rosa, who are not living in NY at this moment. Her mother separated from Marina's father and moved to the United States. As a single mother of three children needing to work exceedingly long hours in a sweatshop making clothing, it was up to Marina to care and be responsible for her younger sisters, including feeding them, making sure they did their homework, and were well behaved. She said, "I had to grow up very fast." She became the mother for her siblings and was the reason why she did not want to have children of her own, but held to the belief "in my culture a woman is not considered successful until she becomes a mother." She was also aware that although she was financially stable, her marriage was on the rocks, but she felt the pressure of having a child to "be a complete woman" and ideally be a "happy woman."

Marina described her mother as very traditional in term of Latinx cultural values with a typical immigration history full of hard work and sacrifices. Her mother was not able to learn English well but made sure that her girls learned the language. Her mother's inability to speak English placed Marina as the "protector and provider" for her mother, who consulted her on most important issues, and because she did not make enough money, she is not economically self-sufficient. Her mother suffers from high blood pressure and borderline diabetes, conditions that need regular visits to the hospital on an emergent basis and require Marina to assist her mother with medical regimes that need to be followed, as well with financial needs. The sisters have moved back to their country of origin, but the mother does not wish to go back.

Marina blamed herself for not having enough energy to be the "perfect mother" for her 3-year-old daughter. She felt guilty when her daughter crying in the middle of the night made her angry. Although she was always attentive to her daughter, she was tired and needed her sleep to be highly functional for the demands of her job the next day. She considered her feelings of frustration as not being a good mother, daughter, and/or a good person and resented having to "protect and care for her mother on a regular basis," but at the same time felt very guilty for having these feelings. These stressors and the resulting tension they created interfered with her sleep, brought feelings of anger, made her feel she was not polite and proper, and was snapping at people she interacted with. She went out of her way to be of assistance to her friends and colleagues when they requested a favor, and although she was resentful, she was not capable of saying no to them because she felt this was not appropriate. She said, "this is not who I am." When these dynamics were explored, it was obvious that she was adhering to simpatía.

Marina's narrative related feeling that she was a failure. It also appeared that she lacked the necessary psychological awareness required for the rewriting of her script. In her mind, at an unconscious level, she had incorporated a component of the migration experience of many migrants. She felt she needed to be perfect to be successful. Marina's psychological work required to realistically identify the factual from the idealized while exploring the cultural pressures she had felt were a requirement for total success. For example, Marina was feeling like a failure for not having been able to save her loved ones from the pain experienced upon arrival to this country and for the continuation of this pain for themselves. This pain became her own pain as well. This practice of marianismo was not initially accessible to Marina in a conscious manner. In fact, Marina felt she was being ungrateful and chastised herself for not being *agradecida* or being ungrateful by not appreciating the achievements and opportunities that she was afforded, particularly during the COVID-19 pandemic. Yet, she expressed feeling disempowered, which translated to not being able to provide for her family (i.e., unable to be happy and ready to attend to her mother and not be upset and burdened when her mother visited and needed attention that Marina had no energy to give, albeit loving her mother very much). She felt like a failure because she could not protect her mother who had sacrificed for the family and who was still suffering humiliations in clinics, hospitals, and from others.

Her perceived sense of failure appeared to connect to expectations of societal acceptance or expectations of not being rejected because of her intersectional components that were deemed "undesirable" by the national narratives of either the Latinx or the North American cultures. She felt that she was being punished by the courts for wanting to speak up, but upon exploration, it seems that she was not adhering to the advice from her lawyer which required her to be less vocal and only say what was asked of her. She said that not being vocal was difficult for her because she had seen how traumatized her mother was by lacking a voice. She did not want to be like her mother, a passive and submissive woman, so she would react intensely, particularly when feeling anxious and threatened. During these times while in court, she described getting incensed and angry when she felt dismissed and not recognized as valuable, consciously knowing she was putting herself in a weaker position to demonstrate that she was a fit mother for her child and not emotionally unstable, as Marco had portrayed her to the courts. Rationally, she understood that allowing her anger to surface in court could be detrimental to her case, but she also said that this behavior was difficult to contain and said laughing, "I become like the Incredible Hulk." Rewriting of the script helped her to incorporate assertiveness rather than expressing anger. She was at the same time helped to feel entitled to her anger, not fear her emotions, but to first recognize the gains and/or losses brought by the expression of anger when indiscriminately applied.

The painful memories brought by the experience of migration that included suffering, humiliation, and powerlessness would pop up during moments when she experienced injustices, but through the rewriting of the "script" that she was carrying, she became aware that she was no longer the powerless little girl that arrived frightened in New York at age 12. An understanding of the reality of her experiences and related dynamics was brought to the surface through the conscious awareness of the intergenerational trauma lived by herself and her family.

The application of a liberation/decolonization healing approach was geared toward the psychological empowerment of Marina. First, the promotion of her connection to her cultural unconsciousness was aimed toward the acquisition of a source of power, healing, and liberation (Comas-Díaz, 2020). The facilitation of an exploration of the relevance of her migration history vis a vis, her mother's. These memories brought forgotten conflicts that revolved around "being poor, not fitting with the school peers, difference and being the other, but in her description." In summary, "being different." First, an understanding of my positionality informed me of Marina's views, and I deemed it fit to share my own migration experience and respond to her reply, "so you then understand what I went through?"

To respond to Marina's question regarding my experience, an application of positionality was required; that is a contextual understanding of the traumatic experiences encountered by Latinx women who have experienced oppressions. The healing of the trauma caused by Marina's migration required a centering of history, actual experience, and cultural knowledge of the descendants, vis a vis the complimentary interactions of the two cultures. This understanding incorporated a sharing by me, the therapist, of the tensions produced by dealing with values that not only differ but clash with the psychological definitions of a good self and or a good Latinx woman. My understanding of Marina's inner tensions and appropriately sharing my own experiences and resolutions helped to foster her self-worth and not see the adherence to cultural values as flaws or weakness. This is where orgullo of "ancestry" and "gender" was useful, where Marina attained psychological empowerment that incorporated a valuable perception of self and ancestors rather than allowing these achievements to be misunderstood. My self-disclosure was a helpful example of a liberation/decolonization therapy application. Listening to Marina's testimonio not only validated the actual suffering brought by the migration experience, but incorporated critical thinking that shifted the blame from self to other sources of oppression. *Acompañamiento* or the act of witnessing, advocating, and incorporating critical thinking in a place that offered safety and validation are key definers used by liberation psychotherapists (Comas-Díaz & Torres Rivera, 2020).

Conclusion

The anxiety and feelings of discomfort evidenced and centered around the national narratives portrayed above would not disappear for many Latinxs by attaining corporate or monetary power when the negative effects of migration included unresolved memories of oppression and prejudice with ties to colonialism. The negative descriptors of the history of migration of the Latinx population to the United States in the 20th century can be advanced by consideration that for most migrants, their decision to leave their country of origin is to escape tyrannical regimes and economic imbalances that produced negative effects on the quality of their lives, including traumatic experiences, and a desire to attain a better life. The attainment of success is especially important to the attainment of self-esteem and well-being but is not the only measure to understand feelings of failed experiences.

An important dimension of the definition of success and attainment of wellbeing is the expectation of achieving a better life that would justify the vicissitudes brought by the move that includes feelings of acceptance by others. Unfortunately, for most Latinxs migrating to the United States, regardless of their country of origin in Latin America and the Caribbean, the expected acceptance upon arrival is thwarted by the entanglement with the War on Drugs in Latin America that not only increased prejudice and victimization, but as indicated, this prejudice was extended to all Latinxs, augmenting the level of stress and continuation of trauma (Fields & Fields 2012).

Marina's narratives portrayed a sense of disenchantment, frustration, and disappointment, where she blamed herself rather than the wider society and carried hidden anxiety and pain that were interfering with the attainment of her well-being. It is of upmost importance to recognize that Marina was successful, insightful, resilient, and very bright, but none of these attributes mitigated the negative experience brought by migration. Protective factors embedded within the Latinx culture were used in therapy to help Marina understand the significance of the struggles sustained by her mother with orgullo rather than shame. At the same time, Marina was also able to understand the connection between the unfavorable descriptors of Latinxs brought by xenophobia that can create a negative identification and self-definition of this population at an unconscious level (Eason et al., 2021; Vazquez, 2018). The gaining of this important insight allowed Marina to successfully rewrite her script and attain psychological power. She embraced the vibrant women she had become.

References

Alcántara, C., Casement, M. D., & Lewis-Fernandez, R. (2013). Conditional risk for PTSD among Latinos: A systematic review of racial/ethnic differences and sociocultural explanations. *Clinical Psychology Review, 33*(1), 107–109. https://doi.org/10.1016/j.cpr.2012.10.005

Anzaldúa, G. E. (1987). *Borderlands/La frontera: The New Mestiza*. Aunt Lute Books.

Anzaldúa, G. E. (2002). Now let us shift... the path of conocimiento... inner work, public acts. In G. E. Anzaldúa & A. Keating (Eds.), *This bridge we call home: Radical visions for transformation* (pp. 540–570). Routledge.

Arredondo, P. M. (2018). Entre Fronteras. In L. Comas-Díaz & C. I. Vazquez (Eds.), *Latina psychologists: Thriving in the cultural borderlands* (pp. 194–210). Routledge.

Billing, M. (1995). *Banal nationalism*. SAGE.

Calzada, E. J., Tamis-Le Monda, C. S., & Yoshikawa, H. (2013). Familismo in Mexican and Dominican families from low-income, Urban communities. *Journal of Family Issues, 34*(12), 1696–1724. https://doi.org/10.1177/0192513X12

Cano, S. (2003). *Acculturation, marianismo, and satisfaction with marianismo: An analysis of depression in Mexican American college women* [Unpublished doctoral dissertation]. University of Houston.

Cerdeña, J. P., Rivera, L. M., & Spak, J. M. (2021). Intergenerational trauma in Latinxs: A scoping review. *Social Science & Medicine, 270*, 113662. https://doi.org/10.1016/j.socscimed.2020.113662

Comas-Díaz, L. (2020). Liberation psychotherapy. In L. Comas-Díaz & E. Torres Rivera (Eds.), *Liberation psychology: Theory, method, practice, and social justice* (pp. 169–185). American Psychological Association.

Comas-Díaz, L., Hall, G. N., & Neville, H. A. (2019). Racial trauma: Theory, research, and healing: Introduction to the special issue. *American Psychologist, 74*(1), 1–5. https://doi.org/10.1037/amp0000442

Comas-Díaz, L., & Torres Rivera, E. (Eds.). (2020). *Liberation psychology theory, method, practice, and social justice*. American Psychological Association.

Courtenay, W. H. (2000). Constructions of masculinity and their influence on men's well-being: A theory of gender and health. *Social Science & Medicine*, *50*(10), 1385–1401. https://doi.org/10.1016/S0277-9536(99)00390-1

Crenshaw, K. (1989). Demarginalizing the intersection of race and sex: A Black Feminist critique of antidiscrimination doctrine, Feminist Theory and antiracist politics. University of Chicago Legal Forum.

Cuevas, A. G., Dawson, B. A., & Williams, D. R. (2016). Race and skin color in Latino health: An analytic review. *American Journal of Public Health*, *106*(12), 2131–2136. https://doi.org/10.2105/AJPH.2016.303452

Davila, Y. R., Reifsnider, E., & Pecina, I. (2011). Familismo: Influence on Hispanic health behaviors. *Applied Nursing Research*, *24*, 67–72. https://doi.org/10.1016/j.apnr.2009.12.003

Diaz-Granados, N., Ross, L., Azar, R., Cheng, C., Coulombe, L., & DesMeules, M. (2006). *A literature review on depression among women: Focusing on Ontario*. Report for the Ontario Women's Health Council.

Dreyer, B. P. (2019). Sustained animus toward Latino immigrants-deadly consequences for children and families. *The New England Journal of Medicine*, *381*(13), 1196–1198. https://doi.org/10.1056/NEJMp1908995

Eason, A. E., Pope, T., Becenti, K. M., & Fryberg, S. A. (2021). Sanitizing history: National identification, negative stereotypes, and support for eliminating Columbus Day and adopting Indigenous Peoples Day. *Cultural Diversity & Ethnic Minority Psychology*, *27*(1), 1–17. https://doi.org/10.1037/cdp0000345

Fanon, F. (1963). *The wretched of the earth*. Grove Press.

Fields, B., & Fields, K. E. (2012). *Racecraft: The soul of inequality in American life*. Verso.

Fortuna, L. R., Noroña, C. R., Porche, M. V., Tillman, C., Patil, P. A., Wang, Y., Markle, S. L., & Alegría, M. (2019). Trauma, immigration, and sexual health among Latina women: Implications for maternal–child well-being and reproductive justice. *Infant Mental Health Journal*, *40*(5), 640–658. https://doi.org/10.1002/imhj.21805

Fortuna, L. R., Porche, M. V., & Alegria, M. (2008). Political violence, psychosocial trauma, and the Context of mental health services use among immigrant Latinos in the United States. *Ethnicity & Health*, *13*(5), 435–463. https://doi.org/10.1080/13557850701837286

Fuligni, A. J., & Pedersen, S. (2002). Family obligation and the transition to young adulthood. *Developmental Psychology*, *38*(5), 856–868. https://doi.org/10.1037//0012-1649.38.5.856

Gil, R. M., & Vazquez, C. I. (1997). *The Maria paradox: How Latinas can merge old world traditions with new world self-esteem*. Perigee.

Haverluk, T. (1997). The changing geography of U.S. Hispanics, 1850–1990. *J. Georgr*, *96*(3), 134–145. https://doi.org/10.1080/00221349708978775.

Hofstede, G. (1980). *Culture's consequences: International differences in work-related values*. SAGE.

Hofstede, G. (1991). *Cultures and organizations: Software of the mind*. McGraw-Hill.

Katz, R. (2017). *Indigenous healing psychology: Honoring the wisdom of the First Peoples*. Healing Arts Press.

Marsiglia, F. F., Parsai, M., Kulis, S., & Southwest Interdisciplinary Research Center (2009). Effects of Familism and Family Cohesion on Problem Behaviors among Adolescents in Mexican Immigrant Families in the Southwest U.S. *Journal of ethnic & cultural diversity in social work*, *18*(3), 203–220. https://doi.org/10.1080/15313200903070965.

Memmi, A. (1967). *The colonizer and the colonized*. Beacon.

Mirandé, A. (1997). *Hombres y machos: Masculinity and Latino culture*. Westview Press.

Morales, E. (2015). *Machismo(s): A cultural history, 1928–1984* [Unpublished doctoral dissertation]. The University of Michigan.

Neisser, U. (1994). Multiple systems: A new approach to cognitive theory. *European Journal of Cognitive Psychology, 6*(3), 225–241. https://doi.org/10.1080/09541449408520146

Nir, B. (2018). *Transgenerational transmission of Holocaust trauma and its expressions in literature*. The Academic College of Emek Yezrael.

Noe-Bustamante, L., & Lopez, M. H. (2019). *Latin America, Caribbean no longer world's fastest growing source of international migrant*. Factank. https://www.pewresearch.org/fact-tank/2019/01/25.

Nuñez, A., Gonzalez, P., Talavera, G., Sanchez-Johnsen, G. A., Roesch, L., Davis, S. C., Arguelles, W., Womack, V. Y., Ostrovsky, N. W., Ojeda, L., Penedo, F. J., & Gallo, L. C. (2016). Machismo, Marianismo, and negative cognitive-emotional factors: Findings from the Hispanic Community Health Study/Study of Latinos Sociocultural Ancillary Study. *Journal of Latina/o Psychology, 4*(4), 202–217. https://doi.org/10.1037/lat0000050

O'Mahony, J. M. (2010). A postcolonial feminist perspective Inquiry into immigrant women's mental health care experiences. *Issues in Mental Health Nursing, 31*, 440–449. https://doi.org/10.3109/01612840903521971

Ornelas, I. J., & Perreira, K. M. (2011). The role of migration in the development of depressive symptoms among Latino immigrant parents in the USA. *Social Science & Medicine, 73*(8), 1169–1177. https://doi.org/10.1016/j.socscimed.2011.07.0

Parsai, M., Voisine, S., Marsiglia, F. F., Kulis, S., & Nieri, T. (2009). The protective and risk effects of parents and peers on substance use, attitudes and behaviors of Mexican and Mexican American female and male adolescents. *Youth & Society, 40*(3), 353–376. https://doi.org/10.1177/0044118X08318117

Phipps, R. (2014). *Transgenerational transmission of trauma in second generation Latino children and adolescents* [Unpublished doctoral dissertation]. University of Mississippi.

Rakoff, V. M., Sigal, J. J., & Epstein, N. B. (1966). Children and families of concentration camp survivors. *Canada's Mental Health, 14*, 24–26.

Russo, N. F., & Vaz, K. (2001). Addressing diversity in the Decade of Behavior: Focus on women of color. *Psychology of Women Quarterly, 25*(4), 280–294. https://doi.org/10.1111/1471-6402.00029

Sabogal, F., Marin, G., Otero-Sabogal, R., Marin, B. V., & Perez-Stable, E. J. (1987). Hispanic familism and acculturation: What changes and what doesn't? *Hispanic Journal of Behavioral Sciences, 9*(4), 397–412. https://doi.org/10.1177/0739986387009400

Sharron-del Rio, M. R., & Aja, A. (2015, April 8). The case for "Latinx" – and why this term matters for intersectionality. *Everyday Feminism*, https://everydayfeminism.com/2016/04/why-use-latinx/

Triandis, H. C., Mar?n, G., Lisansky, J., & Betancourt, H. (1984). Simpatía as a cultural script of Hispanics. *Journal of Personality and Social Psychology, 47*(6), 1363–1375. https://doi.org/10.1037/0022-3514.47.6.1363

Umaña-Taylor, A. J., Updegraff, K. A., & Gonzales-Backen, M. A. (2011). Mexican-origin adolescent mothers' stressors and psychosocial functioning: Examining ethnic identity affirmation and familism as moderators. *Journal of youth and adolescence, 40*(2), 140–157.

Valdivieso-Mora, E., Peet, C. L., Garnier-Villarreal, M., Salazar-Villanea, M., & Johnson, D. V. (2016). A systematic review of the relationship between familism and mental health outcomes in Latino population. *Frontiers in Psychology, 7*, 1632. https://doi.org/10.3389/fpsyg.2016.01632

Vazquez, C. I. (2004). *Parenting with pride Latino style: How to help your child cherish your cultural values and succeed in today's world.* HarperCollins.

Vazquez, C. I. (2018). Uprooted and transplanted. In L. Comas-Díaz & C. I. Vazquez (Eds.), *Latina psychologists: Thriving in the cultural borderlands* (pp. 35–53). Routledge.

Zeiders, K. H., Updegraff, K. A., Umaña-Taylor, A. J., Wheeler, L. A., Perez-Brena, N. J., & Rodriguez, S. A. (2013). Mexican-origin youths' trajectories of depressive symptoms: The role of familism values. *The Journal of Adolescent Health, 53*(5), 648–654. https://doi.org/10.1016/j.jadohealth.2013.06.008

Why Am I A Woman? Or, Am I? Decolonizing White Feminism and the Latinx Woman Therapist in Academia

marcela polanco

ABSTRACT
From the perspective of decolonial feminism and the coloniality of gender, in Spanglish, I develop an analysis of the Latinx woman as a racial and gender category of modernity/coloniality. My analysis unfolds through a narrative on my experiences as a Colombian immigrant, Spanglish speaker, and family therapist in academia in the United States. I am guided by an ethic of liberation and the central inquiries for decolonial feminists that contest bourgeois, White, and heterosexual feminism's universal conception of the woman when exploring its European invention and purpose. I discuss modernity's imposition of gender as a Eurocentric colonial system of oppression, inseparable from race and class. I provide a conceptual framework for my analysis that includes an overview of ethics of liberation; decolonial linguistic considerations responding to Anglo, White feminism in untranslatable Spanglish; discussion on decolonial and postcolonial analysis of the Latinx category; and key concepts of decolonial feminism and the coloniality of gender. I seek to make visible the operations of colonial power implicated in the Eurocentric, racialized, gendered, and classist configuration of the Latinx and the woman, to detach from it, and to consider other possibilities of existence.

I adopted the term "Latinx woman" as a social category of analysis of modernity's colonial power. I advanced such analysis from my corporeal experiences. Based on an ethic of liberation (Dussel, 2013), with decolonial intentions, I seek to interpellate myself both as an accomplice of colonial power, unknowingly, and as a European colonial invention: A Spanglish speaker, *immigrante* Colombiana, family therapist, and educator in the academia in United States (U.S.). My analysis is mostly guided by specific inquiries that are central to decolonial feminism and the coloniality of gender, which contest bourgeois White, heterosexual feminism's universal conception of the woman (Curiel, 2017; Escobar, 2017; Espinosa Miñoso, 2019; Lugones, 2008; Maldonado-Torres, 2017; Mignolo, 2000; Quijano, 2000a).

Decolonial feminists critique Anglo, bourgeois White heterosexual feminists' political agenda on advocacy for equality between cis-men and cis-women's rights. The perspectives of the coloniality of gender and decolonial feminism emphasize other explorations White feminists did not consider themselves, which I discuss below. These include making visible the colonial logic or rationality of modernity's installment of gender by Europe as a system of oppression (i.e., the European invention of the woman) inseparable from race. Thus, decolonial inquiries on gender are guided by central questions such as: Why does the category of women exist? And, whose existence (or not) is captured by that category? Or, in my analysis, why am I a woman, Latina, and whose existence am I living? I approach these decolonial inquiries as a Colombiana immigrant in the U.S., family therapist, and faculty member.

I attempt to encuerar and make modernity's colonial power visible as the materialization of systems of oppression operating in my flesh or corporeal existence. I do so by addressing what the coloniality of gender reveals, which is the paradoxical and oxymoronic category of the "Latinx woman." This is, given that, as I discuss below, according to Lugones (2008, 2010, 2016), the category of "woman" only applies to "humans" (i.e., White women), contrary to the category of "Latinx" as an "object." Furthermore, I seek to expose the colonial creation of gender as a Eurocentric system of oppression of modernity and to poner el dedo en la llaga on how Latinx female therapists in academia in the U.S., like myself, might be implicated inadvertently in the further extension and sustainability of modernity's colonial power if the systems of gender and race are not otherwise transgressed. It is my hope to explore openings for alternative configurations to re-exist, detached from the universal idea of gender.

Before advancing my decolonial explorations whereby I story my skin to reveal my capitalist, racist, and sexist configurations as a product of Europe, I introduce the conceptual framework that served me as a lens for such analysis. The introductory conceptual framework includes four interconnected themes: a brief overview of ethics of liberation as a transmodern project; a reflection on decolonial linguistic considerations to decolonize Anglo, White heterosexual feminism in my untranslatable Spanglish; a discussion on the difference between the decolonial option to address the Latinx category in contrast to postcoloniality; and, finally, an overview of the proposals of decolonial feminism and the coloniality of gender to address the questions on the Latinx and woman categories.

Decolonial Projects of Liberation by Us, for Us, and about Us

I take up the principle of liberation by Argentinian philosopher Enrique Dussel (2013) as a foundation from which I attempt to decolonize the categories of the Latinx and woman. For the Puerto Rican decolonial philosopher, Nelson Maldonado-Torres (2011), Dussel's liberation philosophy is a project for critical thought embedded in Abya Yala's history. And it was from this philosophy that Dussel articulated an ethic of liberation that he called transmodernity (Dussel, 2013; Maldonado-Torres, 2011). Transmodernity refers to an ethic of liberation linked to explicit efforts of decolonization for the fulfillment of projects that are distinct or detached from modernity and post-modernity, therefore from modernity's racist, sexist, capitalist, and Eurocentric colonial impositions.

Furthermore, Dussel (2013) adopts liberation as other than emancipation. Liberation consists of a principle with a driving force toward the materialization of an ethical-critical duty of transformation, desde otros lugares than modernity. Successively, the material or practical fulfillment of a project of liberation, according to Dussel (2013), requires creative interventions that respond to the damning and violent modern systems of oppression and domination of the colonized. Therefore, liberation means radical change in the ways in which we, the colonized, are understood and conceived in society and the way in which societies are understood and conceived through the colonized.

Dussel (2013) considers that the principle of liberation is a necessary condition for the reproduction of life in a society with no colonized or enslaved. Also, similar to Maldonado-Torres (2011), he considers that efforts of liberation are advanced by the colonized or enslaved, meaning "us," the humiliated, disavowed, devalued, disregarded, and considered inferior to human beings or lxs condenadxs de la tierra, borrowing from the Black Martinique philosopher and psychiatrist Frantz Fanon (1999). Hence, decolonial projects are advanced by us, for us, and about us. We become radical points of departure for any decolonial reflection (Maldonado-Torres, 2011). Thus, in adopting liberation as a transmodern ethic to advance decolonial projects in relation to the category of the Latina, I follow an interest to disrupt modernity's idea of gender and race. By questioning the European invention of the woman and the Latinx, I seek to detach from the idea of the Anglo European configuration of the woman. This is, instead than to appropriate it, renew it, reassert it, translate it, or worse, to seek our liberation only through the eyes of and the actions by the standard English speaking, bourgeois, White heterosexual woman.

Intervening Linguistically: Dicolonizando en Untranslatable Spanglish

The English language has become lingua franca of modernity (Said, 1997/2006) to maintain a patriarchal social order. It has propagated the West and therefore mutilated the rest. Standard English is linguistic homeland for bourgeois, White heterosexual feminism despite its French origins during the French Revolution. In Spanish, the word "feminism"—and all the work carved in it—has been translated from English and French as *feminismo*. Ironically, in Spanish as well as in French, both gendered European languages, the word was arbitrarily created as a masculine noun, setting it up linguistically to betray itself as *el feminismo*.

Moreover, according to Nigerian scholar Oyèrónkẹ́ Oyěwùmí's (1997) analysis on gender among the Yorùbá people, prior to Western colonization, the Yorùbá did not have a gender system in place. Yorùbá language is gender-free. Because their past and present has been written into English—a gender-specific language—Yorùbá now has a gendered language system. In Abya Yala, the Anglo American and European feminismo has been adopted and translated into Spanish and Portuguese, rendering invisible, in turn, a long history of initiatives in Aymara, Quechua, Kuna, Chibcha, Mapuche, Náhuatl, K'iche', and many other languages spoken by warmikuna (mujeres in Quechua) responding to colonial domination before the French Revolution.

Decolonizing Anglo, bourgeois White heterosexual feminism in untranslatable Spanglish might be considered a creative intervention of liberation. Hence, by writing in Spanglish, I seek to respond to the damning and violent modern systems of oppression and domination from the perspective of language. Spanglish *es* the unsettled frontera del encounter between two imperial or settlers' languages, Spanish and English that millions of us in the U.S. inhabit. Each language represents among other things the colonial wound by linguistic genocide from the encounter between Europe and the Americas, and Abya Yala and the United States. Spanglish could represent a linguistic coalition for decolonial healing. Notwithstanding that each language represents an imperial history, as a fronterizo language, it resists further linguistic cannibalism by delinking from monolingual and normative language purity and purity of knowledges that each carries.

The encounter that Spanglish represents had not gone unnoticed by language purists, however. Spanglish is escandalosx. It disrupts nationalistic arrangements of a linguistic hierarchy (Sommer, 2004) and, as such, its Ingleñoles, Tex-Mex, Rancho, Pocho, Mocho, Chicanx are humiliated, disavowed, devalued, disregarded, and considered inferior to the virginity of standard English and Spanish. Nevertheless, Spanglish persists in everyday life across the U.S., social class and gender as an unruly play of linguistic promiscuity (Stavans, 2003). In our Spanglish, we detach from each language's universal authority and virginidad. Therefore, it offers possibilities for us to liberate ourselves from the colonial prison house of language, their grammarian guards (polanco, 2019; Sommer, 2004), and universal Anglo White feminist knowledges. Spanglish provides us with plurilinguistic engagements with words, imagery, sensing, esthetics, and humor to re-exist legitimately, interculturally, and interlingually (Tisha et al., 2021). Therefore, by writing in untranslatable legitimate Spanglish, I am engaging a transmodern ethic of liberation to overcome the tradition of silence by patriarchal standard Spanish, English, and Anglo, bourgeois White heterosexual feminism that demands translation. In the words of Gloria Anzaldúa (1987); "Until I am free to write bilingually and to switch codes without having always to translate.... I will then overcome the tradition of silence" (p. 81).

Worlds of Difference: Responding to English (Postcolonial) or Spanish (Decolonial) Colonization?

In the mental health professions, important work continues to advance that often use the terms decolonization, postcoloniality, and decoloniality interchangeably maybe as a metaphor to social justice, a response to oppression, or a political project. Since I am writing specifically on decoloniality from Abya Yala for a Special Issue that locates postcoloniality in relation to therapy, I consider it important to discuss my understandings on some of the differences between postcoloniality and decoloniality. Otherwise, homogenizing all colonial histories under the postcolonial rubric might obscure the specific and unique experiences of the various feminist genres as in Black feminism, Chicanxs feminism, Feminismo Campesino, Feminismo Autónomo, or Decolonial feminism. Additionally, advancing projects of decolonization with knowledge about the places, people, lands, and histories they come from might contribute to pluralistic initiatives and coalitions that honors historical differences and interconnectedness.

Postcolonial Studies and Postcolonial Feminism

For the Uzbek-Cherkess Madina Tlostanova based in Moscow and the Argentinian Walter Mignolo based in the U.S. (2012), while decoloniality and postcoloniality are interconnected in terms of their interest on colonial histories and the effects, the latter emerged from different historical experiences, languages, memories, and traditions of thoughts. Postcoloniality centers the analysis on imperial formations since the 1800s during the British colonization of India in English. While it emphasizes the specific colonial experience in British Asia, postcolonial studies emerged in U.S. academia with the influential work of Palestinian American, professor of literature,

Edward Said (1997/2006). Other contributors are Homi Bhabha, Gayatri Chakravorty Spivak, Partha Chatterjee, and Ranajit Guha (Curiel, 2017; Mendoza, 2016).

Postcoloniality presupposes postmodernity, and it is connected to the French poststructuralist ideas by White, males, philosophers such as Michel Foucault, Gilles Deleuze, and Jacques Derrida. The epistemological foundations of postcoloniality are therefore grounded in European philosophy. Their discourses of resistance and analysis of power, agreeing with Tlostanova and Walter (2012), are inherent in and fundamental to modernity. Furthermore, postcolonial scholars critique totalizing narratives of economic determinism and capitalism. They have contributed significantly to changing the content of the analysis of colonial history, capitalism, and Marxist determinism, although the Eurocentric terms by which such analysis unfolded have not been questioned (Tlostanova & Walter, 2012).

According to the Honduran feminist in the U.S. Breny Mendoza (2016), postcolonial feminists address Eurocentrism and racism within White feminism by studying racial systems constructed within colonial contexts. The postcolonial Indian literary theorist Gayatri Chakravorty Spivak, founder of the *South Asian Subaltern Studies Group*, has contributed to an analysis of gendered division of labor within capitalism and critiques Eurocentrism in Western literature and neoliberal global capitalism in radical feminist scholarship. Chandra Talpade Mohanty (2003), on the other hand, has critiqued White feminists scholarly work by demonstrating the homogenization of third-world women as victims, poor, ignorant, uneducated, domesticated, and family oriented, while first-world women are educated, with control over their bodies and sexualities, and free to make their own decisions.

According to Mendoza (2016), the idea of the subaltern is central in the political project of postcolonial feminism. Spivak (1988) departs her analysis from the question *Can the Subaltern Speak?* in her manuscript with the same title. She conceptualizes the term epistemic violence in Western knowledge through the production of the subaltern: the poor, oppressed, third world woman as an essential Other. The subaltern third world woman could only speak through the representation by spokespersons in the order of intellectuals, scholars, or postcolonial thinkers (Mendoza, 2016). Spokespersons do so from a violent rhetoric of ventriloquist representation and empowerment hidden behind seemingly well intended desires to give voice to the oppressed or vulnerable or to rescue poor third world women from third world men. However, agreeing with Spivak, such position not only violates the same premise of the postcolonial critique but reasserts the superiority of who represents the Other, maintaining in turn the superiority of the West.

Based on the above, a postcolonial critique to White Feminism from the category of the "Latinx woman" therapist and academic might entail the revision of such a category from the perspective of the subaltern. Revising the subaltern Latinx third world woman could mean conceiving her not as a third world woman who made it into the mental health system and the academia but as a revolutionary subject instead, following Mohanty's (2003) work. It might also involve the reassertion of the subaltern Latinx as a revolutionary subject who possess qualities White women also have such as autonomy and control. Furthermore, a postcolonial analysis of the Latinx woman could lead to a critique of the politics of representation and empowerment in mental health when considering the question if the Latinx woman can speak or not. These considerations could translate into inquiries of the following order: Do Latinx women have a voice in academia? Are therapists, Latinx women, or otherwise adopting the violent Western rhetoric to "speak for" the Latinx woman vulnerable client, or to give them voice, or to rescue them from Latinx men, or to empower them? Are professions or academic institutions recruiting the Latinx woman to rescue her from her otherwise inevitable poor and oppressed third-world conditions only countered by including her into the first-woman-and-man-world and institutions? While certainly these are interesting questions to consider, they are not at the center of my decolonial analysis here.

Although postcolonial feminists have significantly contributed to decolonial feminism, the understanding of the third world woman from the vantage point of the British colonization in English and Asia is not the same as in Abya Yala, in Quechua, Spanish, or Aymara. Therefore, different questions would arise than the ones above when different terrains of experiences are explored for the decolonial analysis of the Latinx and woman, as I discuss below. In the words of Tlostanova and Walter (2012),

> Our subjectivities, experiences, languages, histories, desires, frustrations, and angers are different from the ones expressed by Foucault, Lacan, or Derrida. Theirs is a different history; their problems are not our problems; and we surmise that our problems are not necessarily theirs.... Postcolonial studies seem to dwell in a skin different from ours and in need of the epistemic frame of Eurocentric modernity (pp. 34–35).

Taco Sin Salsa No es Taco: Decoloniality without Coloniality is Not Decoloniality

The decolonial option dwells in the land and skin wounded since the colonization of Abya Yala by Spain and Portugal in the 1500s. It was then when modernity emerged by Europe positioning itself at the center of the world that they invented as a mirror image of itself, o a su imagen y semejanza to conquer it (Dussel, 2013). Eurocentrism emerged since. Europeans detached the idea of Europe from a specific geographical location or way of thinking of European people by becoming instead a global narrative called Eurocentrism. As modernity's rationality, logic, or dominant narrative, eurocentrism expanded throughout to indoctrinate the majority of the world for more than 500 years. Whereas Europe was not the only empire, it certainly was one that globalized, persisting until today through the imposition of its languages, religion, gender, knowledge, esthetics, and races (Maldonado-Torres, 2017) as well as its institutions such as mental health, research, and academia. So, when I refer to Europe and Eurocentrism, I am referring to modernity's reason as a predominant narrative materialized in our skins, knowledge, senses, lands, and dreams in Abya Yala, as much as in the U.S., Asia, Africa, and Europe itself, in their particular historical ways.

The bleeding wound on the flesh and lands of Aymara, Quechua, K'che', Nahuatl, and Spanish speaking communities—together with many others in Abya Yala and Abya Yala in the U.S.—are homeland for decoloniality. Being one heterogeneous option among many others, decoloniality is grounded on praxis or actional thinking by many rather than on European philosophy or the academia, even though it has reached the academia across various disciplines (Gordon, 1995; Tlostanova & Walter, 2012). Furthermore, decolonials depart from something other than the exploration of the viability or lack thereof of the subaltern's ability to speak. They rather depart from the assumption that communities in Abya Yala have spoken even prior to the 1500s, despite the genocidal expansion of Europe (Mendoza, 2016). Therefore, an emphasis on the subaltern or the subaltern's voice is not of their interest as much as it is to make visible the West's degree of audibility and blindness that keeps it from listening and seeing beyond itself.

As a further and central matter, according to Maria Lugones (2008, 2010, 2016), the decolonial option or project departs from an understanding of decoloniality with coloniality. Without coloniality, decoloniality would not be relevant and at all needed (Quijano, 2000a). In other words, taco sin salsa no es un taco much like decoloniality without coloniality is not decoloniality. Coloniality, as formulated by the Peruvian sociologist Anibal Quijano (2000b), is a decolonial concept that decolonial feminists borrowed. They did so not without critiquing Quijano's underwhelming emphasis on gender, which Maria Lugones developed much more fully in her work on the coloniality of gender. For decolonial feminists, a decolonial project to decolonize White feminism entails a closer look to the coloniality of gender, which is of my interest to explore its effects on the Latinx woman.

The Inseparability of Modernity and Coloniality

For Quijano (2000a, 2000b), modernity and coloniality are interdependent—one cannot exist without the other. Coloniality came to be because of modernity and the other way around, since the colonization of Abya Yala by Europe. Quijano (2000a) conceived modernity as a European persuasive narrative of progress, civilization, and development that could not have persisted during all this time if not because of a hidden structure of colonial power that produced at the same time seeming stagnant, primitive, and underdeveloped communities in need of modernity.[1] That is modernity's paradoxical logic about which I say more below in relation to gender.

Understanding and addressing the complex modernity/coloniality interdependence is at the heart of a decolonial project, therefore any transmodern interventions on the category of the Latina in mental health and academia; however, it is not always clearly discernible or outwardly revealed. Therefore, Quijano (2000a, 2000b) formulated coloniality as a perspective from where to discern a structure of power modernity depends on. This is, what Quijano called the colonial matrix of power, el patron de poder colonial that features in coloniality, which was translated into English by Mignolo as the matrix of colonial power and then back into Spanish as la matriz del poder colonial (Mignolo, 2021). Quijano considered coloniality as una herramienta analítica del poder.

The Matrix of Colonial Power: Control of Sex, Subjectivity, Labor, and Authority

Quijano (2000b) understood power as constitutive of a kind of Eurocentric social relationality. As constitutive, when considering power in relation to the matrix of colonial power, the matriz could be understood in turn as world-making (Vasquez, 2020). Power is therefore not something an individual person inherently possesses (i.e., therapists, researchers, or White men or women "have" power). Neither is power an individual act or what one person owns to dispense on to others (i.e., White therapists colonizing a Latina client). Rather, it is a complex interdependent structure that materializes in the form of a social relationality that created the world most of us continue to live in, favoring some at the expense of others, hence instituting one way of existence through the destitution others (Mignolo, 2021).

Accordingly, power configures dominant kinds of relationalities that construct a social order. Notwithstanding that this Eurocentric social relationality has been replicated around the world as a pattern, it plays out in particular ways in different societies. For example, while the U.S. and Colombia's social order is founded on Eurocentrism, hence race and gender, the systems of social meanings of the category of the Latinx woman or the therapist in the U.S. is not socially the same or applicable in Colombia as I story some of the differences below through my experiences.

Then, the pattern of colonial power that sustains modernity could be understood as a structure historically conceived and constructed by Europe for the globalization of Europe's control and domination. Europe's dispute of control, domination, and exploitation of the world, according to Quijano (2000a), is centered on four codependent basic areas across all forms of social existence or ways of life for over 500 years. The control of these four areas has constituted and maintained the matrix of colonial power, hence modernity. The codependent basic areas, simultaneously present all across social life, are:

1. Sex: the control of reproduction and sexuality (i.e., the invention of gender, hence the idea of the woman);
2. Knowledge and subjectivity: the control of being as race and gender (i.e., Latinx), and control of epistemology, knowledge, and esthetics based on reason, science, and technology according to a Eurocentric rationality, essentialized, codified, and hierarchically structured (superior-inferior);
3. Labor: the control and division of labor according to different kinds of objectified and monetized subjectivities (race & gender); accumulation of wealth at the expense of the exploitation of others and the earth (i.e., therapy and teaching controlled by capital labor); and
4. Authority: emergence of the Nation-State and the institutionalization of being and knowledge (i.e. healing and suffering institutionalized as therapy and science).

A transmodern analysis of the category of the Latinx woman in academia from the perspective of coloniality emphasizes its emergence within the dispute of control, exploitation, and domination of sex, knowledge, subjectivity, labor, and authority. Maria Lugones' (2016) work on the coloniality of gender provides a framework for such analysis, which guided my story below attempting to discern the europeanmake of my existence.

Coloniality of Gender: The Latinx Woman Can't Be Dehumanized

Maria Lugones (2016) adopted and further extended Quijano's matrix of colonial power. She advanced an analysis of the simultaneity of gender, race, capitalism, and Eurocentrism and a critique to White feminism. Lugones articulated the coloniality of gender as a lens whereby the category of gender is not to be taken for granted to advance equality or justice across all genders but rather to examine its inception as a colonial system of oppression modernity depends for its expansion. Therefore, as a system of oppression, Lugones understood gender as the socializable and socialized sexual difference in a Eurocentric hierarchical, dimorphic, and capitalist system.

Moreover, the perspective of the coloniality of gender helped Lugones (2010, 2012) understand White feminism as a project whereby White women wanted everything that White man had, including the authority to exploit others. It also helped her understand that White women suffered their own oppressions within their own isolation, imprisoned at home raising children. Meanwhile, women of color never had those same oppressive conditions. White women and women of color shared very different prisons given their hierarchical categorizations of their identity which emerged from the dispute of the control of sex, authority, labor, and knowledge, placing them under very different conditions within the Eurocentric global social order.

The Eurocentric Fiction of "Identity"

The construction of "identity" has been central for modernity's project of civilization. The structure of the matrix of colonial power has made it possible for Europe to materialize modernity's rhetoric of civilization through the invention or production of fictional identities like the Latinx and White woman or the Indian, Black, Asian, Mestizx, Mulatx. Identity is therefore a Eurocentric invention that consists of a world-making codification of being and knowledge. It is hierarchically arranged, imposing a colonial difference (Mignolo, 2013; Vasquez, 2020) or a social order of a superiority (White woman) and an inferiority (Latina) of what we are, and we are not.

Europe gave itself the right to invent identities and then force them on us by fracturing, infringing on, and disintegrating our existence for its expansionist self-interests (Espinosa Miñoso, 2019; Lugones, 2016). The imposition of the woman exterminated anything or anyone who resisted or did not surrender to such European categorization. Given the manner whereby modernity's identities were invented, imposed, and sustained by the matrix of colonial power, their configuration became a social system of oppression for modernity's livelihood.

Gender as a System of Oppression: The Non-Human White Woman and the Latina Object

The identity of "the woman" is closely tied to the first modern/colonial hierarchical and dichotomous identity since the 1500s that Europe invented as the basic and universal social classification and domination: The Human and non-Human. The human could be a synonym to Euro-Western Man (Lugones, 2016; Maldonado-Torres, 2017; Wynter, 2003). The concept of the Human and humanity has been the anchor of modernity, expelling "nature" out of its domain but legitimizing its domination and exploitation as its resource (Mignolo, 2021).

Instituting the Man-human, Europe destitute the existence of anything or anyone not European, hence making the Indian, Black, Asian, and Latinx as "nature" or Objects that demand no moral or ethical responsibility at the service of Man's exploitation, domination, and control much like the exploitation of land, water, oil, or foods (Gordon, 1995). The human and non-human division marked the superior civilized Man-human and the inferior Object primitive (Latinx), a resource or a machine for production.

According to Lugones (2010), only the civilized were (White) men or (White) women, with gender, as Christian beings of mind and reason, and heterosexuals with bodies. In turn, Indigenous, Black, Mestizxs, and Multxs were the primitive, non-gendered, and without bodies but flesh. We were classified as inferior to humans, devoid of reason or knowledge. They made us into inferior animals, promiscuous, uncontrollably sexual, sinful, and wild. Furthermore, they persuaded us to believe in their idea of our inferiority and primitive conditions, therefore in the need of our transformation, progress, civilization, and development by means of European intervention; as in the migration from the "primitive" Latin America toward the superior, civilized Europe in the United Sates.

Therefore, for Lugones (2010), gender is a mark for humanity, tied to the notion of the White Human. Latinas are marked by Europe as Objects, hence body-less. In turn, our objectification rendered us rape-able, but never raped or subjected to any crime (Lugones, 2016). Only sexual violence y golpes are noteworthy and punishable as rape and a crime when done to a White woman's body. Acts of violence against our flesh are not socially deemed as rape or murder. These acts are considered unremarkable, self-imposed, and not newsworthy. Agreeing with Lugones (2010), "The semantic consequence of the coloniality of gender is that "colonized woman" is an empty category: no women are colonized; no colonized females are women" (p. 745). Therefore, in the grammar of modernity/coloniality, the category of the "Latinx woman" points at a semantic error and intrinsic contradiction since Latinas are not after all mujeres. So, we, Latinas, cannot be dehumanized when we have never been considered humans in the first place. The Eurocentric universal category of woman that White feminism promoted does not include us but further reasserts our invisibility and compromises the integrity and dignity of our existence. As Objects, we exceed feminist's category of woman o *mujer*: "La frase "mujer indígena" es una contradicción" (Lugones, 2012, p. 133).

From decoloniality, rather than postcoloniality or White feminism, the decolonial task at hand in relation to gender or la Latina would be something entirely different than advancing a humanizing project or the reclamation of Western equal rights to White Man and Woman. Rather, an ethic of liberation or a transmodern project invites possibilities to delink or detach from modernity/coloniality's Eurocentric fictional Human category, identity, race, and gender so our existence is no longer disputed and controlled as resources to reproduce White Men's children or their knowledges, i.e., therapy, research, or pedagogies to continue maintaining their expansionist institutional legacy. My exploration of such possibilities is out of the scope of this paper, yet to engage in those explorations. First, it is important to discern our position and complicity with the matrix to know what we are responding to and from what to detach from. Hence, I advance a decolonial analysis on my existence as I know it now as product of Europe and, at the same time, in complicity with Europe's violent expansionist tactics.

My Europeanmake

I was born *en* 1973 to heterosexual parents that came from families with racial and economic privileges, social justice sensibilities, as well as classist and racists practices. I am from la Confederación Muisca, en el Norte of what we now call Bogotá en Colombia, Abya Yala. The name given to the Nation-State Colombia is an ongoing painful reminder of the tangible European expropriation of our territories, bodies, senses, languages, knowledges, imaginations, dreams, and communities. The name Colombia was given to "honor" Christopher Columbus, and it means "The Land of Columbus," La Tierra of a White, Catholic, European, male: Colón. My ancestry is Southern European due to the colonization in the 1500s, as well as Black, and Indigenous Muisca, and Pijao. My feign Southern European identities attached to my corporeal configurations go hand in hand with the Anglo, Northern European epistemologies and their translations into Spanish that settled in my consciousness, languages, perspectives, and ways of engaging through my private, Westernized, and Catholic education.

Although my ancestry is as much Indigenous as it is Southern European and Black, the amount of Spanish blood running under my wounded flesh have sufficed to serve me as the single and universal guide to lead the way through the only world I got to know and understand in the image and likeness of Europe. My Black and Indigenous ancestry were violently kept hidden in a seeming archaic and primitive existence, echoing the sound of a genocidal silence. The predominance of my Southern European ancestry and consequent storycide of my Indigenous and Black legacies also recruited me, blindly, to further execute the European project to exploit and benefit from anything not European.

During my urban upbringing in Colombia, Indigenous, Black, and Campesinas in my everyday social life came across as criminalizable domestic workers o sirvientas in my family and friends' households (Cumes, 2019). They were exploited as "objects" by "us" for our benefit and privileged lives. I don't recall their names or caring to know about their lives, families, or communities. I do recall that they were responsible to ensure my comfortable and clean living while I pursued my private British and Catholic education. While they were washing my school uniform at an outrageously low economic price, I was being educated at an outrageously high economic price about how primitive and barbaric Indigenous and Black people were, and how relieved we ought to be by having been saved by the White Catholic God who, in their eyes, civilized us from such demeaning and inferior conditions of existence. No one outwardly revealed that their seeming social justice, notwithstanding genocidal White Catholic God, recruited us and turned us equally and intimately violent against ourselves in the intimacy of our own homes and communities. The hidden in plain sight violence toward our Indigenous, Black, and Campesinas ancestors and community members, and exploitation of their conditions of poverty that we created, were required for our progress and upward mobility. Although two decades after, the conditions of domestic workers are better protected by the Nation-State's neoliberal rhetoric of equality, rights, and feminist advocacy, certainly the work and integrity of Indigenous, Black, and Campesinas still has no value —they still do not sit at the dinner table.

In my mid 20 s, I migrated to the Europe in the U.S. in the year 2000, willingly and on my own. My bilingual Catholic and private Westernized education in Colombia prepared me to migrate, giving me the English language and Western eyes through which I could only speak of and see my homeland criminalized and deemed barbaric and violent, hence inferior to the progressive, democratic, human rights driven superior Europe in the U.S. Hence, I took residence in a land with a history of British colonization and slavery, blind to the 400 years of barbaric, violent, and racist foundations of the U.S.' society.

Within the social order of things in the U.S. and the borderlands between Colombia and the U.S., my existence has been reconfigured through 20 years of immigrant life. Similar to Colombia, I am simultaneously sexualizable and sexualized in the U.S.; but unlike Colombia, in the U.S., I am racially marked, monetized, and criminalized as a "cis-Latina" or "Hispanic," brown immigrant, and middle class. Perhaps not in spite of but more so due to Colombia's private, Catholic, bilingual, and classist heteronormative schooling system, I have no religious affiliations. Hablo two imperial languages, Español Colombiano, and 20 years-old U.S. immigrant English or gringlish. Living in community with Mexican Americans and Chicanxs people, I have come to learn to better address the pinche colonial linguistic hierarchical fractures by speaking, thinking, sensing, and dreaming in Spanglish/Inglañol.

Unlike the life caminos of thousands of immigrants from Abya Yala, who arrive in this country in precarious conditions, and in great part due to the U.S. economic and military occupation in our land, my immigration journey has led me to live an advantageous urban life. After paying thousands of dollars in legal fees, I became a "naturalized" U.S. citizen years after my first arrival and when Colombia was criminalized by the West as one of the most violent countries in the world; a position that the West at this time has allocated to Afghanistan.

When arriving in the U.S., leaving behind the racial benefits I did not know I had in Colombia, I became the "Object." I was marked as colored, Indigenous, or Black when working as a waitress underpaid, exploited, sexualized, humiliated, and not allowed to sit at the dinner table of the White people I was serving at restaurants owned by White, European U.S. Americans in New York and Florida. Yet, I found myself under such conditions as one among other choices I knew I had, which the Indigenous and Black sirvientas, who served my family in Colombia, did not.

Despite my Latina Colombian immigrant configuration in the U.S., few aspects have been whitely advantageous to me such as the English language, a Westernized education, hence understanding of immigration law, and possibilities to continue my education in this country. However, my advantages are not always believable. My U.S. passport, doctoral degree, and English language do not always surpass the finalized social stories my racialized, sexualized, and gendered flesh tell instead both in public and private life.

For example, before the Covid pandemic, I befriended Angélica from México who recently migrated to San Diego. We met at the gym of the university I work at. We used to run into each other every day in the locker room before spinning class at 6:00 am. Angélica was very surprised not only to learn that I worked at the university but that I had a desk and computer all to myself. She asked a lot of questions about the software I was using. I later understood that she was interested in applying for a job at the university hoping to change her cleaning job at the gym for an office position. Last time we met, she asked me to teach her few computer features that she suspected I may have learned at my advantageous "secretarial" job that could help her prepare for her application.

José, a Mexican immigrant I had the fortune to meet a couple of years ago when I hired him to paint my mortgaged 650 sq. ft. studio, after our first brief encounter, he quickly told me how lucky I was to have gotten the job of the "cuidadora" of the studio in this area. He assured me that I was going to be safe in the neighborhood as the studios' keeper. I see him from time to time on his way to various painting jobs nearby. Up until this day, it has not come to his mind the possibility that I could be the person responsible for the mortgage instead. Perhaps he would have given me a discount had he known. It has not come to my mind to say otherwise and question the authenticity of his perspectives, much like Angélica's who otherwise I fear would have had a heart attack.

Something similar has unfolded in my interactions with Rogue, an African American person in my neighborhood who sleeps outside, and I met during the pandemic. I visit him almost daily at the park during my walks with Nala. Nala is my animal companion that I "rescued," benevolently a la Colón, from her animal conditions at the local "Humane Society" animal shelter to give her a domesticated, human-like, and civilized urban life. Rogue shares stories of police harassment he endures daily. His jaw dropped after months had passed, and I was still walking around this "expensive neighborhood of white people," as he aptly calls it. He still cannot believe that I was able to sustain my rent in this area all throughout the pandemic, given that all the factories and restaurants around from where he imagined my income might have come had closed due to the pandemic's economic impact. "I can't believe it either," I said. That certainly would not have been the case twenty years ago when I first migrated.

In spite my criminalizable, sexualizable, racialized, monetized, and gendered corporeal europeanmake, I live an unbelievably comfortable life in this country parallel to the various lives Angélica, José, and Rogue created about me. Similar to Colombia, my advantages depend on the disadvantages of others. I benefit from the expropriated and gentrified territories of the Kumeyaay peoples in San Diego, California. This city borders con Tijuana, México; it has five U.S. military bases and is considered among the most expensive cities in the country, yet with a high percentage of people who, like Rouge, sleep outside. I actively participate in, therefore sustain, Eurocentric capitalist institutions centered on the commodification of life and exploitation of the land through salaried work, mortgage-financing, the federal student loan system, and consumerist market.

I am also a commodity of the global market of knowledge. My earnings come from institutions dedicated to legitimizing the production of knowledge in standard English through Eurocentric patriarchal science, racialized professional education, and the Anglo exclusionary elitist publication industry. I paid taxes to the U.S. government Internal Revenue Service as a single person (heterosexually divorced) in 2020 of over 100,000 US dollars in income. My income from my university job salary represents 18.8% less than the earnings of a White male in academia in the U.S. system of higher education (American Association of University Professors, 2020); and aproximadamente 22,000% more than the earnings of Indigenous and Black gente who, from a Eurocentric economically configured existence, live in poverty in Abya Yala. While my income is outrageously disproportional to alguna gente in Abya Yala—who may work (if at all) and/or live under impoverished conditions, some enduring the effects of Colombia's armed conflict, others falling victims of femicide, or the exploitation of their own communities by families like mine—I participated in a task force of women of color at my university which agenda included advocating against "our unjust" salaries, seeking pay increases in relation to the centered advantageous White male criteria.

In my impossible pursuit to whiten myself toward becoming (Man)-Human—hence less primitive and more European—enjoying the persuasive comforts of capitalism that modernity extends through my professional and academic positions, I keep the violent implications of doing so hidden in plain sight. I have become academia and the mental health system's sirvienta. I serve the university as a tenured associate professor who would never sit at the table unless I exterminate anything that does not resemble their Human, European scholarly Anglo work, research, pedagogies, methodologies, technologies, interventions, and scientific rhetoric.

In the family therapy field, Anglo, Euro-Men and Women are out there writing their evidence or practice-based scientific modern and postmodern epistemological and ontological world-making criteria. As their sirvienta, I color their knowledge in multiculturalism for global export to assure the sustainability of their research, pedagogy, and interventions among my colored communities. While doing so, I am also serving them to further advance the institutionalization of healing as a Westernized profession that centers White Man, North Eurocentric, heterosexual epistemologies of relationality as marriage, family, and therapy. I am a member of the faculty team of a master's program in marriage and family therapy at a Westernized university where Angélica wants an office job. I help recruit European-made colored people into a Westernized Anglo family therapy program to "produce" colored-skin, White-practicing therapists skilled in Eurocentric professionalism, research methodologies, assessments, and therapy interventions to hide our objectified colored and primitive flesh, humiliated Spanglish, and inferior knowledge as sabiduria.

Finally, within the capitalist division of labor in the U.S., I profit from the monetized value of my scholarly agenda on decoloniality, feminism, and an ethic of liberation that seeks to question and detach from the very same racists, sexists, and capitalist's systems that my unbelievably comfortable livelihood depends on as much as it depends on my own exploitation and the exploitation of the lives of gente como Angélica, José, and Rogue.

Closing Remarks

My transmodern or ethic of liberation intentions to adopt decoloniality as a perspective to address the question on the Latina and the woman, rendered the world my flesh dwells on paradoxical. When considering the inseparable modernity/coloniality conditions within which the Latina is embedded, I can better discern the Eurocentric configurations of my existence inseparable from the dispute of race, gender, sex, and knowledge. This is a first step for advancing a decolonial project whereby pluriversal possibilities of thinking, doing, sensing, and dreaming are rendered available, delinked from a centered Europe (Mignolo, 2013). According to Mexican, Sociologist, Rolando Vasquez (2020) based in the Netherlands, projects oriented by decoloniality include four stages:

1. Address the historical reality of modernity whereby the Latinx and woman codifications are discerned as linked to the modern/colonial fictional renditions, violently and hierarchically established and naturalized unquestionably by Europe for self-fulfilling reasons.
2. Address the Latinx and woman from the perspective of coloniality or the matrix of colonial power to make more palpable all otherwise legitimate possibilities of existence disposed, erased, and exterminated by the invention and imposition of the idea of the Human and woman, hence the creation of the body-less Object.
3. Discern the inseparability between modernity/coloniality and consequently the imposition and settlement of the colonial difference whereby the advancement of some depends on the exploitation of others and objects, i.e., therapist's upward mobility depending on social suffering. Discerning such paradoxical conditions, according to Vasquez, raises the ethical question on how we are "complicit and implicated in the suffering of others and the wasting away of the body of Earth" (p. 136).
4. The ethical question on our complicit participation in the further sustainability of the colonial difference, open possibilities beyond resistance and critique, and rather toward re-existence by detaching from the center and periphery dichotomy and the European episteme and esthetics as the only way of being.

I tried to address the first three points Vasquez proposes. Therefore, I have come to understand the question on the Latinx and woman as a colonial semantic error—I was made a Latina in the U.S., not a woman, to be a resource and serve, hence sustain the White project in mental health and academia, among other things. Therefore, as long as we continue being Latinas, so does the White project of modernity. Ignoring this interdependency is required for the sustainability of ourselves as Europe's Objects whereby White men and women remain the only parameters of reference of life according to their norms, races, genders, languages, spaces, institutions, sensibilities, dreams, values, and Western rules. Addressing the interdependency, on the contrary, implicates the fourth step above that demands actional thinking to redesign ourselves linguistically, apart from Euro-identities, and inseparable from the Earth. Perhaps inhabiting Spanglish could offer a border-sentipensate way, dwelling *ni aqui ni alla* to re-exist in the otherwise.

Acknowledgements

I would like to thank Sociologist, Alejandro Montelongo from Aguascalientes, México for the invaluable contributions to an earlier draft of this manuscript.

Note

1. See polanco and Tisha (2021) and Tisha and polanco (2021) for an analysis of this interdependence between modernity and coloniality within the context of the mental health system, i.e., mental health interdependence of psychiatric mental illness and the configuration of the suicidal person.

Disclosure statement

No potential conflict of interest was reported by the author(s).

References

Anzaldúa, G. (1987). *Borderlands-La Frontera: The new mestiza* (2nd ed.). Aunt Lute.
American Association of University Professors. (2020). *Data snapshot: Full-time women faculty and faculty of color*. https://www.aaup.org/sites/default/files/Dec-2020_Data_Snapshot_Women_and_Faculty_of_Color.pdf
Cumes, A. E. (2019). La "india" como "sirvienta:" Servidumbre doméstica, colonialismo y patriarcado en Guatemala. In A. S. Monzón (Ed.), *Antología del pensamiento crítico guatemalteco contemporáneo* (pp. 569–606). Aura Estela Cumes.

Curiel, O. (2017). Género, raza, sexualidad: Debates contemporáneos. *Intervenciones en Estudios Culturales, 4,* 41–61.

Dussel, E. (2013). *Ethics of liberation: In the age of globalization and exclusion.* Duke University Press.

Escobar, A. (2017). *Designs for the pluriverse: Radical interdependence, autonomy, and the making of worlds.* Duke University Press.

Espinosa Miñoso, Y. (2019). Hacer genealogía de la experiencia: El método hacia una crítica a la colonialidad de la Razón feminista desde la experiencia histórica en América Latina. *Revista Direito e Práxis, 10*(3), 2007–2032. https://doi.org/10.1590/2179-8966/2019/43881

Fanon, F. (1999). *Los condenados de la tierra.* Gebara.

Gordon, L. R. (1995). *Fanon and the crisis of European man: An essay on philosophy and the human sciences.* Routledge.

Lugones, M. (2008). Colonialidad y género. *Tabula Rasa, 9*(9), 73–101. https://doi.org/10.25058/20112742.340

Lugones, M. (2010). Toward a decolonial feminism. *Hypatia, 25*(4), 742–759. https://doi.org/10.1111/j.1527-2001.2010.01137.x

Lugones, M. (2012). Subjetividad escalva, colonialidad de género, marginalidad y opresiones múltiples. En La Paz: Conexión Fondo de Emancipación (Ed.), *Penando los feminismos en Bolivia* (pp. 126–137).

Lugones, M. (2016, July 24). The Human. [Video]. Vimeo. https://vimeo.com/224880187

Maldonado-Torres, N. (2011). Enrique Dussel's liberation thought in decolonial turn. *Journal of Peripheral Cultural Production of the Luso-Hispanic World, 1*(1), 1–30.

Maldonado-Torres, N. (2017). Frantz Fanon and the decolonial turn in psychology: From modern/colonial methods to the decolonial attitude. *South African Journal of Psychology, 47*(4), 432–441. https://doi.org/10.1177/0081246317737918

Mendoza, B. (2016). Coloniality of gender and power: From postcoloniality to decoloniality. In L. Disch & M. Hawkesworth (Eds.), *The Oxford handbook of feminist theory* (pp. 1–24). California State University.

Mignolo, W. D. (2000). *Local histories/global designs: Coloniality, subaltern knowledges and border thinking.* Princeton University Press.

Mignolo, W. D. (2013). Geopolítica de la sensibilidad y del conocimiento. Sobre (de)colonialidad, pensamiento fronterizo y desobediencia epistémica. *Revista de Filosofía, 74*(2), 7–23.

Mignolo, W. D. (2021). *The politics of decolonial investigations.* Duke University Press.

Mohanty, C. T. (2003). *Feminism without borders: Decolonizing theory, practicing solidarity.* Duke University Press.

Oyěwùmí, O. (1997). *The invention of women: Making an African sense of Western gender discourses.* University of Minnesota Press.

polanco, m. (2019). En defensa de Spanglish family therapy supervision in the era of English. In L. Charles & T. Nelson (Eds.), *Family therapy supervision in extraordinary settings: Illustrations of systemic approaches in every day clinical work* (pp. 1–12). Routledge.

polanco, m., & Tisha, X. (2021). Andean decoloniality and mental health. In J. N. Lester & M. O'Reilly (Eds.), *The Palgrave encyclopedia of critical perspectives on mental health* (pp. 1–12). SHERPA/RoMEO.

Quijano, A. (2000a). Colonialidad y modernidad/racionalidad. *Perú Indígena, 13*(29), 201–246.

Quijano, A. (2000b). Colonialidad del poder y clasificación social. *Journal of World System Research*, 1(3), 342–388.

Said, E. W. (2006). *Orientalismo* [Orientalism] (M. L. Fuentes, Trans.). De bolsillo. (Original work published 1997)

Sommer, D. (2004). *Bilingual aesthetics: A new sentimental education*. Duke University Press.

Spivak, G. Ch. (1988). Can the subaltern speak? In C. Nelson & L. Grossberg (Eds.), *Marxism and the interpretation of culture* (pp. 66–111). Macmillian.

Stavans, I. (2003). *Spanglish: The making of a new American language*. Harper Collins.

Tisha, X., Chang, M., Hogan, L., & polanco, m. (2021). Storying the Aesthetics of Nuestras Linguistic Borderlands: A Tapestry de Solidarity. In M. Polanco, N. Zamani, & Ch. K. Da Hee, (Eds.), *Bilingualism, culture, and social justice in family therapy*. Springer.

Tisha, X., Polanco, M. (2021). An autopsy of the coloniality of suicide: Modernity's completed suicide. *Health*, 26(1), 120–135. https://doi.org/10.1177/13634593211038517

Tlostanova, M. V., & Walter, D. M. (2012). *Learning to unlearn: Decolonial reflection from Eurasia and the Americas*. The Ohio State University Press.

Vasquez, R. (2020). *Vistas of modernity: Decolonial aesthetics and the end of the contemporary*. Mondriaan Fund.

Wynter, S. (2003). Unsettling the coloniality of being/power/truth/freedom: Toward the human after man, its overrepresentation—An argument. *The New Centennial Review*, 3(3), 257–337. https://doi.org/10.1353/ncr.2004.0015

Conclusion—Latinx Feminist Liberation Practices: Integration and R/Evolution

Lillian Comas-Díaz and Carrie L. Castañeda-Sound

The Women's Liberation Movement developed in the Global North during the early 1960s, and unfortunately, paid no attention to Black, Indigenous, and other Women of Color. Additionally, it did not address Global South women's issues such as political oppression, economic exploitation, and cultural-gender domination. Specifically, it ignored the need for decolonization (Macleod, et al., 2020; Mohanty, 1991, 2003). Consequently, a feminism of color surfaced to decolonize feminism (Espinosa Miñoso, 2020) and to address the needs of women of color and women in the Global South (Barreno, et al., 1975). We define the emergence of feminism of color as a re-surfacing process because women of color's wisdom have been buried in history. Therefore, we need to *archeologize history* to uncover *herstory*.

The herstory of Women of Color is as old as time. Indeed, the first healer was a woman shaman (Yakushko, 2017), as well as priestess, warrior, and leader. To illustrate, the first published writer was a woman from the Global South—Enheduanna—a princess-priestess-warrior-poet from Mesopotamia (https://theconversation.com/hidden-women-of-history-enheduanna-princess-priestess-and-the-worlds-first-known-author-109185). Regrettably, the intersection of sexism, racism, patriarchy, and heteronormality has erased many Global South women's contributions. Latinx feminist liberation practices are one way to right such a wrong. Specifically, these practices illustrate the powerful ways many Latinx women engage in healing, decoloniality, liberation, and social justice action.

Feminism of color, particularly Latinx feminism, addresses Kuumba's (1994) urgent need to decolonize feminism. To combat women of color's oppression, feminists of color commit to radical hope, decoloniality, and liberation. Interestingly, liberation psychology was born in the Global South to address the needs of oppressed populations (Martín-Baró, 1994). Living in El Salvador, Ignacio Martin-Baró—a Jesuit priest and social psychologist—integrated liberation theology into emancipatory psychology (Comas-Díaz & Torres-Rivera, 2020). As the architect of liberation psychology, he connected with Latin American liberation sources, such as Brazilian Paulo Freire's (1970) pedagogy of the oppressed. Likewise, *pensadores* (thinkers) from Central America, the Caribbean, and South America clamored for decolonial and liberation movements to address the needs of oppressed and marginalized populations. However, early liberation psychologists did not concentrate on the needs of women and or women of color. Indeed, feminist liberation psychologists such as M. Brinton Lykes and Geraldine Moane (2009) were early articulators of the need for liberation psychologists to address women's issues. Like Elizabeth S. Fiorenza's (1975) criticism of theology of liberation's absence of feminist applications, Ada Maria Isasi-Dıaz (1996)—a Latinx feminist liberation theologizer—denounced theology of liberation, regardless of its Latin American roots, as being silent regarding Latin American women's issues.

The contributors to this edited book articulated feminist liberation practices while addressing Latinx women's needs. Specifically, they shared how Latinx feminists re-write herstory to create spaces for healing, decoloniality, and liberation. Specifically, feminist liberation practitioners recognize that Latinx females are born with an ancestral wound—one that is re-activated and aggravated by the exposure to intersectional oppressions. Since many Latinx females contend with colonial mentality and speak with a colonial accent, as such, are raped by gender and racial-xenophobic discrimination. As they cope with oppression, several Latinx women become pregnant with a thirst for liberation. To address such yearning, cultural *parteras* (midwives) minister ancestral knowledge and wisdom to Latinx females. Likewise, *abuelas* (grandmothers), mothers, aunts, *madrinas* (godmothers), sisters, *amigas del alma* (sisters of the heart), and *mentoras* (female mentors) become vessels of ancestral healing, decolonization, and liberation. Indeed, Latina *abuelas* are channels of female spirituality (Norat, 2005). Similarly, *promotoras*—Latina paraprofessional health workers—promote health and well-being in their communities (Lujan, 2008). Thus, many Latinx women engage in decolonization when they reconnect with Indigenous cultural traditions (Diaz, 2022).

Liberation psychologists syncretize, transform, and evolve their practices (Comas-Díaz & Torres-Rivera, 2020). Liberation psychology concepts include *testimonio, acompañamiento,* Spirit, *and artivism. Testimonio*—a Latin American healing practice—is a first-person narrative of the experiences with personal and collective oppression (Aron, 1992). *Acompañamiento* (accompaniment) means that the psychologist/healer stands alongside the sufferer to witness, nurture *conscientización* (critical consciousness), and assist in the recovery of her discounted knowledge and wisdom (Watkins, 2015). Rooted in participatory action (Fals Borda & Rahman, 1991), *acompañamiento* provides a guide to the liberation path (Martín-Baró, 1994; Watkins, 2015). Spirit relates to a profound interconnection to the sacred, one that includes everyone and everything, such as nature, environment, and cosmos. Given that most Indigenous and African cosmovision identify spirituality as a fundamental factor in healing through the relation with the inner healer (Mehl-Madrona, 2003), spirituality becomes a source of radical hope. Finally, artivism—the creation of art for social justice purposes (Sandoval & Latorre, 2008) is a Latinx form of promoting empowerment, decoloniality, and liberation. To illustrate, *arpilleras* (burlaps)—colorful patchwork weavings made by groups of Latin American women known as *arpilleristas* to oppose governmental oppression—were popularized under the Chilean Augusto Pinochet dictatorship. Additionally, feminist liberation psychologists developed PhotoVoice as a means of empowering Indigenous females and other women of color to take photos of their lived realities and to facilitate their development of critical consciousness (Women of PhotoVoice & Lykes, 2000). Likewise, Latin America has a long history of artistic murals and many other art forms addressing the need for social justice.

As dissident daughters of liberation theology, womanists (African American feminist women) and *mujeristas* (Latinx feminist women) promote decolonial and liberation practices (Bryant-Davis & Comas-Díaz, 2016). Moreover, Lillian Comas-Díaz and Thema Bryant-Davis (2016) coined the term *womanista* to designate women of color who support global feminism of color. The number of *womanistas* is increasing throughout the world (Chavez-Dueñas & Adames, 2021). When *mujeristas* and womanistas recover their historical memories, they drink from their ancestral, cultural, and gendered fountains. Some of these sources include *dichos*, (proverbs)—a form of flash therapy (Comas-Díaz, 2012), cultural rituals such as Days of the Dead for grieving and connecting with ancestors, *baños* (spiritual cleansings), *sobos*, (spiritual massages), *limpias* (exorcising bad energy), *yerbas* (healing herbs), and *peregrinaje* (spiritual pilgrimage), among many others. Likewise, Latinx folk healing practices such as *curanderismo* (Latin American Indigenous healing), *espiritismo* (Latin American spiritualism mixed with Indigenous healing), *Santería* (Afro Caribbean Oricha divinities camouflaged under Catholic divinities), and *Santerismo*—a syncretism of *Santería* and *espiritismo*; among others, are sources of healing and liberation (Comas-Díaz, 2012). Indeed, *curanderismo* (Del Castillo, et al., 2012), and *espiritismo* (Olmos & Paravisini-Gebert, 2003), have been identified as decolonial methods.

Resisting oppression, many Latin Americans transformed imposed colonial Catholic religious symbols into icons of liberation. To illustrate, La Virgen de Guadalupe—a Black/Brown Indigenous Madonna—has been declared the mother of the oppressed (Castillo, 1997). Guadalupe first appeared to the Indigenous Juan Diego on the site of the temple of the Aztec goddess Tonantzin, to herald the liberation of Mexico (Castillo, 1997). Mexicans won their independence carrying banners of Guadalupe's image (Comas-Díaz, 2014). Similarly, many Black and Indigenous Madonnas, such as the Brazilian Virgen La Aparecida and Virgen de Copacabana, in addition to the Cuban Virgen de la Caridad del Cobre (Virgen Mambisa), among various others, were key icons in several Latin American countries' independence wars.

Latinx cultural and folk healing are grounded in spirituality. Interestingly, females occupy central positions among many Latinx folk healing practices. Moreover, feminist Latinx spirituality is empowering, decolonial, liberatory, and transformative at both personal and collective levels. To illustrate,

Spirita—a womanist *mujerista* spirituality—redefines feminist of color spirituality as protest, resistance, and r/evolution (Comas-Díaz, 2008). Rooted in liberation psychology, the Spirita path entails a psychospirital journey to amalgamate revolution with a spiritual evolution. Consequently, Spirita stages include (1) awareness of and rejection of oppression, (2) embracing sacredness, (3) engaging and practicing collective healing, (4) joining in solidary with all oppressed people, and (5) fostering r/evolution. Similarly, Rayburn and Comas-Díaz (2008) identified the WomanSoul quest as a feminist journey through a connection with liberation spirituality. Hence, WomanSoul psychospiritual stages include (1) spiritual awakening, (2) recovery of ancestral spiritual wisdom, (3) development of critical consciousness and empowerment, and (4) collective liberation.

To make the sacred tangible (Alexander, 2006) feminist Latinx women syncretize ancestral healing into other spiritual orientations for decolonial and liberation purposes. In this fashion, many Latinx women rescue and use psychospiritual practices that have been historically associated with females, such as healing, shamanism, card reading (*La Baraja* and Tarot) (Comas, 2021), Indigenous and Aboriginal oracles, among others into their psychospiritual practices. Of interest, growing numbers of feminist Latinx women baptize themselves as *brujas* (witches) as an empowering, decolonial, revolutionary, and liberatory act (Flores, 2017). Many of these *brujas* are second generation Latinx who transform ancestral shadows into spiritual activism (Monteagut, 2017). Specifically, *bruja* feminism is an act of political resistance (Flores, 2017). Moreover, feminist Latinx women follow the Spirita path and the WomanSoul journey to develop spiritual psychic gifts such as intuition, prophecy, extrasensory perception, *la facultad*, and others. *La facultad* is a psychospiritual ability to correctly perceive power differentials from an oppressed perspective (Anzaldúa, 1987). Finally, as they restore their cultural wisdom, feminist Latinx women integrate their ancestral spirituality into feminist liberation methods to infuse transformation and evolution. As such, they use decolonial liberation practices to re-author their lives and to emancipate. Since feminist theology is a critical theology of liberation (Fiorenza, 1975), several feminist Latinx women engage in spiritual activism. The commitment to social justice action with a spiritual vision, spiritual activism is a feminist Latinx construct (Anzaldúa, 2002).

In conclusion, grounded in their connection to the sacred, feminist liberation Latinx women oppose networks of power and work towards empowerment and decolonization. Rooted in ancestral memory and in psycho-spiritual wisdom, feminist liberation Latinx women engage in ethical and political action to promote collective liberation and global wellbeing.

References

Alexander, M.J. (2006). *Pedagogies in Crossing: Meditations on Feminism, Sexual Politics, Memory, and the Sacred.* Duke University Press.

Anzaldúa, G. (1987). *Borderlands/La Frontera: The New Mestiza.* Spinster/Aunt Lute.

Anzaldúa, G.E. (2002). "Now let us shift..the path of conocimiento..inner work, public acts". In G.E. Anzaldúa & A.L. Keating (Eds). *This Bridge We Call Home: Radical Visions for Transformation.* (pp. 540–570). Routledge.

Aron, A. (1992). Testimonio, a bridge between psychotherapy and sociotherapy. *Women & Therapy, 13,* 173–189.

Barreno, M.I., Horta, M., & Velho da Costa, M. (1975). *The Three Marias: New Portuguese Letters.* Translated by H.L. Land. Doubleday.

Bryant-Davis, T. & Comas-Díaz, L. (2016). Introduction: Womanist and Mujerista Psychologies. In T. Bryant-Davis and L. Comas-Díaz (Eds.). *Womanist and Mujerista Psychologies: Voices of Fire, Acts of Courage.* (pp. 3–25). American Psychological Association.

Castillo, A. (Ed). (1997). *Goddess of the Americas: Writings on the Virgin of Guadalupe.* Riverhead Books.

Chavez-Dueñas, N.Y. & Adames, H.Y. (2021). Intersectionality awakening model of Womanista: A transnational treatment approach for Latinx women. *Women & Therapy, 44*(1–2), 83–100. https://doi.org/10.1080/02703149.2020.1775022

Comas, L. (2021, May 1). *Bruja, espiritista* or psychologist. https://witchesandpagans.com/sagewoman-blogs/an-invitation/bruja-espiritista-or-psychologist.html

Comas-Diaz, L. (2008). Illuminating the Black Madonna: A healing journey. In C. Rayburn & L. Comas-Díaz (Eds). *WomanSoul: The Inner Life of Women's Spirituality.* (pp. 85–95). Praeger.

Comas-Díaz, L. (2012). *Multicultural Care: A Clinician's Guide to Cultural Competence.* American Psychological Association.

Comas-Díaz, L. (2014). *La Diosa:* Syncretistic Folk Spirituality among Latinas. In T. Bryant-Davis, A. Austria, D. Kawahara, & D. Willis (Eds.). *Religion and Spirituality for Diverse Women: Foundations of Strength and Resilience.* (pp. 215–231). Praeger/Greenwood.

Comas-Díaz, L. & Bryant-Davis, T. (2016). Conclusion: Toward Global Womanist and Mujerista Psychologies. In T. Bryant-Davis and L. Comas-Díaz (Eds.). *Womanist and Mujerista Psychologies: Voices of Fire, Acts of Courage.* (pp. 277–289). American Psychological Association.

Comas-Diaz, L. & Torres-Rivera, E. (Eds.) (2020). *Liberation Psychology: Theory, Method, Practice, and Social Justice.* American Psychological Association Press.

Del Castillo, R., Wycoff, A. & Cantu, S. (2012). *Curanderismo* as Decolonization Therapy: The Acceptance of *Mestizaje* as a *Remedio* NACCS Annual Conference Proceedings. 7. https://scholarworks.sjsu.edu/naccs/2012/Proceedings/7

Diaz, J. (2022). *The Altar Within: Radical Devotional Guide to Liberate the Divine Self.* Row House.

Enheduanna (https://theconversation.com/hidden-women-of-history-enheduanna-princess-priestess-and-the-worlds-first-known-author-109185).

Espinosa Miñoso, Y. (2020, July 1). Why We Need Decolonial Feminism: Differentiation and Constitutional Domination in Western Modernity. Afterall Articles. www.afterall.org/article/why-we-need-decolonial-feminism-differentiation-and-co-constitutional-domination-of-western-modernit

Fals Borda, O., & Rahman, M.A. (1991). *Action and Knowledge: Breaking the Monopoly of Power with Participatory Action Research.* Apex Press. http://dx.doi.org/10.3362/9781780444239

Fiorenza, E.S. (1975). Feminist theology as a critical theology of liberation. *Theological Studies, 36*(4), 605–626.

Flores, A. (2017). Why Young Markers are Proudly Reclaiming Bruja Feminism. ReMexcla. https://remezcla.com/features/culture/bruja-feminism-culture-makers-latinx/

Freire, P. (1970). *Pedagogy of the Oppressed.* Seabury.

Isasi-Díaz, A. M. (1996). *Mujerista Theology: A Theology for the Twenty-First Century*. Orbis.
Kuumba, M.B. (1994). The limits of feminism: Decolonizing women's liberation/oppression theory. *Race, Sex & Class, 1*(2), 85–100. www.jstor.org/stable/41680222
Lujan, J. (2009). Got Hispanic clients: Get a *promotora*? *The Internet Journal of Allied Health Sciences and Practice, 7*(3), Article 4, https://nsuworks.nova.edu/ijahsp/vol7/iss3/4/
Lykes, M.B. & Moane, G. (2009). Editors' introduction: Whither feminist liberation psychology? Critical explorations of feminist and liberation psychologies for a globalizing world. *Feminism and Psychology, 19*(3), 283–297.
Macleod, C.I., Bhatia, S., & Liu, W. (2020). Feminisms and decolonizing psychology: Possibilities and challenges. *Feminism and Psychology, 30*(3), 287–305. https://doi.org/10.1177/0959353520932810
Martín-Baró, I. (1994). *Writings for a Liberation Psychology* (A. Aron & S. Corne, Eds. and Trans.). Harvard University Press.
Mehl-Madrona. L. (2003). *Coyote Healing: Miracles in Native medicine*. Bear & Company.
Mohanty, C.T. (1991). Under Western Eyes: Feminist Scholarship and Colonial Discourses. In C. Mohanty, A. Russo, & L. Torres (Eds). *Third World Women and the Politics of Feminism*. (pp. 51–80). Indiana University Press. http://links.jstor.org/sici?sici=01903659%28198421%2F23%2912%3A3%3C333%3AUWEFSA%3E2.0.CO%3B2-Y
Mohanty, C.T. (2003). *Feminism without Borders: Decolonizing Theory, Practicing Solidarity*. Duke University Press.
Monteagut, L.E. (2017). Second generation *bruja*: Transforming ancestral shadows into spiritual activism. USF Tampa Graduate Theses and Dissertations. https://digitalcommons.usf.edu/cgi/viewcontent.cgi?article=8623&context=etd
Norat, G. (2005). Latina grandmothers. Spiritual bridges to ancestral lands. *Journal of the Association for Research on Mothering, 7*(2) 98–111.
Olmos, M. F. & Paravisini-Gebert, L. (2003). *Creole Religions of the Caribbean: An Introduction from Voodu, and Santería, to Obeah and Espiritismo*. New York University Press.
Rayburn, C. & Comas-Díaz, L. (2008). A WomanSoul Quest. In C. Rayburn & L. Comas-Diaz (Eds). *WomanSoul: The Inner Life of Women's Spirituality*. (pp. 261–265). Praeger.
Sandoval, C. & Latorre, G. (2008). Chicana/o Artivism: Judy Baca's Digital Work with Youth of Color. In A. Everett (Ed.). *Learning, Race, and Ethnicity: Youth and Digital Media*. (pp. 81–108). MIT Press.
Watkins, M. (2015). Psychosocial accompaniment. *Journal of Social and Political Psychology, 3*(1), 324–341. https://doi.org/10.5964/jspp.v3i1.103
Women of PhotoVoice/ADMI & Lykes, M.B. (2000). *Voices e Imagenes: Mujeres Mayas Ixsiles de Chajul/Voices and Images: Mayan Women of Chajul*. Guatemala Magna Terra.
Yakushko, O. (2017). Witches, charlatans and old wives. *Women & Therapy, 41*(1–2), 18–29.

Index

Page numbers in **bold** refer to tables and those in *italic* refer to figures.

abolition feminism 89–91
Adames, Hector 4–5
Adams, G. 54
African Americans 56
AfroIndigenous Latinas 69
AfroLatinas 69
Aguilar, A. 42
American Civil Liberties Union (ACLU) 94
American Psychological Association (APA) 53, 97
ancestral knowledge 74–6
anti-colonial existence 79
Anzaldua, G. 36
Attitudinal Familismo 113–14

Bernal, Delgado 11
Bernstein, Elizabeth 89
Black feminism 130
Black Indigenous Womxn of Color (BIWOC) 89
Black Lives Matter Movement 11, 17
borderlands concept 36–7; coloniality 42; historical, intergenerational and community trauma 43; overcoming adversity 43; resilience 43
border thinking 36
bottom-up approaches 53
Bryant-Davis, T. E. 65

Chavez-Dueñas, N. Y. 43
Chavez, Nayeli 4–5
Chicanxs feminism 130
cognitive process 37
coloniality 36
Comadre approach 62
Comas-Díaz, L. 50, 54, 58, 65
"The Connectivity Bridge" 106–7, 111
concientización process 54
conscientization 91
control of sex, subjectivity and labor 134–5
Cooper, Brittney 70
Cordell, Nina 72
CoreCivic, private detention company 91
Critical Race and Ethnic Studies 16–17
critical reflection 95

critical social analysis 18–21
cultural domination 2
Customs and Border Protection (CBP) 93

decolonial feminism 130
decolonial feminists 127
decolonial healing concept 15, 17–18
decolonial love concept 15
deideologizing process 54
Department of Homeland Security (DHS) 86
De Robertis, C. 25
De Sousa Santos, B. 35, 38–41
Dicolonizando en Untranslatable Spanglish 129–30
Domínguez, D. 5
Dussel, Enrique 128

ecology of knowledge 41
ecology of productivity 41
economic exploitation 2, 3
emancipatory frameworks **88**
Emotional Emancipation Circles 3
emotional process 37
envision transformation 57–8
Espiritismo (spiritism) 58
Essed, P. 73
eurocentrism 133
experiential and somatic therapy models 38

Falicov, C. J. 58
Fanon, Frantz 108, 128
Feminismo Autonomo 130
Feminismo Campesino 130
feminism of color 147
feminist liberation therapists 3
Fernández, J. S. 4
Fields, Karen 110
The first Nepantla moment 47
folk psychology 39
freedom dreaming 89
Freire, Paulo 38

generational trauma 105–6
GEO Group, private detention company 91

Ginwright, S. 25
Grosfoguel, Ramon 92
Guatemalan refugees 57

Healing Circles 3
Hip Hop 3
Hofstede, G. 109
Holocaust survivors 56
Huber, Perez 44

identity, eurocentric fiction 136
Ignacio Martín-Baró 91
immigrant detention 90, 94–5; before 92–3; apprehension 93–4; individual level 95–6; institutional level 97–8; multi-level reflection strategies 95; mutual aid level 96–7; policy level 98–9
Immigration Customs Enforcement (CBP) 93
immigration industrial complex 85–7, *86*
imperial feminism 1
Indigenous Latinas 69, **75**
international sisterhood 1
Intersectionality Awakening Model of Womanista Treatment Approach (I AM Womanista) 5, 70
Interviews/entrevistas (2000) 36

Kaba, Mariame 96
Keating, A. L. 37
Kelley, Robyn 89
King, E. 37, 38
Kuumba, M. B. 1, 2, 147

La Lucha: critical consciousness and engaging 64–5; and social justice 59
Laria, A. J. 59
LatCrit theory 16–17
Latinx asylum seekers 87
Latinx migrant womxn. *see* immigrant detention
Latinx studies 16–17
Latinx women: cultural values 109–11; defined 105; and descendants 105; Indigenous and Blacks populations 106; postcolonial psychotherapy 108–9; seeking psychological help 108; traumas 105–6
Lewis-Fernández, R. 59
liberation principle 128
liberation psychology 53–4, 91–2, 148
Lugones, M. 6, 127, 135, 136, 137
Lykes, M. Brinton 148

Maldonado-Torres, N. 128
Marianismo and Machismo 111–12
Markus, H. 54
Martín-Baró, I. 54
Mayan League (2020) 71
Memmi, Albert 108
Mendoza, B. 131
Mendoza, Breny 131

middle-to-late phase of therapy 63–4
Miehls, D. 37, 38
Mignolo, W. 36
migration process 87
Mirandé, A. 112
Moane, Geraldine 148
modern/colonial/capitalist world-system 85
modernity and coloniality 134
Mohanty, C. T. 2, 131, 132
monoculture: of classification and production 40–2; of knowledge 39; of linear time 39–40
Mosley, D. V. 31
Mujerista approach 54
mujerista liberation psychology: critical reflexivity among readers 12; critical social analysis 18–21; and decolonizing standpoint 10; healing 10; Latinx students 16; mutual recognitions 22–5; perspectives 12; radical hope 25–9; social condition/place metaphorical blinders 11–12; on *Testimonio* 12–15
multi-level reflection strategies 95

National Latinx Psychological Association 97
Native Americans 56
non-human white woman and Latina object 136–8

oppression trauma 105
Orgullo and Simpatía 114–16

Patrón (Blueprint) 57
Perez-Chavez, Jessica 4–5
personal reflection 95
Pilar Hernández-Wolfe's (2022) 4
political subjugation 2
postcolonial studies and feminism 130–2
post-migration process 87
prison industrial complex (PIC) 90
promotoras 3
psychospirituality 58–9, 64
psychotherapy 60–1

Queer BIWOC 89
Quijano, Anibal 36, 133, 134

racial-gendered colonialism 72–4, 76–7, 76–9
racism 72
Rakoff, Vivian M. 105–6

Sabin, M. 57
The second Nepantla moment 47–8
Secure Communities Program 86
sexual orientation marginalization 3
Singh, A. A. 54, 100
Society for the Psychology of Women 97
Spanglish 130
Spivak, G. 131
Spoken Word 3

spokespersons 131
Steady, F. C. 1

Testimoniando El Presente essay assignment 11, 16–17, 34
testimoniantes 4
Testimonio 44; *mujerista* liberation psychology 12–15; *see also* decolonial healing concept
Theron, L. 43
The third Nepantla moment 48–50
Tlostanova, M. V. 131, 132
Town Hall Project's Mutual Aid Hub (2020) 97

traditional Indigenous cultures 71–2
transmodernity 128

Ungar, M. 43

Walsh, C. 36
Walter, D. M. 131, 132
Western feminists 1
Women of Color (WOC) 70, 147
women's liberation movement 147

xenophobia 3

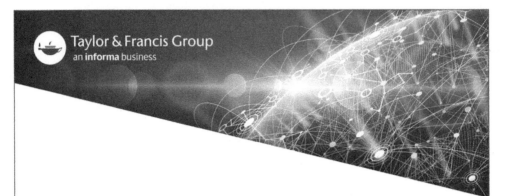